The Art of Managing Things

Second Edition

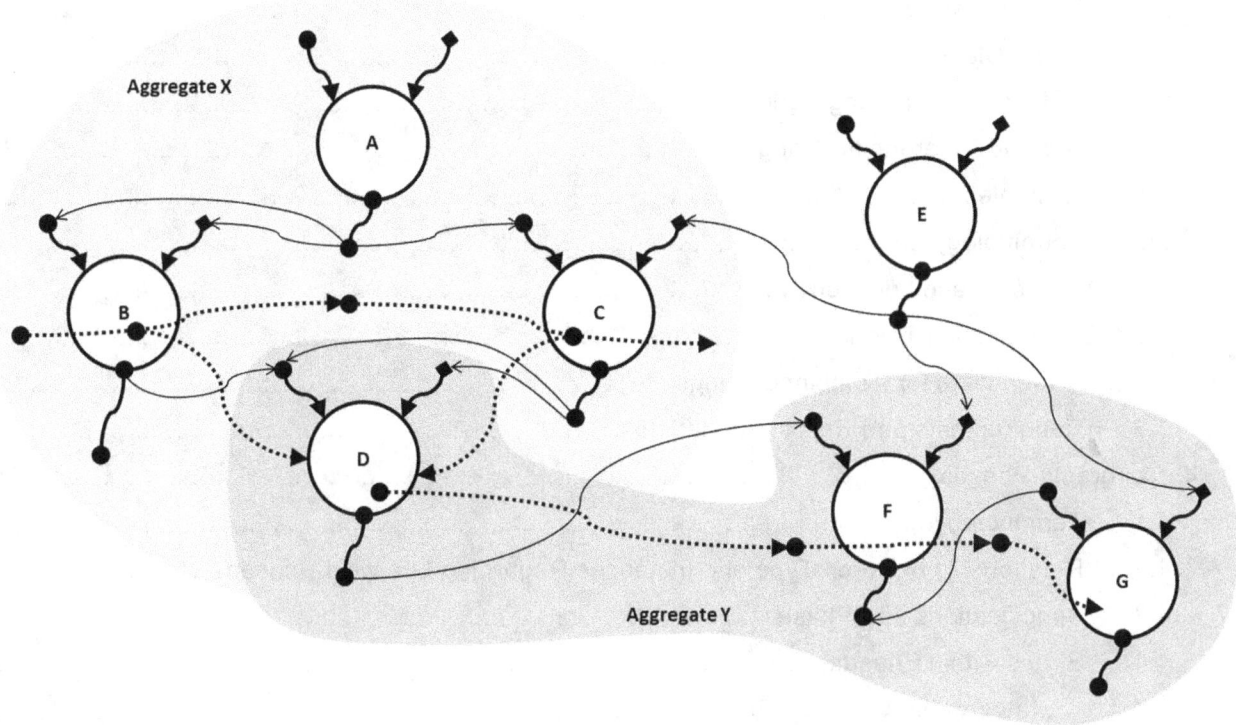

by Stephen Fratini

Contents

Figures

Tables

Preface

This book is intended for people and organizations looking to manage collections of related things in a systematic manner, with a common foundation and with common patterns across areas such as catalog management, inventory management, identification and naming, ordering, configuration, lifecycle management, security, assurance and billing. To be clear, this book is a framework and does not provide a detailed account of each management area. However, many references are provided where the reader can find more detailed information.

While based on the common terminology and framework presented in Sections 2 through 8, the various concepts and patterns in Sections 11 and 12 can be used separately. Thus, a green-field scenario is not necessary for those looking to make use of the concepts and patterns in this book. Further, it is quite possible to pick and choose several of the concepts and patterns while effectively making use of only those items in a given situation.

Those already familiar with management concepts may find my thoughts on anti-layering (Section 6.4.4) and antifragility (Section 6.5) to be of interest (as I challenge some common beliefs). For those not familiar with management concepts, this book can serve as an initial overview.

The concept for this book has been in my head for at least a decade. My motivation for writing the book comes from years of participation in and contribution to various standardization efforts in the general area of telecommunications management. Each time a new set of management standards are started, the same process occurs, i.e., define some common concepts and patterns, and apply the ideas to a new area that needs to be managed. The problem is that many times the concepts and patterns are reinvented without taking a proper look at what has been done before (albeit for another area). This is the "not invented here" pattern.

In this book, I have taken up the task of recording the management concepts and patterns that I have learned over some 30 years in the telecommunications industry while using one consistent terminology. Further – and I have discussed this often with my colleagues – the concepts and patterns used for telecommunications management are quite generic and pretty much apply to any type of thing (there is even an example about a brick later in this book). That explains the usage of "thing" in the title.

The following is a short-list of the industries where the concepts and patterns in this book can be applied: telecommunications, smart grid, smart cities, computer networks, fintech (financial technology), manufacturing, transportation, warehouse (inventory management in particular) and airline.

Past efforts to collect management patterns have had mixed success. For example, the Telecommunication Standardization Sector of the International Telecommunication Union (ITU-T) work on systems management (see ITU-T Recommendation X.700 [1] and the other specifications in the ITU-T X.700 series) were a good start but the work is focused on telecommunications, and further, the specifications have not been updated to reflect current trends. My view is that there needs to be a cross-industry effort to collect management concepts and patterns. My hope is that this book will serve as a basis (or at least a starting point) for such an effort.

Regarding the book's cover (i.e., statues at Easter Island), some have made comments to the effect "this is a nice photo but what's does it have with your book?" The point is that even though the famous statues were constructed long ago and far away, many of the concepts and patterns in this book can be applied (and probably were applied in some form at the time). For example:

- Each statue was invented (concept), planned, built, put into operation so to speak and in some cases retired. See Section 4 concerning lifecycle phases.

- Probably someone kept track of all the statues and the various types of statues. See Section 11.3 on inventory and catalog management.

- The workers who built the statues needed to be compensated in some form. See Section 11.1 regarding billing.

- The statues needed to be monitored for problems and then repaired. Known design problems with earlier statues where likely corrected and applied to newer statues. See Section 12.6 on metrics and Section 12.7 root cause problem analysis.

The point is that many different types of things need to be managed. This need to manage collections of things is not new. However, a systematic approach to management (crossing many industries and types of things) has not been put to paper. This book is my humble attempt to do so.

Stephen Fratini
Sole Proprietor of The Art of Managing Things
Eatontown, New Jersey (USA)
Email: sfratini@artofmanagingthings.com
LinkedIn: www.linkedin.com/in/stephenfratini
Twitter: @ssfratini

Acknowledgments

As noted in the preface, I have discussed many of the issues covered in this book with my colleagues in the telecommunications industry. These discussions have been a key motivation in writing this book.

I'd also like to thank the reviewers for their time and effort in making comments and improving the quality of this book:

- Reviewers of Edition 1: Michel Besson, Dave Hood, Alan Pope and Yuval Stein

- Reviewers of Edition 2: Paul Jordan, Yuval Stein, David Milham, Tony Clark and Vincent Fratini.

1 Introduction

1.1 Overview

This book is about concepts and patterns for managing things.

- **Pattern** – a model used as an archetype or original for imitation
- **Concept** – general idea or understanding of something.

The things under consideration include static objects without intelligence (e.g., optical fibers, telephone poles, bricks), entities with electronic interfaces (e.g., physical components within the Internet of Things (IoT)) and composite entities comprised of intelligent and non-intelligent things (e.g., automobiles, airplanes, IP routers).

"Management" includes the entire lifecycle of a given instance or type of thing, starting from the identification of an idea for a new type of thing to the eventual retiring of the thing.

The book is kept at a conceptual level. Further details concerning the various concepts and patterns can be found in the many references.

1.2 Suggestion on How to Read

The book is divided into several parts:

- Sections 2 to 8 cover the foundations that underlie the concepts and patterns covered in Sections 11 and 12, respectively.

- Section 9 provides an information model that summarizes some of the key concepts from the previous sections and also some concepts that are covered in more detail later in the document.

- Section 10 includes a healthcare application ecosystem example with the intent of illustrating some of the key concepts in the previous sections of the document.

- Section 11 covers management areas such as billing, capacity management, catalogs, inventory and several other areas.

- Section 12 describes common patterns that can be applied to one or more of the management areas.

In terms of reading the document, it is recommended that Sections 2 to 9 be read first. The various subsections in Sections 11 and 12 can be read in any order. However, there are considerable cross-references among the subsections in Sections 11 and 12. So, reading one subsection may lead the reader to several other subsections.

2 Basic Terminology

2.1 Definitions

This section provides basic definitions that are used throughout the book. Additional definitions are provided, as needed, in subsequent sections of the book. There is also an Index of terms at the end of the book (with references to the page where the term is defined).

Some of the terms are first introduced via the examples below. This is followed by more formal definitions.

Consider a brand/model of pocket knife (a **type** of **thing**), e.g., "Acme Pocket Knife – Model X123." Each knife is an **instance** of some **type** of knife. The specification of a type defines the common characteristics for all instances of the type. Some **characteristics** may be optional while others are mandatory. There may also be default values for some characteristics, e.g., if not specified by the consumer, the knife retailer will provide a pocket knife with a red outer shell by default. The type specification for a knife might also be published in a catalog to help **consumers** make purchasing decisions. The knife maker (**provider**) has a **factory** that produces instances of the knife (perhaps a process that is partially automated with some human intervention). The knife **agent** (i.e., owner) takes care to wash the blade after each use and occasionally sharpen the cutting edge.

An IP router is a type of composite thing with electronic interfaces. Various aspects of IP router instances may be handled by different **agents** (also things). In Figure 1, the Security Agent (represented as the box with a dashed-line boundary) covers security for all the IP routers shown in the diagram (represented as black circles). For example, the security agent controls access rights to the IP routers. There are two configuration agents (boxes with the solid boundary) with Configuration Agent #1 handling half of the IP routers and Configuration Agent #2 handling the other half.

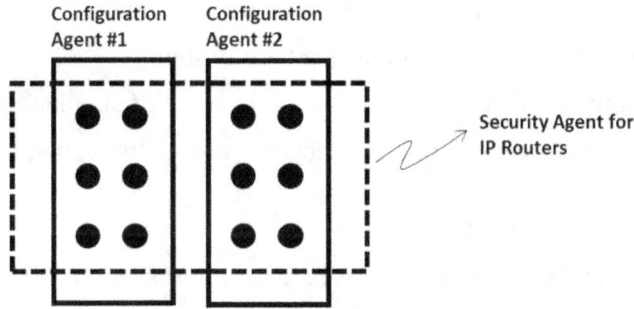

Figure 1. Configuration and Security Agents Controlling Access to IP Routers

Agent – a thing that provides access to the capabilities offered by a set of things

- Access can be technical or legal (contractual).
    - Technical access concerns functions that can be performed on a set of instances, e.g., retrieval (inventory), modification, deletion and other specialized functions.
    - Legal access concerns agreements that permit technical access.
- In other words, an agent provides a façade to a set of things relative to a given aspect or set of aspects, e.g., configuration, assurance, security or accounting (usage).
- A thing can have several agents where each agent covers a different aspect of the thing.

- This definition can be further specialized to cover various kinds of agents, e.g., gatekeeper (general access control), business manager, lifecycle manager, assurance manager, or factory.

Capability – [Author's note: I decided not to define this term beyond what one would find in the dictionary. For example, The Free Dictionary by Farlex provides the following definition of capability: "the quality of being capable; ability."]

Characteristic – a distinguishing quality, feature or trait of a thing.

- For example, a brick has the characteristics of volume, dimensions, mass and color.

Consumer – a role played by a thing when it uses or requests the use of a capability offered by another thing.

Factory – a thing that can create instances of one or more types of things.

- A factory is a kind of agent that transforms the specification of a thing (input) into an instance of a thing (output) with requested characteristics.

Feature – an externally visible characteristic or capability of a thing.

Instance (of a thing) – a realization of a given type.

Instance Agent – a thing that serves as an agent for a set of instances.

Instantiate (a thing) – the act of creating an instance of a type. The word is also used as a noun (i.e., instantiation) in this document.

Manage – to have charge of; direct or administer; regulate or limit toward a desired end. [Author's note: I tried to avoid defining "manage" as its definition has a difficult history within the area of telecommunications. However, several reviewers thought it was critical to define the term. In the end, I compromised and decided to use several innocuous dictionary definitions.]

Provider – a role played by a thing when it fulfills or offers a capability to another thing.

Specification – a thing that defines (or describes) a type of thing.

Specification Agent – a thing that serves as an agent for a set of specifications.

- For example, a catalog system that offers access to detailed software component descriptions is a specification agent.

Thing – anything that can be managed.

Type – the collection of all instances (potential or realized) that share a common set of characteristics.

- The distinction between "specification" and "type" is a bit subtle. Think of a specification as a description in a catalog (perhaps a description of a type of camera). The collection of all cameras based-on the specification is the type.

- It is possible to have a specification for a type with no realized instances. Conversely, it is possible to have a type but no specification, e.g., a type of animal or plant that has not yet been described. The type exists (with many instances) but there is no specification.

Figure 2 shows a type with multiple instances. Instances are members of a given type. The type is defined (a priori) or described (a posteriori) by a specification. Hexanchus vitulus – a newly classified species of Sixgill Shark – is an example of a type.

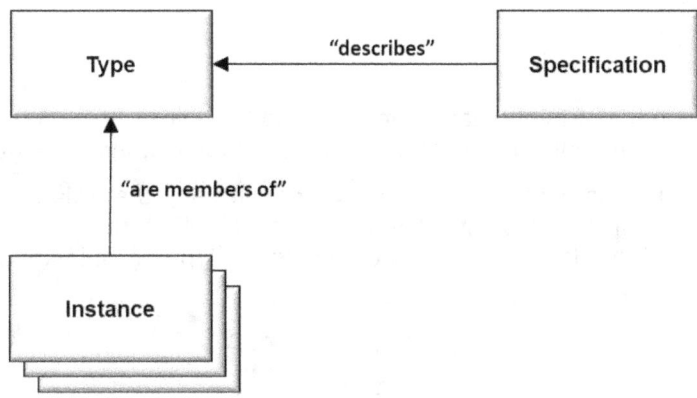

Figure 2. Specification, Type and Instance

While not used in this document, there is also the related concept of a "class." From Dictionary.com, the concept of a "class" is defined as "a number of persons or things regarded as forming a group by reason of common attributes, characteristics, qualities, or traits; kind; sort." This is similar to the definition of "type" given above. However, in the world of object-oriented design, a distinction is made between "type" and "class." The following explanation of the distinction between "class" and "type" is taken from *The Object-Oriented Database System Manifesto* [2]:

> A *type*, in an object-oriented system, summarizes the common features of a set of objects with the same characteristics. It corresponds to the notion of an abstract data type. It has two parts: the interface and the implementation (or implementations). Only the interface part is visible to the users of the type, the implementation of the object is seen only by the type designer. The interface consists of a list of operations together with their signatures (i.e., the type of the input parameters and the type of the result).

> The notion of *class* is different from that of type. Its specification is the same as that of a type, but it is more of a run-time notion. It contains two aspects: an object factory and an object warehouse. The object factory can be used to create new objects, by performing the operation *new* on the class, or by cloning some prototype object representative of the class. The object warehouse means that attached to the class is its extension, i.e., the set of objects that are instances of the class. The user can manipulate the warehouse by applying operations on all elements of the class.

2.2   Creating an Instance of a Manufactured Type

For a given type of thing, the following steps take place to create instances:

- (Concept) Define a specification for the new type, e.g., a virtualized firewall for the Internet or a new type of shovel.

- (Build Factory) Build a factory to create instances of the given type or modify an existing factory to create a new type (could be a physical factory or just software that creates object instances).

- (Place Specification in a Catalog or similar) Assign a type agent, e.g., a catalog application, to provide access to the new specification.

- (Instantiation Requests) Make requests to the factory to create instances of the given type.

- (Manage Lifecycle) Manage the various aspects of the instances via the agents assigned to the instances.

2.3 Thing Classification

Thus far, three general kinds of things have been defined, i.e., specifications, agents and things that are neither specifications nor agents (referred to as "regular" things in Figure 3).

Figure 3 shows a classification of things. The arrows indicate an "is a" relationship, e.g., a Specification is a kind of Thing. In Object-Oriented Design (OOD) terminology, this kind of relationship is known as "inheritance." Inheritance applies to types (not instances).

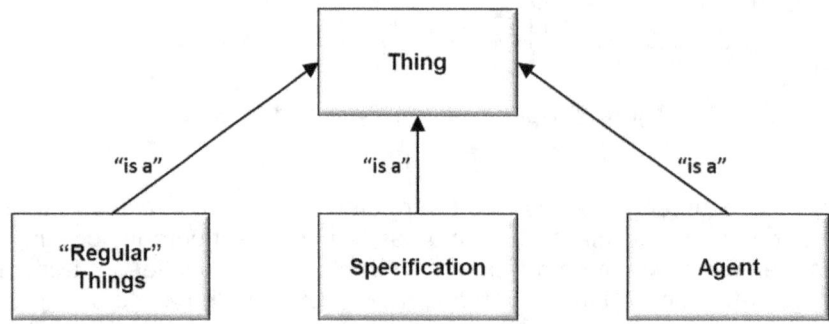

Figure 3. Classification of Things

2.4 Agent Classification

Agents provide access to sets of things in the context of an area of concern such as creation (factory), assurance (repairs) or security.

Figure 4 shows a classification for some of the kinds of agents discussed in this book. The arrows indicate an "is a" relationship, e.g., a Factory is a kind of Agent, and Security Agent is a kind of Instance Agent. While not shown in the figure, there are many additional relationships among the things in Figure 4, e.g., factories have specifications which are handled by specification agents, and instances of a factory can be managed by assurance and security agents.

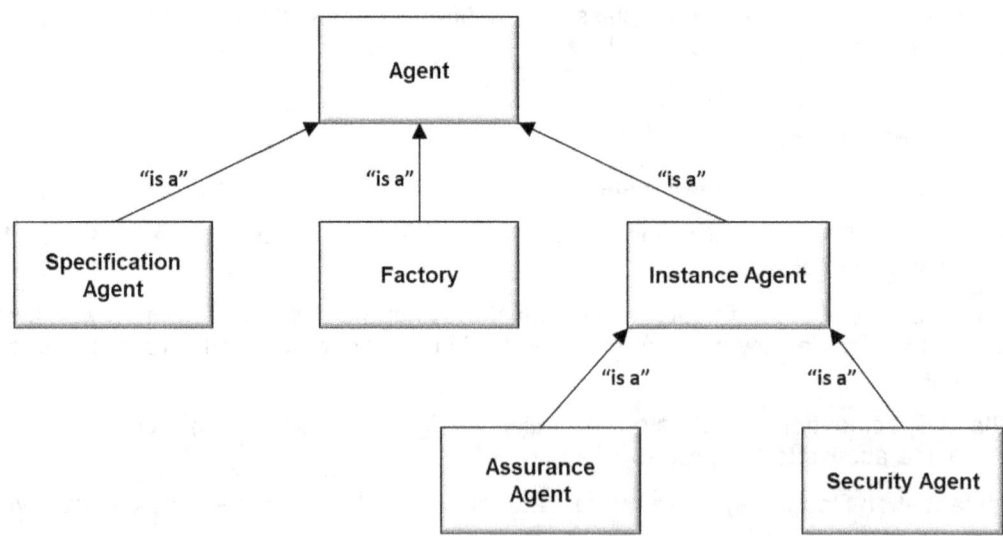

Figure 4. Classification of Agents

2.5 Relationships among Agents

Agents can be stacked in the sense that one agent provides capabilities to other agents.

In Figure 5, Agent Y provides capabilities to Agent X. Agent Y allows Agent X to make configuration requests on the things for which Agent Y serves as an agent. Agent X, in turn, could also act as a provider to yet another agent, e.g., Agent Z.

For example, Agent Y might handle IoT devices in a building. Agent X might handle some IoT devices directly and make use of (or just monitor) IoT devices handled by Agent Y and several other building-level agents (not shown in the figure). So, Agent X acts on a larger geographic area than Agent Y. Agent Z might act on yet a wider geographic area.

Usage of the term "stacking" (as opposed to "layering") is intentional. The grouping of things into layers is discouraged (see Section 6.4.4).

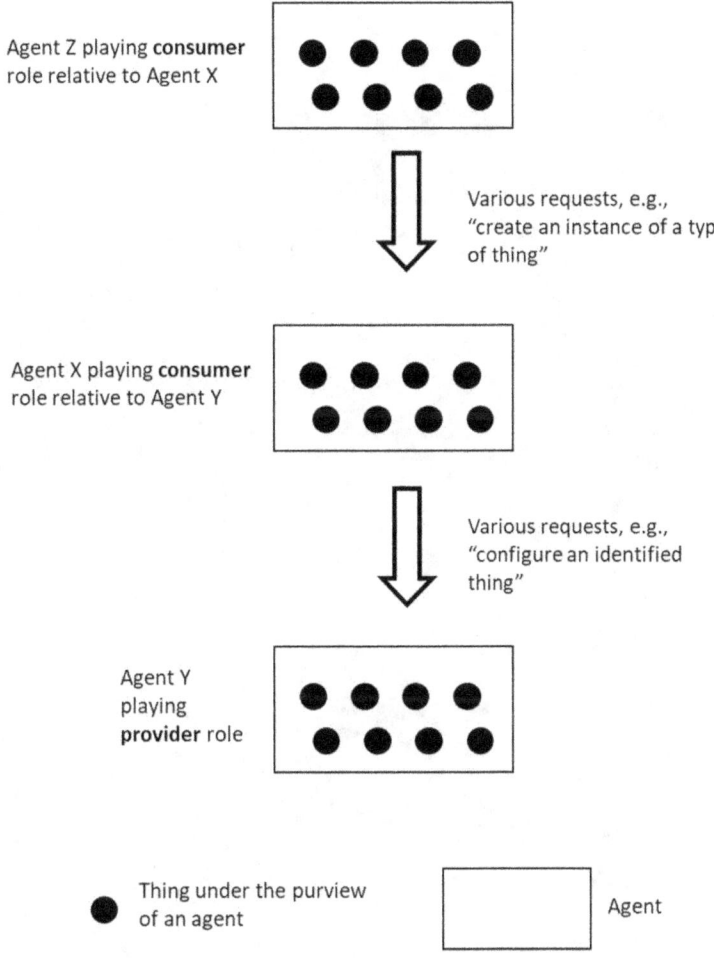

Figure 5. Stacking of Agents

An agent is also a thing. To emphasize this point, Figure 6 is offered as an alternative representation of an agent and its subtending things.

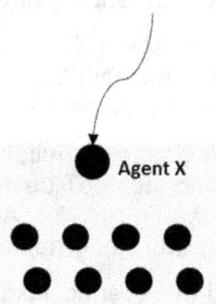

Figure 6. Alternate Depiction of Agent and Subtending Things

3 Locating and Referencing Things

This section concerns concepts such as naming, identification, addressing and location. These terms are often mixed together. For example, consider the definition of "identifier" in Wikipedia (note that "name" is used in the definition of "identifier."):

> "An identifier is a name that identifies (that is, labels the identity of) either a unique object or a unique *class* of objects, where the "object" or class may be an idea, physical [countable] object (or class thereof), or physical [noncountable] substance (or class thereof)."

In telecommunications management standards, "identifier" is distinguished from "name" where the unique label for a thing is its identifier while its name is a secondary label which may or may not be globally unique.

3.1 Examples

For things to communicate, they need to be able to identify each other and there needs to be a communication medium (which can be viewed as a kind of agent). However, mutual identification is only needed for 2-way communication. Even things that do not communicate (e.g., a library book) still require unique identifiers.

In the simplest case, one thing directly interacts with another (with no agent in between other than the communications medium), e.g., two people talking to each other, with their voices carried over the simple medium of air.

In Figure 7, Thing A sends a modify request to Thing B.

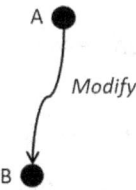

Figure 7. Direct Interaction between Things

For A's request to reach B, there are several options:

- (Addressing) Thing A provides the communications medium with an address for B, and the communications medium delivers A's request to the address. An address provides sufficient information for a communications medium to locate a thing. However, it is possible for a thing to change addresses. A thing may also have more than one address at any given time.

- (Identification) Thing A provides the communication medium with a unique identifier for B. The communication medium maps the identifier to the current address for A and then delivers the request to B. Addressing and identification are not the same thing. For example, it is possible to have a unique identifier for a person (perhaps his or her name, or an identification number as issued by a government) but not know that person's address and thus have insufficient information to communicate with the said person. Conversely, it is possible to have the address for a thing (at a given point) but not have that thing's identification information. For example, consider junk mail that is sent to an address using the identification "Current Occupant" or a robocall system that has addresses (phone numbers in this case) but does not know the identity of the people that it is pestering.

- (Broadcast and Filter) Thing A broadcasts and B filters the medium for messages of interest. For example, someone drowning in a pool screams for help, and one or more people at pool-side attempt a rescue.

In Figure 8, Thing A wants to send a request to Thing B but there are several agents between A and B.

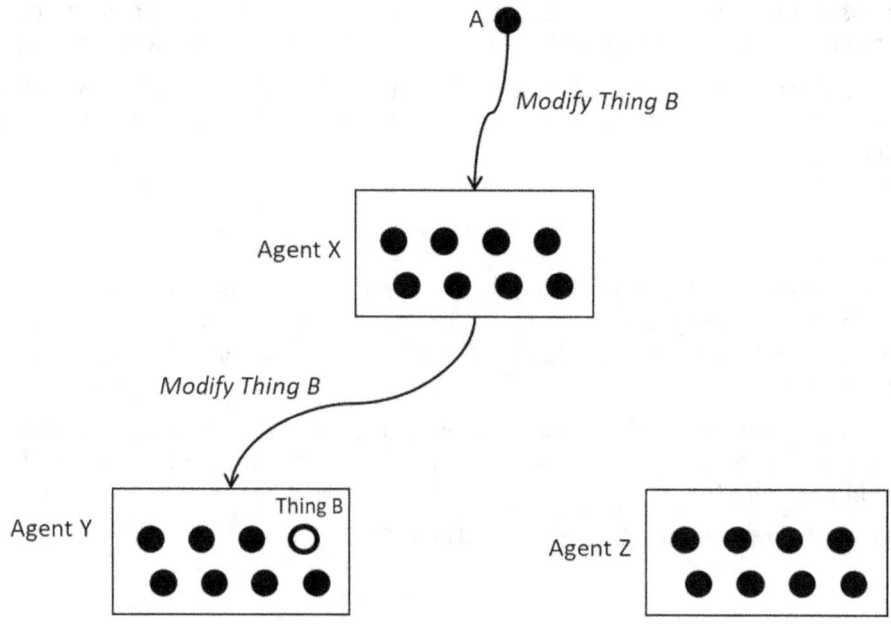

Figure 8. Interaction between Things via Agents

In this case, the following step could be used to get the request from A to B:

- Thing A provides the communications medium with an address or identification for Agent X, and the communications medium delivers A's request to Agent X. The request itself identifies Thing B as the intended recipient. The communications medium does not need to know the identity of Thing B.

- Agent X examines the request from Thing A and determines that Agent Y provides access to Thing B.

- Agent X determines the address for Agent Y and sends Thing A's request to Agent Y via the communications medium. As before, the communications medium does not need to know the identity of Thing B.

- Agent Y coordinates the modification to Thing B and sends a response back to Thing A (via Agent X).

In Figure 9, Thing A wants to modify a subset of the characteristics of all things that meet given criteria. For example, Thing A might be a configuration management system in a telecommunications network that needs to reconfigure equipment instances (e.g., optical switches) of a given type that have been configured incorrectly. It is not known what equipment instances have been configured incorrectly but this can be determined by matching the given criteria against the current characteristic values of each equipment instance. For example, if for a given equipment instance characteristic L equals 31 and characteristic M equals 7, then a match has been found and the equipment instance needs to be reconfigured.

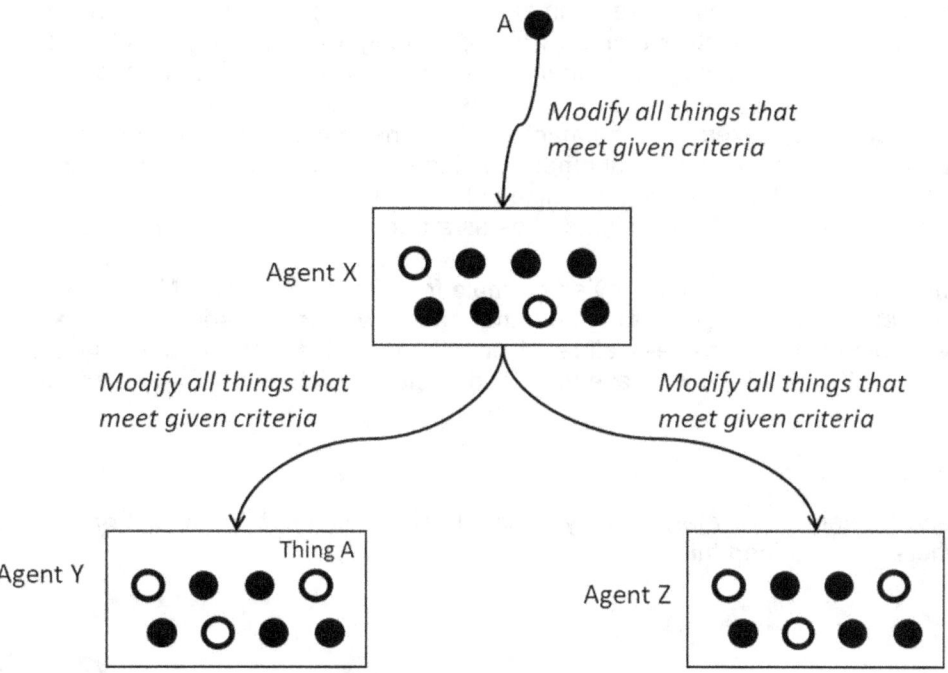

Figure 9. Identifications of Things via Search Criteria

The following steps are used to propagate the request from A to the appropriate things that need to be modified:

- Thing A determines that Agent X has access to all the things that could possibly match the given criteria. If this were not the case, Thing A would need to send the request to several agents.

- Thing A determines the address of Agent X and uses the communications medium to forward the request to Agent X.

- Agent X applies the criteria to the things directly under its control and requests that the things matching the criteria make the appropriate modifications.

- Agent X determines that Agents Y and Z may also have access to things that meet the criteria. In this case, Agent X effectively acts as an intermediate agent to Agents Y and Z.

- Agent X already knows the addresses of Agents Y and Z. Therefore, Agent X can use the communications medium to forward the request from Thing A to Agents Y and Z.

- Agents Y and Z apply the criteria to the things directly under their control and request that the things matching the given criteria make the appropriate modifications.

- Agent X collects the responses from Agents Y and Z, combines this with the actions it has taken internally and sends a response to Thing A. Alternately, Agent X could have sent several responses to Thing A, i.e., one response concerning the things directly under its purview, one response for the things under Agent Y and other for the things under Agent Z. Message exchange patterns are discussed further in Section 12.5.

In other cases, a thing may not have or need a unique identifier. For example, consider a part in a washing machine such as the agitator (the thing that goes back and forth to help clean the clothing). A repair person only needs to know where the washing machine is located (i.e., house address for the owner of the washing machine) and the part number for the agitator. With this information, the part can be replaced. In other words, a unique identifier is not needed because the agitator is unique within the addressed domain of the washing machine. But if the washing machine design had two agitators then they would no longer be unique within the addressed domain and would likely require unique identifiers such as Agitator #1 and Agitator #2.

On the other hand, the broken washing machine could be in a common laundry room in an apartment building (along with several other washing machines). In this case, the repair person would need to be told which washing machine is broken (perhaps via a tag on the machine saying "Out of Order"). The "Out of Order" sign serves as a temporary identification.

[Author's note: I was going to do a similar example for the Tire-Pressure Monitoring System (TPMS) in an automobile, but then found out that each tire pressure sensor emits a unique Id that is easily readable using an off-the-shelf receiver. With the advent of the Internet of Things (IoT) even small insignificant things will have unique identifiers which can be read electronically.]

3.2   Terminology

The subsections below cover terminology for labels and location, the concept of combining things, and identifiers for combined things.

3.2.1   Labels and Location

The following definitions concern references to things:

Address – a label that provides sufficient information to communicate with a thing.

- The address for a thing and its location are not necessarily bound. With dynamic IP addressing, for example, different IP addresses are assigned to the same location at various times.

- A thing can have multiple addresses at the same or at different times.

- If a thing is not able to communicate (e.g., a library book or a brick), then it would not need an address (based on the definition given here).

Identification Context – the scope or circumstances under which an identification scheme applies.

- For example, the United States uses a 9-digit social security identifier for all citizens. Within the United States, social security identifiers are unique. If another country or organization used 9-digits identifiers, there would be no guarantee or expectation that the identifiers did not overlap the social security numbers used in the United States because the context is different.

Identification – a collection of characteristics that reference one or more things in a context.

- The matching criteria in Figure 9 are an example of identification.

- Identification and the associated classification of types can be particularly complex. For example, biological taxonomy has taken centuries and is still under debate (see the Wikipedia article entitled "Taxonomy (biology)" [1]).

Identifier – a label that unambiguously references one and only one thing within a context.

Location – the position of a thing relative to a given physical coordination system.

- Some examples of coordinate systems:
  - geographic coordinate system consisting of latitude, longitude and elevation
  - celestial coordinate system (geocentric or heliocentric; polar or rectangular coordinates).

- The location of many but not all things can be identified by a single point. For things that span a long distance (such cables, electrical conduits and fences), area (the surface of a lake) or volume (a planet), a single location may not be sufficient. In such cases, the location needs to be described by a geometric shape within a coordination system.

- Yet other things move from location to location (e.g., car, school bus, people, wild animals). Even in these cases, it is possible to equip a moving thing with a tracking device and thus have access to the current position of the thing.

- In some cases, an address can be associated with a location, e.g., a street address.

Name – a label that references a thing.

- An identifier is an example of a name, but a name is not necessarily an identifier since it does not necessarily need to be unique in a context.

- For example, in the context of the United States federal government, someone's social security number is their identifier. Several people with the same name will have unique social security numbers.

Figure 10 depicts relationships among labels, names, identifiers, addresses and location. For example, the author of this book has the name "Stephen Fratini" and as a citizen of the United States, he has a unique social security number (an identifier). The author has several addresses. His house address is linked to a location but not necessarily his location. His email address is not linked to any location.

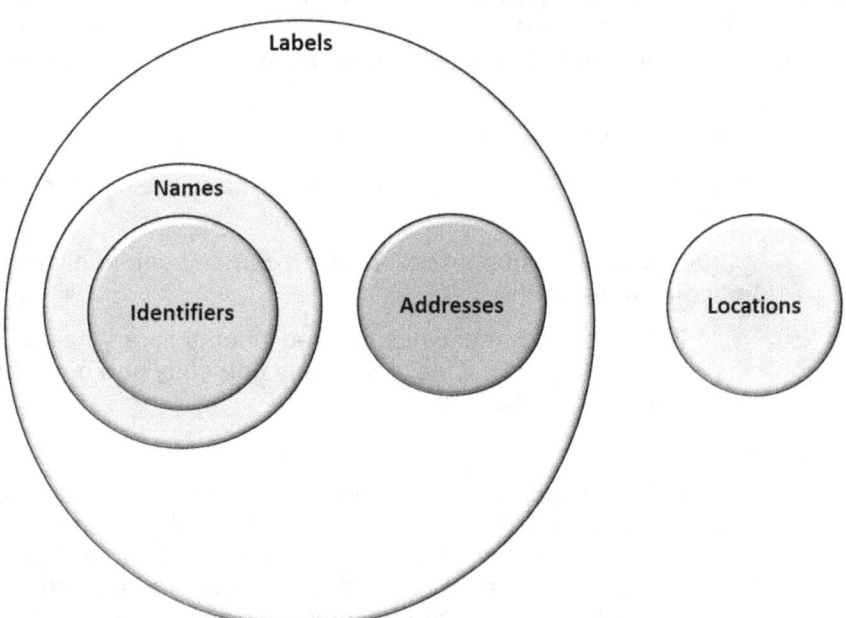

Figure 10. Venn Diagram concerning Labels and Locations

As an example of the above definitions, consider a specific copy of a book in a library. In the analysis that follows, a distinction is made between the book (type) and a given copy of the book (instance). The input information for the example is taken from a web page hosted by Simon Fraser University, where an explanation is provided concerning how to locate a book (in the library) given its call number (defined below).

- Type information

- o Identification Context: Planet Earth
- o Type: ISBN-10: 1554583578 or ISBN-13: 978-1554583577
    - The ISBN is usually printed as a bar code on each instance of a given book type.
- o Name of Book: *Borrowed Tongues: Life Writing, Migration, and Translation*
- o Other identification information that can help to reference the book:
    - Author: Eva C. Karpinski
    - Publisher: Wilfrid Laurier University Press
    - Date of Publication: May 1, 2012
- o Address:
    - While one does not communicate with a book (referring to the definition of "address" given previously), it is possible to contact the author. The author's contact information could serve as an address for the book (type).

- Instance information
    - o Identification Context: Simon Fraser University W.A.C. Bennett Library
    - o Identifier: this is usually handled via a bar code that is attached to a book by someone on the library staff.
    - o Call Number (typically put on the spine of a book by someone on the library staff) – For the example at hand, the call number is "PR 8923 W6 L36 1990 c.3." A call number can be thought of as a key to determine the desired or default location for a book.
        - "PR 8923" indicates the subject area.
        - "W6 L36" identifies a specific title within the range of books in the given subject area.
        - "1900" is the date of publication which can be used to distinguish among editions of the book.
        - "c.3" is the copy number which is used when a library has several copies of the same book (type). If there was only one copy of a given book, this field would not be needed.
    - o Location:
        - When a given book instance is on the shelf and in its proper place, the call number can be used to locate the book. Typically, each library will have a map or some sort of directions to help users find the location of a book based on the call number, e.g., "call numbers starting with P are on the 5th floor of the W.A.C. Bennett Library in Burnaby." The mapping between call number and desired location in a library can change, e.g., all the books with a call number that starts with P could be moved to another floor or even to an annex of the main library. So, the call number plus a location mapping guide is necessary to know the desired location of a book.
        - If the book is out on loan, the library would know who has the book but not the exact location, noting there is no guarantee that the person who checked out the book is at their home address (or whatever address is associated with their library card).

- If the book has been taken off the shelf and then put in a stack for library staff to re-shelve (in its proper place), then the location is temporarily unknown.
- If the book was taken off the shelf and then put back in the wrong place, the book could be very difficult to locate which is why many libraries have warning signs, not to re-shelve books.
  - o Address: not applicable, unless the book has some sort of electronic tracking chip.

3.2.2 Combining Things

The concepts of association, composition and aggregation are covered more fully later. However, to more fully explain compound identifiers, the definitions of these concepts are needed here.

Association is a weak relationship among things where the things have independent lifecycles and there is no owner.

- For example, the relationship between a lawyer and a client is an association. The lawyer can be associated with multiple clients at the same time, and one client can be advised by several lawyers. Each of these things has their own lifecycle and there is no owner. The things that are part of the association relationship can be created and destroyed independently.

Aggregation is a kind of association among several things in which the things have independent lifecycles. However, in this case, there **is** an owner. A thing can belong to several aggregations at the same time.

- For example, a person may belong to several clubs (sports, chess, reading, etc.) where the club is the aggregation (taking the role of "owner"). The club and its members still have independent lifecycles.

Composition is a kind of aggregation in which the parts cannot belong to more than one composition at a time.

- In some cases, the following condition is added: the parts cease to exist if the whole (the composite) is destroyed. This condition is an optional characteristic of composition. As an example, consider a house and its rooms. If the house is destroyed, so are the rooms. The rooms cannot exist by themselves.

As depicted in Figure 11, all compositions are aggregations, and all aggregations are associations.

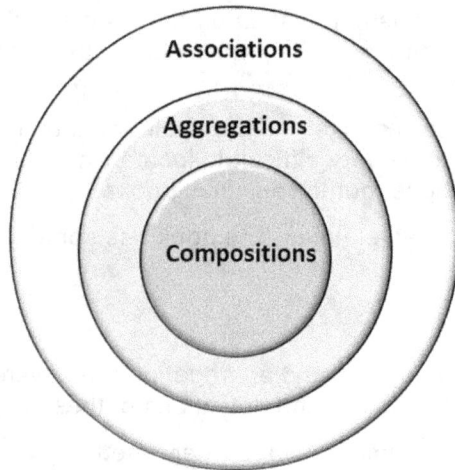

Figure 11. Venn Diagram concerning Associations, Aggregations and Compositions

The above definitions work well in the realm of Object-oriented Design (OOD) since one can mandate that when a given composite is deleted, so must its parts. In the physical realm, the distinctions are not as clear cut. For example, while a car is typically considered to be a composite, some of the parts of a "destroyed" car may still be reusable in other cars. Even if all the parts of a car are demolished, the various metals and plastics can be recycled and used in other things.

When in doubt (concerning definitions), the best approach is to say exactly what is required for a given situation and not spend endless time perfecting the definitions.

3.2.3 Identifiers for Combined Things

In the case of a composite thing, there are several options for assigning identifiers to the components:

- If the composite completely encapsulates the components (with no visibility to the outside), it may not be necessary to have identifiers for the components.

- If the components are externally visible, use compound names for the components, e.g., an ordered pair such as (Id for Composite, Id for Component). In this case, the component identifier only needs to be unique in the context of the composite. This approach has the advantage of shorter names for the components and no need for a universal identification authority (or mechanism) to provide identifiers for the components.

- It is also possible to assign universally unique identifiers to both the composite and each of its components. This may be the trend for things with electronic interfaces, e.g., IoT.

In the case of aggregates, and especially when the components can belong to several aggregates, one approach is to assign identifiers to the components that do not depend on the identifier of the aggregate. On the other hand, it is possible to define an aggregate solely for the purpose of assigning identifiers and use compound names for the components based on the name of the "identifier" aggregate. This approach would still allow the components to belong to several aggregates.

The above definitions of composition and aggregation are in keeping with earlier versions of the Unified Modeling Language® (UML®). However, the latest version of UML [4] defines composition as a specialization of aggregation as follows: "Composite aggregation is a strong form of aggregation that requires a part object be included in at most one composite object at a time. If a composite object is deleted, all of its part instances that are objects are deleted with it." In this definition, composition is posed as a stronger form of aggregation.

3.3 Requirements and Recommendations

It is recommended that the following requirements be followed when assigning identifiers to things.

- **Id_R1**: The identifier for a thing shall be stable, i.e., not changing over time.

    - It is possible to create an identifier for a thing before it exists, e.g., vehicle Ids can be created for cars that have not yet been created. Similarly, it is clearly possible to retain memory of an identifier when the associated thing no longer exists. It is an implementation issue whether to reuse identifiers from things that no longer exist.

- **Id_R2**: The identifier for a thing shall be opaque, i.e., there shall be no information embedded in the internal structure of the identifier.

    - The problem with putting business related information in an identifier is that the business information needs to change as the business requirements change which, in turn, forces changes to the identifier (an undesired side-effect) thereby violating requirement Id_R1.

    - A better approach is not to assign any meaning to identifiers and to use separate characteristics as needed.

- **Id_R3**: In an identification context, a thing shall have exactly one identifier.

- **Id_R4**: Identifiers for things shall **not** be based on the identifier of an associated agent.

    - Assigning identifiers such that the agent identifier is part of a compound identifier for the associated things is a potentially costly error. If the agent changes, then the names of the associated things need to change.

Keep in mind that not all things need identifiers (see the previous example concerning the agitator in a washing machine). Further, it is possible for one thing to make a request on another without knowing its identifier, e.g., via matching criteria on a set of characteristics (see the example related to Figure 9).

4 Lifecycle Phases

4.1 Terminology

A thing, be it a type or instance, passes through several phases. Depending on the phase, different management processes and activities will be required. Figure 12 shows the lifecycle phases and some of the possible state transitions for a thing. The phases are defined as follows:

- **Inventing Phase** – a lifecycle phase where either a new type of thing is conceptualized or the concept for an existing type of thing is modified.

    o   This phase can also apply to instances of (typically complex) things. For example, there could be an inventing phase for a new instance of a Content Distribution Network (CDN). To be clear, this would be about the concept of a new CDN instance and not the design. A content provider may be considering entry into another geographic area and requires a CDN in the new area. In the inventing phase, the content provider might consider tradeoffs such as whether to build the CDN or lease from another provider. Another example would be an architectural design concept for a new building (an instance).

- **Planning Phase** – a lifecycle phase where a type or instance is designed, and scheduled for construction and deployment according to a plan.

- **Building Phase** – a lifecycle phase where the plan for construction and deployment of a thing is executed.

- **Operating Phase** – a lifecycle phase where a thing is fulfilling its intended purpose.

- **Retiring Phase** – a lifecycle phase that results in a thing no longer fulfilling its intended purpose.

Some things will only touch on some of the phases. For example, a Virtual Machine (VM) instance may come into existence to support the scaling-up of a workload and then be terminated as soon as it is no longer needed. In this case, the VM instance has no inventing or planning phases, and very short and relatively insignificant building and retiring phases. The interesting part of the lifecycle for the VM instance is its operating phase. To be clear, the VM type does need to be invented, planned and built (in the sense of creating a factory that can spawn VM instances).

On the other hand, a custom-made rocket (used to launch a satellite) might have long and detailed inventing, planning and building phases but very short operating and retiring phases.

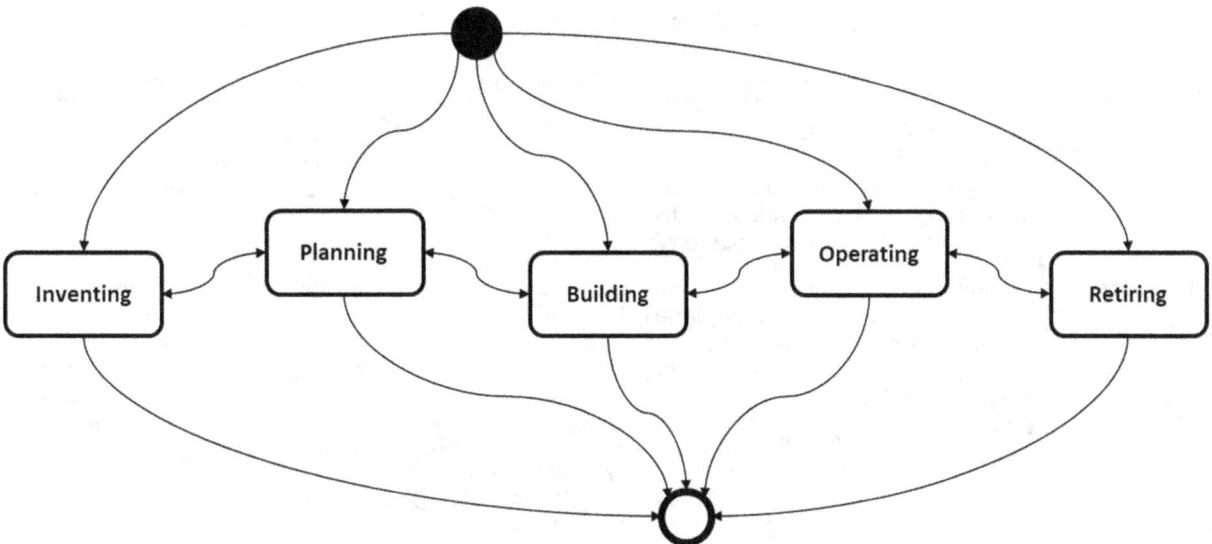

Figure 12. Lifecycle Phases and Transitions for a Thing

The diagram in Figure 12 should not be construed as a waterfall process model. It is possible to have multiple parallel cycles regarding a given type of thing. Consider the example of an adventure jacket with special pockets for hiking-related equipment. There could be one cycle related to an initial trial concerning a prototype version of the jacket with limited distribution. If the trial goes well, a parallel cycle could be started for a mass-market version of the jacket. While the mass market version of the jacket is being sold (Operating phase), another cycle could be started to plan the next version of the jacket.

The above leads to the question of whether the same version of a type can be in multiple phases. This is conceivable. However, there would need to be a strong governance process in place to handle such situations. For example, it may be possible to continue with the inventing phase for a given type/version while planning is also taking place. In this case, given that planning has already started, only limited changes may be accepted from those working on the inventing phase. If a proposed change negatively impacts the planning schedule, the change could be deferred to a later version of the type. See Section 12.9 for further details on versioning.

4.2   Relationship between Type and Instances Regarding Lifecycle Phases

The lifecycle phases for a type of thing and the associated instances are separate but related. Consider the example of a new type of airplane, as described in Table 1. The lifecycle for the new airplane type is managed by the airplane manufacturer while the lifecycle for an instance of the airplane type is managed by an air carrier company. In the Planning phase for an airplane instance, the air carrier orders an airplane instance from the airplane factory (which is in the Operating phase). See the circled items in Table 1.

Table 1. Airplane Type and Instance Phases

	Inventing	Planning	Building	Operating	Retiring
Type	Determine the concept for a new type of airplane	Determine a plan for building a factory to produce instances of the new airplane type	Build the airplane factory	Operate the airplane factory	Eventually, retire the airplane factory
Instance	Consider the idea of offering service in a new region, which may involve the purchase of airplanes	Determine what type of airplanes to use, airports to serve and flight corridors Order new airplanes	Build new terminals or secure existing terminal space at the selected airport Receive and test new airplanes	Operate in a new region, using newly purchased airplanes	Possibly withdraw from the region if not profitable and either retire or re-assign airplanes

4.3 Specifications and Phases

The specification for a type of thing will vary, depending on the phase. In one approach, the specification increases in detail as the type moves from the inventing phase to the planning phase and so on. In this approach, the information accumulates in the same specification. Alternately, separate specifications can be kept for each phase of a given type.

The following is an example of the information (segmented per phase) that might be included in the specification for a type:

- Inventing phase: purpose statement, intended audience, market information, description of capabilities that are to be offered to consumers

- Planning phase: pricing, licensing strategy, deployment scenarios (information needed to create an instance of the given type)
  - In order to build the type factory (next phase), it is necessary to know how the instances are to be created (i.e., deployment scenarios). Further details on factories and deployment scenarios can be found in Section 11.5.

- Building phase: determination of metrics to be collected (for instances of a given type), determination of conditions that result in alarms
  - Metrics and alarms (for instance) could be decided during the planning phase for the associated type, but this could be deferred until the building phase for the type.

- Operating phase: consumer reviews and objective performance measurements could be associated with the specification (it is debatable whether such items are part of a specification)
  - The specification should be stable for a given type and version at this point.

- Retiring phase: the date when new instances cannot be created, the date when existing instances are no longer supported and subsequently terminated.

In terms of the type repository (catalog), various approaches are possible. For example, an organization may want to have one catalog for types that are in the inventing phase, another catalog for types that have passed the inventing phase but do not yet have any associated instances (planning and building phases) and another catalog for types that do have existing instances (operating and retiring). Catalogs are discussed further in Section 11.3.

4.4 States within Phases

The phases defined above can be divided into states. For the sub-divisions of the phases, states are used. A state indicates the present condition of a thing with respect to its lifecycle (e.g., "accepted," with emphasis on the past tense) whereas a phase is a distinct period in the lifecycle of a thing (e.g., "building") that covers several states. In both cases (phases and states), there are conditions for entering and leaving. [Author's note: I could have just used one term here ("state" or "phase") but decided that "phase" was more expressive for the top-level processes. If this bothers you, just think of the phases as top-level states that have sub-states.]

The states defined in this section are not intended to be prescriptive or exhaustive, but rather, just some examples to better understand the structure of each phase. State transitions within a phase are typically a mesh (can go from any state to another).

Each state is defined in the past tense (indicating what needs to have happened for the thing to enter the given state).

In terms of maintenance and knowledge of the state for a thing, responsibility will depend on the state and the type of thing. Clearly, before a thing exists, its state would need to be maintained by another thing. Once a thing exists and assuming sufficient intelligence, the thing itself could possibly be responsible to keep track of and report on its state.

4.4.1 States within Inventing Phase

The following states, within the Inventing phase, are defined:

- Conceptually Defined – the general idea of the invention (new type or modification of an existing type) has been discussed, considered and defined.
    - o This state could also apply to instances. For example, a Communications Service Provider (CSP) may want to consider the idea of offering instances of an already existing type of service in a new geographic area.

- Invented – the invention proposal has been fully explored and tested, and is ready to be taken to the next step.
    - o For types, this state may entail an extensive investigation and study of the concept, e.g., prototyping, trials, market research, patent searches, and subsequent patent filings. In the case of a trial, the "trial-type" would traverse the planning, building and operating phases while the "production type" may still be in the Conceptually Defined state until the trial is completed. So, there is one state machine for the "trial-type" and another for the "production type." As noted, this is not a waterfall process model.
    - o This state can also apply to instances. Using the example above, the CSP may do an economic study to see if it makes monetary sense to offer instances of a given service type in a new geographic area, and if so, file a tariff with the appropriate governing body.

4.4.2 States within Planning Phase

The following states are defined within the Planning phase:

- Proposed – a requirement for the thing (type or instance) has been identified, but the associated characteristics or deployment details have not been decided.

- Feasibility Checked – a check has been done to see if the proposed thing can be built as requested.
  - This state is most prominent in the Planning phase, but one could argue that all phases have some element of a feasibility check.
- Designed – the characteristics of the thing and its deployment details have been completely defined, but nothing has been built or ordered in support of the thing.
- Requested – an order for building a thing has been made. In the case of a type, the order is for a new factory or update to an existing factory that can create instances of the type.
  - This state potentially involves several parties (organizations), e.g., the party that has designed and requested the given thing, and the party that builds and delivers the given thing. This relates to the Delivered state in the Building phase.

4.4.3   States within the Building Phase

The following states are inspired by things (equipment) in a telecommunications network but have been generalized to fit other situations.

- Built – the thing has been constructed.
- Delivered – the thing has been acknowledged by the requesting party as having been received.
  - This could entail delivery of a physical thing (e.g., a new car, a washing machine, kitchen cabinets), the allocation of a logical resource (Voice over IP connection), or the download of software and associated electronic license codes.
  - In some cases, the Delivered state does not apply. Consider, for example, an office building or a bridge. Such things are built on site and not typically "delivered." However, the various components may have a Delivered state. It is true, however, that the management of the building or bridge is transferred from the construction company to the owner once construction is complete. This transfer can be considered as a sort of delivery.
- Unit Tested – the thing has been verified to function as required in an isolated environment.
  - Unit testing is common in software development. The new code is first tested in isolation to make sure it does what it was designed to do and then tested in the software system in which it is to run.
- Integrated (or Installed) – the thing has been connected or placed into the environment in which it is to function.
- System Tested – the thing has been verified to function as required in its intended environment.
  - Depending on the type of thing involved, there could be several iterations of integration and system test. For example, a new type of component in an electric grid might first be integrated into a test environment, system tested (in the test environment) and if all goes well, the component would be integrated and then system tested in the actual electric grid.
- Accepted – the thing has been approved to be activated in the actual environment in which it is to function.

4.4.4   States within the Operating Phase

There are several dimensions to the state of a thing in the operating phase. Administrative and operational states have a long history in the telecommunications industry. For example, see ITU-T Recommendation X.731 [5]. Variations of these states are used in this document, as described below.

4.4.4.1   *Administrative States*

The Administrative state of a thing is typically set (or request to be set) by an external thing (e.g., a designated agent). It is sort of an On / Off switch. The following administration states are defined:

- Activated – the thing is enabled to process consumer requests.

    - It is possible for a thing to be Activated but in the operational state "Not Working" (as defined in the following subsection).

- Deactivated – the thing is disabled and forbidden from fulfilling any consumer requests.

    - The thing may still be able to respond to management requests.

Some models for "administrative state" (e.g., ITU-T Recommendation X.731) define a Shutting Down state. This can be used if a thing still has active consumers when a decision has been made to deactivate the thing. While in the Shutting Down state, the thing can still provide service to existing consumers (for a time) but would not be allowed to accept new consumers.

4.4.4.2   *Operational States*

The Operational state gives an indication of how well (or how fully) a thing is functioning. Earlier models of the operational state (e.g., the model in ITU-T Recommendation X.731) only allowed for two values, e.g., enabled (working) and disabled (not working). In a collection of things where relationships among things are based on contracts (see Section 12.3), it is more important to know whether the thing is currently meeting its contract with respect to each consumer.

A discrete operational state variable (such as the one defined below) can provide some information but for complete operational information, one or more continuous measures may be needed (possibly on a per contract basis). For further discussion on measurements, see Section 12.6.

- Working – the thing is completely functioning as intended.

- Meeting All Contracts – the thing is presently meeting all the contracts promised to each of its consumers but is not completely functional.

    - An example would be a thing that when fully operational can support five consumers but presently can only support three consumers. However, the thing currently only has three active consumers, so the thing is fulfilling its contracts.

- Meeting Some Contracts – the thing is meeting only some of its contracts with its consumers

- Meeting No Contracts – the thing is not meeting any of its contracts with its consumers

- Not Working – the thing is completely non-functional.

The Working and "Not Working" states apply even when a thing is not under contract with any consumer.

4.4.4.3   *Relationships between Administrative and Operational States*

If the administrative state of a thing is set to "Deactivated," it cannot provide service to any of its consumers, regardless of the operational state.

If the administrative state of a thing is set to "Activated," it may be able to provide service to its consumers, depending on its operational state.

4.4.5 States within the Retiring Phase

There are several issues to be considered regarding the Retiring phase of a thing:

- While a decision may have been made to retire a given thing, there may also be a requirement to keep the thing operational for consumers that currently have contracts with the thing. No new contracts will be allowed, and once the current contracts expire or are cancelled, the thing can be retired.

- In some cases, retirement may just be a resting place for a thing until it is needed for another purpose.

The following states, within the Retiring phase, are defined for instances of things:

- Discontinued (or Deprecated) – the thing can continue to fulfill existing contracts to consumers but is not allowed to accept any new contracts.
  - The administrative state should still be set to "Activated."

- Halted – there are no contracts associated with the thing, and any new contract is to be rejected.
  - The administrative state should be set to "Deactivated."

- Removed – the thing has been uninstalled from its previous environment.
  - In this state, the thing can still be reinstalled in its previous environment, or ownership can be transferred to another entity.

- Terminated – the thing can no longer be used.
  - However, the components of a compound thing can be reused.

The above pertains to the retiring phase of an instance of a type of thing. Types also have a retiring phase. For example, a clothing company may want to retire a type of overcoat. The first step might be to remove the item from its catalog and at the same time, stop production of new instances of the overcoat. Retailers would continue selling instances until they run out of stock. The factory where the overcoat is made simply switches over to making another type of overcoat. For other types of things (perhaps automobiles), it is possible that the factory would be closed or retooled to make a different model of automobile.

The following states, within the Retiring phase, are defined for types of things:

- Discontinued – no new orders will be accepted for instances of the type, and the type should be removed from all catalogs. Existing orders will, however, be fulfilled.
  - The administrative state for the type should still be set to "Activated."

- Halted – there are no existing orders for instances of the type, and any new orders are to be rejected.
  - The administrative state for the type should be set to "Deactivated."

- The Removed and Terminated states are not applicable to types.

4.5 Example

In the following example, the various phases of a car are represented from various points of view.

The car (call it Car X) is first identified as part of a planning process by the car manufacturer (perhaps as part of a batch of similar cars that meet certain demand predictions). The top-left of Figure 13 shows the phase diagram for Car X from the perspective of the car manufacturer. The car manufacturer plans, builds and then gets Car X into an operating state.

Eventually, Car X is transferred to a car dealer. The phase diagram from the perspective of the car dealer is not too interesting. Within the Operating phase, the car dealer may decide to put the car on the showroom floor and thus, effectively, put Car X into the "Deactivated" Administrative state.

Car X is sold by the car dealer to a customer. From the first owner's point of view, Car X traverses the Operating and then Retiring phases. Within the Operating phase, the car may alternate among various Operational states. The first owner may, at some point, decide to sell Car X and store the car in a garage while it is up for sale. Car X is now in the Retiring phase for the first owner.

Car X is sold to its second owner and goes through similar transitions as it did with the first owner.

At the bottom of the figure is yet another phase diagram which represents the point of view of the Department of Motor Vehicles (DMV). The DMV tracks the car from the time it arrives at the car dealer until it is eventually retired to a junkyard (either for spare parts or to be crushed for disposal and recycling).

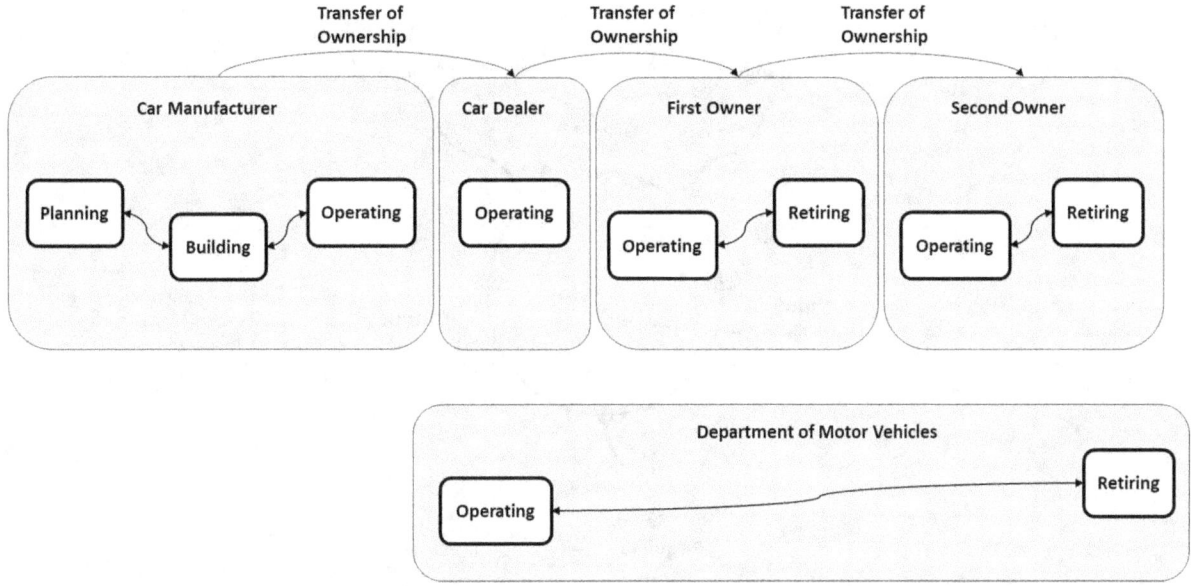

Figure 13. Phases for an Automobile from Different Viewpoints

5 Composition, Aggregation, and Coordination

In this section, a general (externally visible) structure for a thing is defined. This recursive structure is used to facilitate the construction of more complex things from simpler things (components) using composition or aggregation. As used in the document, **Component** is a supporting role played by one thing in relation to another thing.

The section concludes with a discussion of approaches for coordinating the interactions among collections of things.

5.1 External View of a Thing

To combine things for some common purpose (e.g., bricks to form a building, or software objects to build a software system) there needs to be some common conventions and structures for the type of things involved. The common conventions and structures will vary depending on the type of things involved and the intended purpose of the combination (could be achieved by either aggregation or composition). In any case, it is possible to define a very general structure for a thing which can be further specialized as needed.

Figure 14 depicts the general structure of a thing (external view).

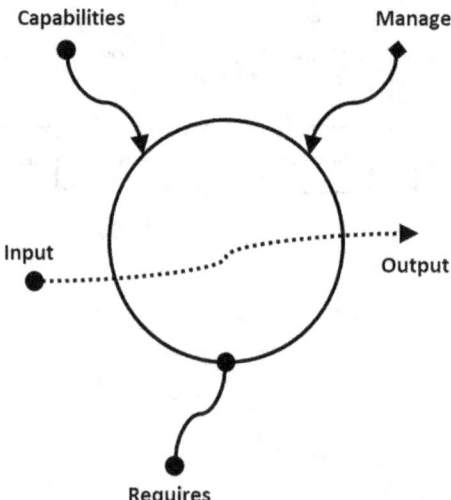

Figure 14. General Structure of a Thing (external view)

The external view of a thing is exposed by the following types of interfaces:

- Capabilities – what the thing offers to other things via a message exchange (e.g., request-reply pattern). The Capabilities interface is based on message exchanges such as electronic messages, voice commands, hand gestures, blinking lights, etc.

- Management (or Manage for short in some of the diagrams that follow) – allows for administration of the thing, e.g., configuration, accounting and usage collection and reporting, assurance management, and control of access right to the capabilities. The Management interface is based on message exchanges.

- Input / Output – a flow that is transformed by a thing. The Input / Output interface is not based on message exchange but rather on streams of things such as data. The entry and exit points from a thing related to a flow are called **ports**. Examples include a firewall acting on a stream of IP packets, a water purifier acting on a stream of water, and an AM/FM radio transforming a radio signal into a stream of sound.

- Requires – what the thing needs from other things to function properly. The Requires interface is based on message exchanges.

The message-based interfaces (i.e., Capabilities, Management and Requires) are comprised of one or more types of **operations** that follow various exchange patterns. Section 12.5 provides further details on message exchange patterns.

Some examples of the external interfaces offered or used by things are shown in Table 2. In some cases, a type of interface is not supported or minimally supported (the associated cell in the table is left blank in such cases).

Table 2. Examples of the External Structural Aspects of Things

Type of Thing	Capabilities	Manage	Input / Output	Requires
Acoustic Guitar	Makes sounds when strings are plucked and (sometimes) pressed against frets	Strings can be tuned via turning of the tuning pegs		Air is required for the sound to travel
Electric Guitar	Sounds produced with actions similar to an acoustic guitar Volume control Tone dial (potentiometer) used to cut-out higher frequencies Whammy bar allows the guitar player to temporarily vary the string tension thereby changing the pitch to create a vibrato, portamento or pitch bend effect	Strings can be tuned via turning of the tuning pegs Since the action of the whammy bar is temporary, it is listed under Capabilities rather than Manage (this is a debatable point)		Air Electricity Speakers

Type of Thing	Capabilities	Manage	Input / Output	Requires
Firewall (telecommunications)	Supports requests to retrieve security threat and attack logs Some of the firewall's capabilities are not accessed via a message exchange but rather through the Input / Output aspect, e.g., detection of a computer worm may trigger a firewall to send packets to a tarpit (to slow the attack)	Various firewall options (e.g., tarpit) can be configured either via a message exchange or in some cases via conditions identified in the traffic flow which could, for example, lead to more stringent traffic monitoring during an attack	Input: traffic flow Output: input flow minus any packets that violate security rules	Power supply Network connectivity
Water Filter			Input: tap water Output: purified water	Pitcher into which the water filter is placed
USB Memory Stick	Supports request to store a file (e.g., via dragging the file with a mouse motion), retrieve a file, delete a file, rename a file	Some USB memory sticks have a write lock which can be toggled On and Off	Input: file being uploaded to a memory stick Output: file being downloaded from memory stick	USB port (e.g., on a laptop computer)
AM/FM Radio (hardware versus app on cell phone or tablet)	Band / channel selection Volume control		Input: radio waves, external audio Output: music, talk, etc. from various radio stations	Batteries or electricity Air to carry the input and output
Dictionary App on Cell Phone or Tablet	Supports requests for word lookup	Ability to install a new version of the app		Underlying OS on which the app runs External dictionary if the app is not self- contained

Variations of the structure shown in Figure 14 are possible. For example, a thing may have several interfaces of a given type (as shown for Thing X in Figure 15). The multiplicity of interfaces allows for the separation of concerns. In other cases, some interface types may be absent for a given type of thing. For example, Thing Y in Figure 15 does not have Input / Output interfaces.

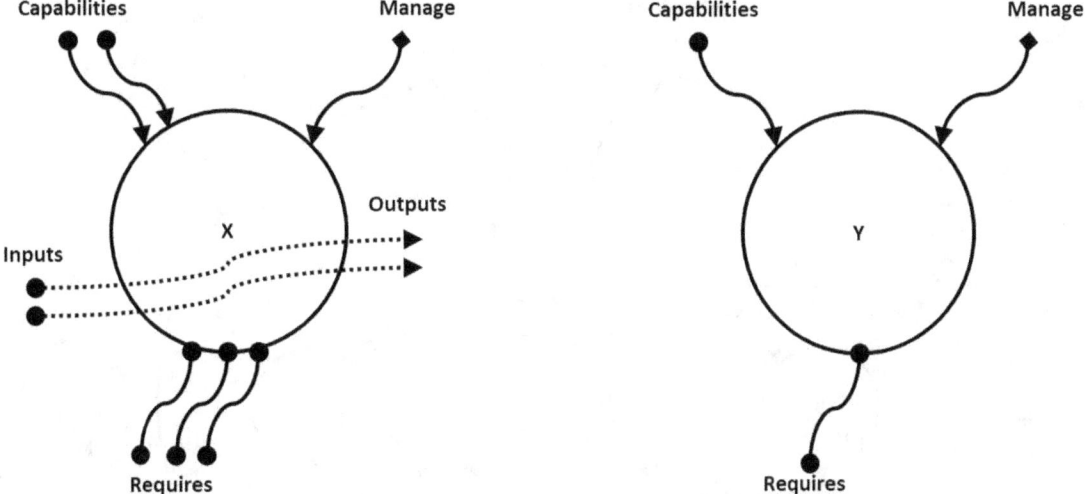

Figure 15. Structural Variations

5.2   Composition

To compose things, it is not sufficient that the things to be composed have a common structure (such as that shown in Figure 14). It is critical to use common interfaces (and associated information models) but even this is not sufficient. The thing offering services to other things must also have sufficient capacity and supply to handle the needs of the things it serves. For example, it doesn't help if an online hardware store supports an electronic ordering interface but does not have in stock the items required by its customers.

Consider the composition example in Figure 16:

- Things B and C are different types of firewalls that check for different issues (perhaps B checks at the IP layer and C checks at the link layer and below, e.g., Ethernet and optical transport). For more information on the layering of information exchange, see the Open Systems Interconnection – Basic Reference Model [6].

- Thing D is a tarpit that B and C use to divert packets during security attacks.

- Thing A coordinates the activities of B, C, and D, and exposes capability and management interfaces externally.

- The thin arrows among the things represent usage relationships. For example, A uses both the capability and management interfaces of B and C. As noted, this is not sufficient. For example, it doesn't help if A can request that B monitor a given input stream, but the stream is at a bit rate higher than what B can monitor. Similarly, it doesn't help if the tarpit capability of D is much smaller than what is required by B and C.

- For this example, assume the internals (in this case, Things A, B, C, and D) of the composite thing (call it the "advanced firewall") are opaque to things external to the composite. This type of hiding or encapsulation of the internals is the basis for an intent-based approach (see Section 12.4 for more details on intent-based interfaces).

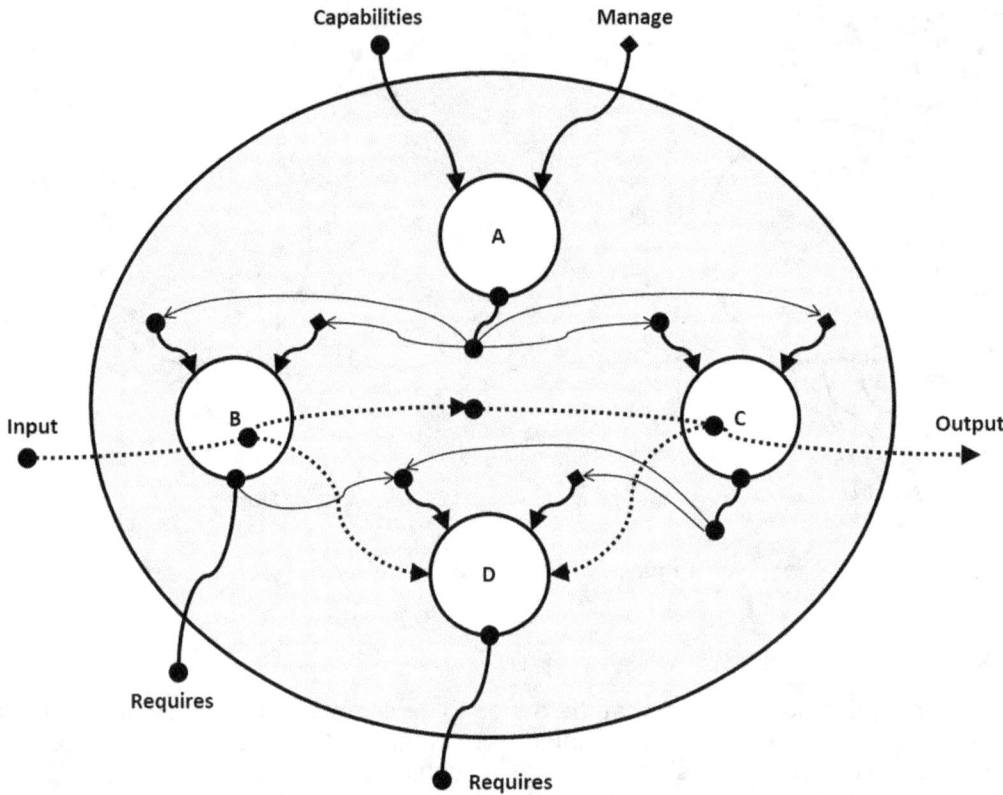

Figure 16. Example of Composition – Advanced Firewall

While the advanced firewall may be a composition (as defined in Section 5.2) during its lifetime, when the advanced firewall is retired, it may be possible to recover components A, B, C or D, and use them in other compositions or aggregations. So, composition and aggregation also depend on the phase of the thing. Another example is an AM/FM radio which is treated as a composite during its lifetime but can be dismantled for spare parts when it is retired (basically an aggregation during its retirement phase).

5.3 Aggregation

The basic requirements for forming aggregations are the same as for composition:

- common interfaces
- common information models
- sufficient capacity and supply of capabilities.

Aggregation is a weaker form of combining things, as described in Section 3.2.2.

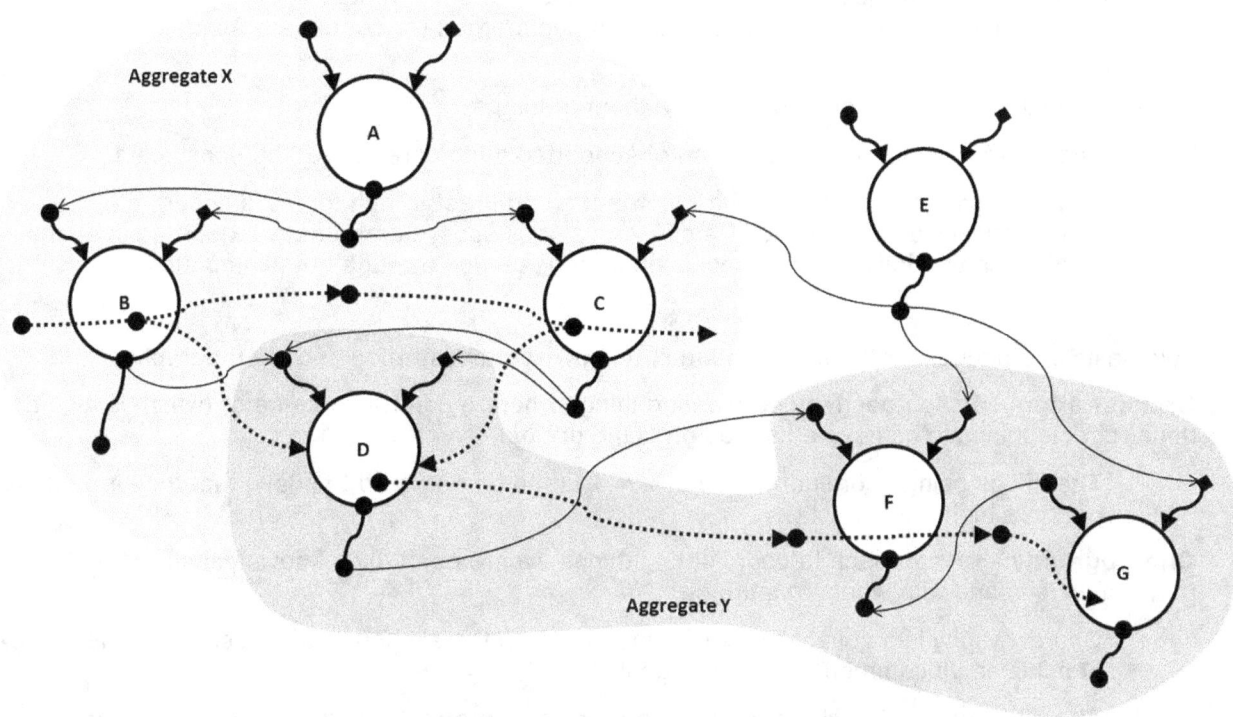

Figure 17. Example of Aggregation

Figure 17 depicts a situation with several aggregations:

- Aggregation X is similar to the advanced firewall in Figure 16.

- Aggregation Y provides further analysis of security attacks and additional tarpit capacity, as needed.

- Thing E knows how to configure firewalls, tarpits, and other security applications.

- Thing D is in X and Y, which would not be possible if either X or Y were compositions.

- Thing D has an internal tarpit and can also do analysis on the packet streams sent to it by Firewalls B and C.

- Thing F is a security attack analysis application. Anything that D cannot handle, it sends along to F. Thing D can forward packets to F (via Input / Output stream) and provide already compiled analysis via the Capabilities interface to F (thin arrow from D's Requires interface to F's Capabilities interface). Thing F uses analysis reports from D as a basis for further analysis.

- Thing G is a tarpit used by F.

5.4   Coordination

5.4.1   Terminology and Concepts

For things to collaborate on a higher-level task, coordination and an associated environment are required. The following terms relate to the coordination of things:

Ecosystem of Things (or just "ecosystem") – a supporting environment within which a collection of things can thrive (function properly), interact and be merged (or coordinated) into more complex things.

- The supporting environment is also a thing or things.

- The environment and the collection of supported things are part of the ecosystem.

- Example ecosystems include the following: a coral reef, a rain forest, a desert, a commercial cloud environment, a city, a business ecosystem (a network of organizations involved in the delivery of a specific product or service through both competition and cooperation).

Two basic approaches for the coordination of things are orchestration and choreography.

Orchestration – an approach to coordinating things where a central coordinator (which is also a thing) directs things to achieve a desired outcome or goal.

- The things being coordinated do not "know" (and do not need to know) that they are taking part in a higher-level activity.

Choreography – an approach to coordinating things, where each thing knows exactly when to perform actions and with whom to interact.

- Choreography is a collaborative effort focusing on the exchange of messages in the context of achieving a common outcome or goal.

- All participants in the choreography need to be aware of the common outcome or goal, actions to perform, communications to exchange, and the timing of communication exchanges.

- Choreography, in contrast to orchestration, does not rely on a central coordinator.

Coordination can occur at several phases regarding a desired outcome or goal. For example, a composer or music arranger creates a plan (a musical score in this case). During the performance of the musical score, the conductor leads the orchestra members. So, in the planning phase, the composer or music arranger is the central coordinator, and in the operating phase (when the music is performed) the conductor is the central coordinator. However, a conductor is unlikely for a chamber orchestra and almost never for a small ensemble. In these cases, choreography would be used of the method of coordination.

In this book, the term **coordination** (or the phrase "outcome-oriented coordination") is used as a more general concept that covers orchestration, choreography or various combination of the two.

Coordination within a composition or aggregation can be based on orchestration, choreography or a mixture of the two approaches.

5.4.2   Unintended Interactions among Components: Functional Aspects

In this set of problems, the composition or aggregation of components causes unintended (as well as undesired) interactions. It is assumed that the components are in the same ecosystem.

5.4.2.1   Undesired Request Sequences

A common unintended dependency among things is a request loop, i.e., a series of requests that eventually circle back to the originator of the initial request. For example, consider a dependency chain such as A → B → C → D → A where → means "depends on" or "makes use of the capabilities offered by" and A, B, C, and D are things in a composition or aggregation. In this example, a request from A to B will eventually get back to A via a request from D.

First, it should be noted that the presence of a loop may not necessarily cause a problem. In this case, nothing needs to be corrected. However, if the looping can potentially cause issues (see Figure 18), the first step would be to isolate the problem. One approach for the detection of loops (or undesired dependencies among things in general) is for the ecosystem's environment to support the tracing of interactions, e.g., via a log of requests between things that can be consulted after the fact to determine loops. Another approach is to embed the traceability information in the requests.

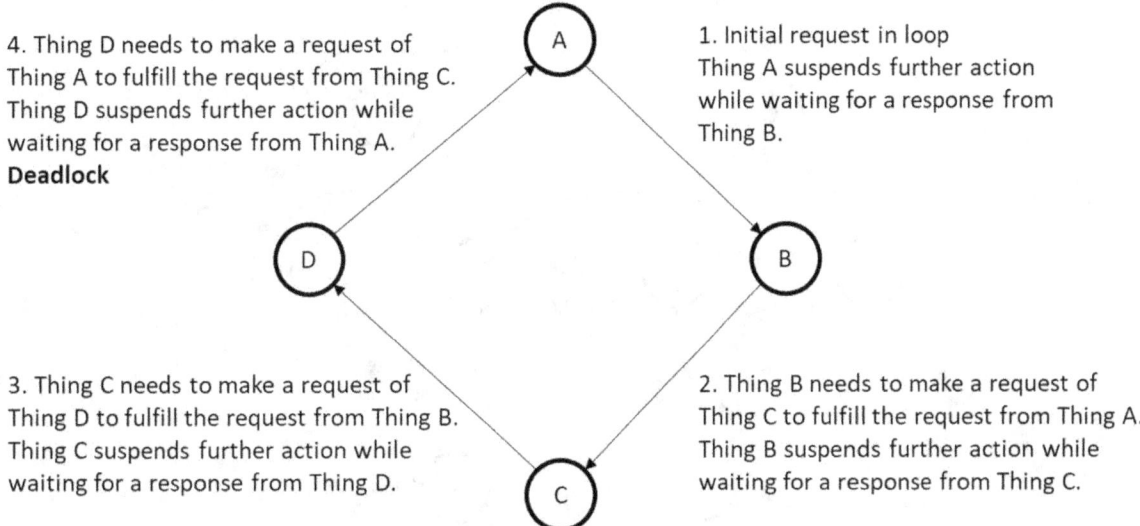

4. Thing D needs to make a request of Thing A to fulfill the request from Thing C. Thing D suspends further action while waiting for a response from Thing A. **Deadlock**

1. Initial request in loop Thing A suspends further action while waiting for a response from Thing B.

3. Thing C needs to make a request of Thing D to fulfill the request from Thing B. Thing C suspends further action while waiting for a response from Thing D.

2. Thing B needs to make a request of Thing C to fulfill the request from Thing A. Thing B suspends further action while waiting for a response from Thing C.

Figure 18. Looping that Results in a Deadlock Condition

In terms of correcting (i.e. eliminating) the loop, there are several options:

Option 1 (Choreographed Request Routing) Each request message would contain a list of the previous requests related to the initial request. In the loop example above, the request from B to C would also show that the request started from A to B. The request from C to D would also show the previous requests, i.e., A → B → C. If D is designed to avoid loops, it would know not to make a request to instance A but rather to another instance of the same type as A.

This approach can be applied to more complex request graphs. Consider the situation shown in Figure 19, with a potential request loop, i.e., C → F → G → C. Assume that the loop is problematic and thus, unwanted. Using Option 1, Thing G knows that the request it received from F followed the path A → B → C → F → G and if G makes a request back to C, a loop will be created. In this case, G would simply find another thing of the same type as C (assumed to be J in the example) and make a request to that thing.

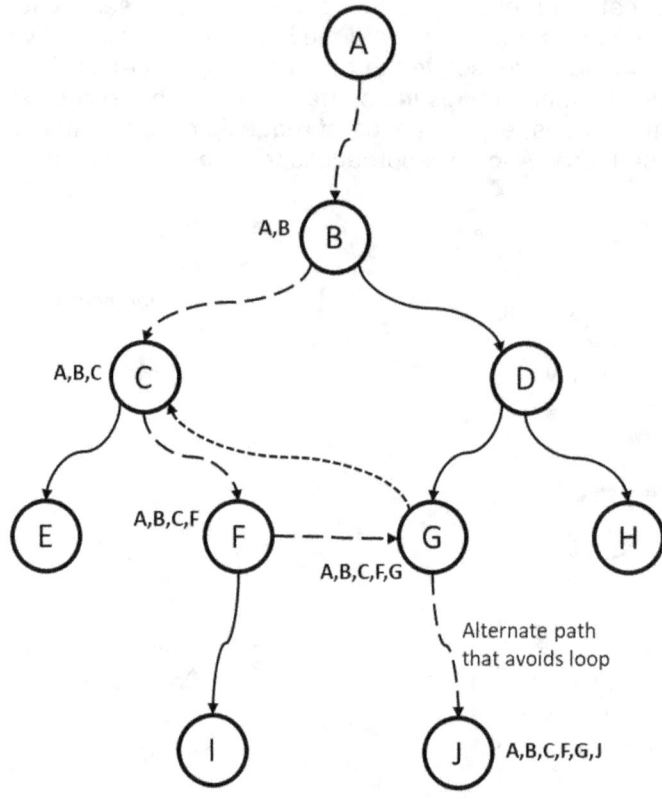

Figure 19. Request Graph with Potential Cycle

Further, this approach may be applied to other undesired request graphs. For example, perhaps it is desired to restrict Figure 19 to a tree structure. (A **tree** is an undirected graph in which any two vertices are connected by exactly one path.) In this case, F would not make a request to G but rather to another thing of the same type of G, thereby preserving a tree structure for the request graph (which is a subgraph of the graph shown in the figure).

Option 1a (Traceability Info Constructed from Request Logs) In this variation of Option 1, the paths of active request sequences are logged rather than carried in the requests. The log is consulted by the various things in a request sequence to help avoid unwanted patterns such as loops.

Option 2 (Orchestrated Request Routing) In this approach, a third-party (an orchestrator) could track and guide request patterns. Consider the example in Figure 18. Each thing would first consult the orchestrator before sending a request. At Step #4, Thing D would consult with the orchestrator before sending its request. The orchestrator would detect the potential loop if the request is sent to Thing A and consequently, direct Thing D to sends its request to another thing (same type as Thing A) to avoid a deadlock situation.

Option 3 (Design-time Approach) One design-time approach is to use type variations to avoid looping or other undesired request patterns. Consider a looping example: A → B → C → D → A. Assume that Thing A is an instance of Type X and Thing D is an instance of Type Y. In this case, one could define a variant of Type X (call it Type X1) and then redesign Type Y so that all instances of the new type use instances of Type X1. This would prevent D from making a request of A (since A is not of type X1).

Another design-time approach would be to make the things in an ecosystem non-blocking, i.e., capable of proceeding with activity (responding to other requests) while waiting for a response to a given request.

Options 1, 1a and 3 assume something of an open environment where the details of various request flows (i.e., instances, their types and the type of requests) are made available to all the things (and their suppliers) involved in the request flow. This may not always be desired. For example, consider an application ecosystem where the application suppliers **do** want their applications to be used by others but **do not** want to give away the details of the applications. Consider the example depicted in Figure 19. Assume the things are software applications (each from a different supplier) and the suppliers do not want to share the details of their implementations in the sense that they don't want their potential competitors to know what other things and associated operations they use in support of their application. In this case, Options 1, 1a and 3 would not work since these approaches reveal the details of the request flows. For example, after several iterations of a request from Thing A to Thing B (or thing of the same type as B), Thing J could eventually figure out that Thing A use Thing B (or more precisely, uses instances of the same type as B), Thing B uses things of the same type as Thing G and Thing H, and so on. However, Option 2 (if performed by a trusted third-party) would protect the various suppliers from revealing their usage requirements. With Option 2, a thing would only have knowledge of one level downstream (things and associated operations that it uses) and one level upstream (things that use it).

5.4.2.2 Deadlock and Livelock

Deadlock and livelock are two well-known examples of unintended consequences that can occur among things that were designed separately and then put together in a common environment.

Deadlock is a situation in which each thing in a group is waiting for some other thing to act (such as sending a message or more commonly releasing a lock) before proceeding.

The Wikipedia article on Deadlock [6] describes techniques for detecting and resolving deadlocks.

Livelock is a situation in which each thing in a group takes ineffective action based on the observed actions of other things in the group. For example, consider two people approaching each other on the street and each moving back and forth to get out of the way of the other, with neither person moving forward.

5.4.2.3 Version Compatibility Issues

To verify that an instance of a given type can interact with (i.e., make use of the offered capabilities of) an instance of another type, it may be necessary to also verify the versions of the types supported by the respective instances. For example, an instance of Type A (v1) may work fine with an instance of Type B (v2) but not with any instances of Type B (v3).

To resolve version mismatch issues, several elements are needed to mitigate the problem:

- Accurate type definitions need to be maintained in a repository and imposed on associated instances. So, if instances of Type A (v1) work fine with instances of Type B (v2) but not with instances of Type B (v3), this needs to be reflected in the associated type definitions. Instances of Type A (v1) need to be designed to only use instances of Type B (v2).

- Further, it would be helpful if all the components in an ecosystem followed the same set of rules for backward and forward compatibility. This topic is covered further in Section 12.1.

5.4.2.4   Conflicting Interactions

It is possible for multiple consumers of a thing to make conflicting requests. In the world of telephony, there is a similar problem (known as "feature interactions") among supplementary services (call waiting and "forwarding to voicemail" interactions).

Figure 20 shows a situation where several submitters (contributors) to an online dictionary are making conflicting definitions for a new term. To resolve such situations, the online dictionary could be designed to log multiple entries when there is a conflict, and on some regular basis, prepare an automated report of terms whose definitions need to be evaluated by a team of experts.

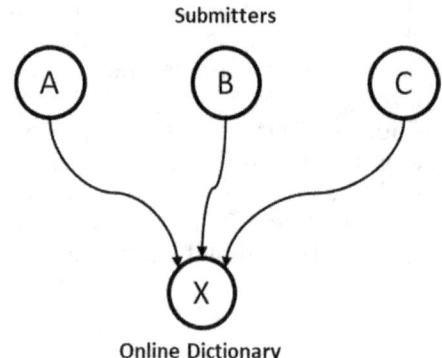

Figure 20. Conflicting Additions to an Online Dictionary

For such problems, the first line of attack is to define the behavior of a thing to detect conflicting requests and act accordingly, e.g., reject requests that cause conflicts. This is a bit limiting since the potential conflicts need to be known when the type is being designed. As new conflicts are discovered, the type can be updated to a new version that is able to handle the conflicts. This only partially solves the problem since it may be difficult to update existing instances to support the new type version. A more flexible solution is to use policy management. As new conflicts are discovered, additional policies can be added (without the need to create new versions of the types involved in the issue). Of course, the types and associated instances would need to be "policy enabled" (i.e., the capability of interacting with a policy management agent). See Section 12.2 for more details on policy management and other behavior adjustment techniques.

5.4.3   Unintended Interactions among Components: Non-functional Aspects

The scenarios in this section are similar to those in Section 5.4.2, except that the conflict is with regard to supply, capacity, latency, resiliency and other non-functional characteristics.

5.4.3.1   Capacity Problems

While a collection of interacting things may match-up fine from a functional standpoint, there can be non-functional issues that compromise the interactions. For example, consider the case where A → X, B→ X and C → X are fine functionally (where → means "depends on the capabilities offered by"), but in terms of capacity, X is overbooked and cannot satisfy the demands of A, B and C at the same time.

The basic solution entails the enforcement of well-defined contracts among interacting participants. For the example above, a well-defined contract may cause X to reject a request from C, if X is already at capacity while serving requests from A and B. The rejection could entail some sort of compensation to C in keeping with a previously agreed contract. Alternately, it may be that C has agreed to a higher level of service from X than that provided to A or B. So, when C makes a request to X, lower priority requests (in the process of being fulfilled) could be delayed or rejected, or resources could even be deallocated from A or B and then reassigned to C.

Contracts are discussed further in Section 12.3.

5.4.3.2   Latency Problems

There can be latency issues among a collection of interacting things that are otherwise fine from a functional matching point of view. The latency issues can be due to the location of the things in a composition or aggregation. Excess latency can also be caused by the added processing time when a request by one thing (the initiator of some interaction) is handled by too many intermediate things in transit from the initiator to the ultimate receiver of the request.

Well-defined contracts are the first line of defense here.

5.4.3.3   Resiliency Problems

Resiliency issues present another type of non-functional issue.

Consider Aggregation G shown on the left-hand side of Figure 21. The intention is for the Aggregation G to be fully redundant beyond the initial entry point (Thing Z). The primary flow is Z → A → B → C → X and the backup is Z → D → E → F → X. Having X in both flows compromises the redundancy arrangement. This could possibly happen if the sets { A, B, C } and { D, E, F } are managed by different agents.

Even harder to detect and correct is the situation shown on the right-hand side of Figure 21. From the point of view of Aggregate H, the two paths are redundant within the aggregate (shaded region) and exit the aggregate on distinct paths to Things R and S. Usage of Thing X by Things R and S takes place outside of the aggregate's view. Further, Thing R may know nothing about Thing S and vice versa. So, telling Thing R (or Thing S) that redundancy is required may not help. A broader view of the situation is required to solve the problem.

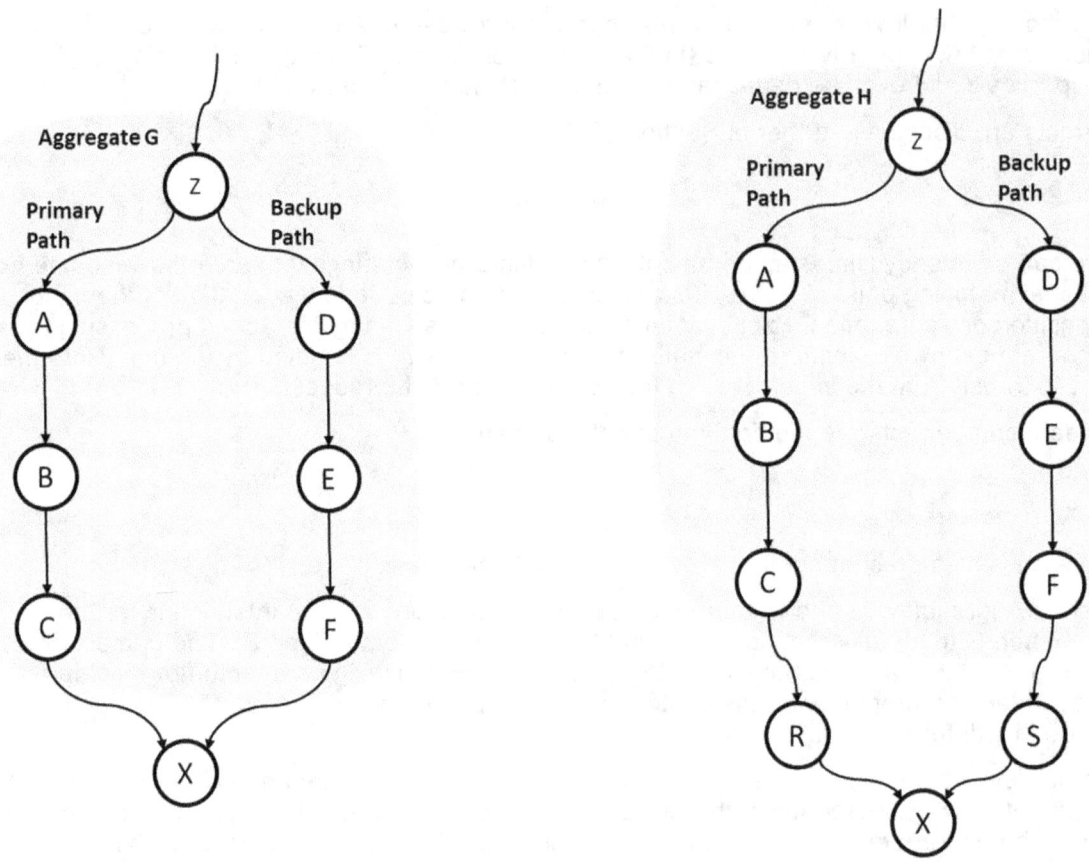

Figure 21. Failed Attempt at Redundant Paths

Another example might be someone (Mr. Marino) going to two different financial experts to get advice about forming a business. Mr. Marino is hoping to compare the responses and then decide about how to form his new business. However, unknown to Mr. Marino, the financial advisors both make use of the same attorney for legal advice and withhold their client's name when communicating with the attorneys. This results in Mr. Marino getting almost the same legal advice from both financial advisors (at least partially defeating the purpose of going to two financial advisors).

The above resiliency problems require some sort of tracing to detect the issue. While this is not necessarily a loop detection and resolution issue, the techniques in Section 5.4.2.1 still apply here (but with some modifications).

In other cases, resiliency can be guaranteed via a contract offered by one thing (provider) to another (consumer). This could be an intent-based contract where the provider takes care of the details (see Section 12.4 for more on intent-based approaches). In this case, the consumer may only be told, for example, that their access to some capability is guaranteed to be available 99.9999% of the time and if not, there is some compensation to be paid back to the consumer. In other cases, resiliency can be coordinated by the consumer using affinity and anti-affinity rules. An example of an affinity rule would be a request to place virtual machines A and B on different computing platforms which are at different physical locations (to address resiliency issues). An example anti-affinity rule would be to require that both virtual machines be on the same compute node (perhaps to reduce latency). Affinity and anti-affinity rules are common in various open source computing platforms such as OpenStack®. Affinity and anti-affinity rules are also used in network virtualization standards such as Network Functions Virtualization (NFV), see European Telecommunications Standards Institute (ETSI) standard ETSI GS NFV-IFA 010 [8].

5.4.4 Business, Financial and Governments Issues

There can be business and financial related issues when combining components.

Licensing (and associated payments) is an issue in application ecosystems (e.g., NFV in the telecommunications industry). The expiration of a license for a common component (e.g., a security authentication application) could halt many other things that incorporate or make use of that component. Thus, license management should be a major concern in an ecosystem. The topic of license management is discussed further in Section 11.6.

Another issue concerns the unintended crossing of geographic, administrative or legal boundaries regarding the components in a composition or aggregation. For example, consider an aggregation with the following dependencies among the components: A → B → C → D → E where there is a mandate to have all the components within one domain (e.g., a given country), which is the case for A, B, C and D, but perhaps E is in another domain and that goes undetected. This could be an issue if the aggregation is, for example, a government agency that requires all the components and associated data be located internal to the country. This type of problem can be detected by request tracing and the examination of appropriate characteristics concerning the things involved (in this case, the "location" characteristic). Such problems can be prevented from reoccurring by either changing the behavior of the things involved (e.g., by creating an updated version of an application that has sufficient intelligence to avoid boundary issues) or by assigning policies that must be followed.

6   Platforms and Domains

This section covers environments (referred to as "platforms") that facilitate interactions among a collection of things within a domain of interest.

6.1   Terminology

For things to interact and to be combined into more complex things, a common environment is needed. The environment must include a medium for communications. The environment may also include common things to facilitate interactions among the things in the environment (e.g., a brokerage or matching service, authentication, and capacity management of underlying resources such as compute and storage in the case of digital environments). The common things are referred to as being native to the environment.

In Section 5.4, the concept of an ecosystem of things was defined. In this section, the related concept of a platform is discussed. A platform (or several platforms) can be part of the supporting environment for an ecosystem. However, an ecosystem can exist without any platforms. While ecosystems can entail natural collections of things such a coral reef, platforms are typically created by humans and usually involve inanimate things such as software applications. Some exceptions to the above statement include termite mounds, underground ant colonies, and beaver dams.

Platform – a supporting environment for a collection of things.

A platform serves as an agent for one or more aspects of the things in its environment. It is possible for different aspects of a thing to be managed by several platforms.

A platform is not to be confused with the concepts of composition and aggregation. A platform supports many combinations of things for various purposes and allows for things to be included in or removed from its environment. On the other hand, composition or aggregation is more of a fixed arrangement of things for a single purpose. A platform can support many compositions and aggregations.

Closely related to the platform concept is the concept of a domain. Informally, a domain or set of domains defines the scope or coverage of a platform. In *Domains: A Framework for Structuring Management Policy* [9], the following definition of domain is given:

> A domain is an object which represents a collection of objects which have been explicitly grouped together to apply a common management policy.

In this book, a variation of the above definition is used.

A **domain** is a collection of things that are grouped together under a common set of policies.

6.2   Concepts

6.2.1   Platform-based Business

A related concept to "platform" is a platform-based business, which is defined in Platform Revolution [10]:

> A platform is a business, based on enabling value-creating interactions between external producers and consumers. The platform provides an open, participative infrastructure for these interactions and sets governance conditions for them. The platform's overarching purpose: to consummate matches among users and facilitate the exchange of goods, services, or social currency, thereby enabling value creation for all participants.

A platform business model is a collective where the members of the collective provide value (e.g., car rides, rental rooms, merchandise, video content) and the platform owner or caretaker facilitates matching between the providers (i.e., collective members) and consumers. The platform owner does not typically provide the items that are sold or rented to the consumers. It is possible, however, for the collective members to also be consumers. This model differs a pipeline (or linear) business model where the business owner providers the things of value that are sold or rented to consumers.

Some additional reading on the topic of business platform models can be found in the references [11], [12] and [13]. There is a wealth of information on platform-based businesses on the website of Innovation Tactics [14].

6.2.2   Criteria for Domain Selection

Domains can be based on many different criteria. The following is a non-exhaustive list of such criteria:

- geographic, e.g., weather stations in a geographic basin or valley
- governmental/legal boundaries, e.g., residential properties in a tax-levying area such as a county
- administrative boundaries, e.g., assets in an administrative region as defined by a given business
- type of thing or category of things (i.e., collection of similar types of things)
- management function, e.g., assurance, lifecycle management, security
    - This criterion would typically be used with several other criteria, e.g., an assurance domain for various types of telecommunications network equipment.

A domain can be based on multiple criteria. For example, consider a domain of parking meters (a type of thing) in a given region (e.g., a set of blocks in a city) that are group together for the purpose of collecting electronic payment information. The region is defined by the company that collects the payment information.

Other factors that can limit or impact the scope of a domain include the following:

- Latency, e.g., the region covered by a cell tower and associated equipment may be limited by latency issues. In this example, the collection of things (cell phones) in the domain is constantly changing.
- Capacity, e.g., a platform (automated or manual) may only be able to handle so many things which, in turn, limits the size of the domain.

6.2.3   Platform – Domain Relationships

A platform facilitates a desired outcome or set of outcomes on one or more things within a domain. This is essentially an intent-based statement that relates the concepts of "platform" and "domain." A platform represents a governance boundary for the management of a set of things. The set of things is defined by one or more domains.

In some cases, a domain is mandated and the associated platform needs to adapt to the domain. For example, consider the domain consisting of the set of residential properties in a county, and the platform that handles property tax billing and collection for the county. The platform must be able to cover the given domain as properties are added and replaced. Further, it may possible for the platform instance to cover several counties, if proprietary information can be segregated per county and the platform is sufficiently flexible to handle multiple billing and collection processes (which may vary per county).

In other cases, the platform may put restrictions on the size of a domain. For example, a cloud computing and storage platform may be designed to handle a given load of processing and thus needs to be replicated to handle large loads. In this example, the domain is not a discrete number of things but rather defined by the processing capacity of the platform. The things, in this case, are "processing workloads" of many different sizes.

6.2.4 Examples

The examples in this section are meant to further illustrate the relationship between platforms and domains. Various drawing styles are used to emphasize different points.

In Figure 22, Platform Z facilitates interactions among the things in Domain X and (separately) facilitates interactions among the things in Domain Y. If allowed by governance rules, Platform Z could also facilitate cross-domain interactions.

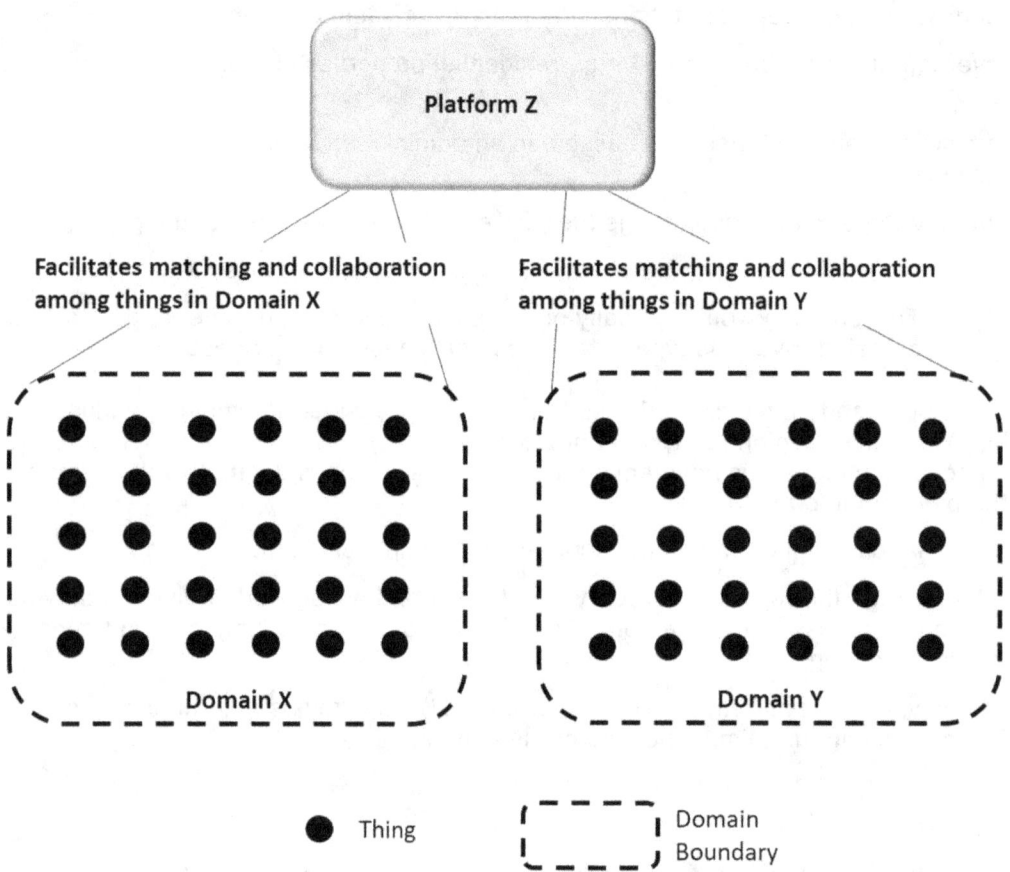

Figure 22. Platform Covering Several Domains

Figure 23 is an alternate representation of the situation shown in Figure 22. In this drawing style, the domains covered by a platform are shown as being within the platform. This style is used in the subsequent sections of this document where the things managed by a platform are shown as being within the platform (see, for example, Figure 28 and Figure 29).

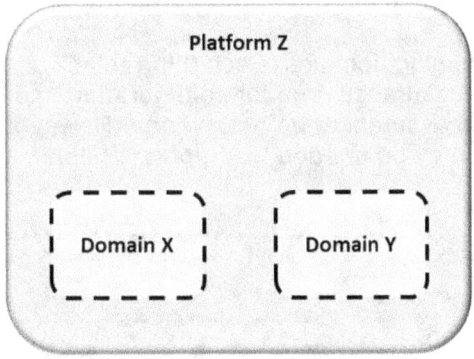

Figure 23. Alternate Depiction of a Platform Covering Several Domains

Yet another way of representing the relationship between platforms and domains is shown in Figure 24. The scenario is taken from the telecommunications industry. In this scenario, there are three network segments each of which is represented by a domain. For each domain, the figure shows what platforms facilitate interactions within the domain.

- There is a separate platform for assurance in each domain, i.e., Platform A for the Radio Access Network (RAN) Domain, Platform B for the Backhaul Network Domain and Platform C for the Core Network Domain.

- In the case of configuration, Platform D covers the RAN and Backhaul Network Domains, and Platform E covers the Core Network Domain.

- For inventory, a single platform (i.e., Platform F) covers all three domains.

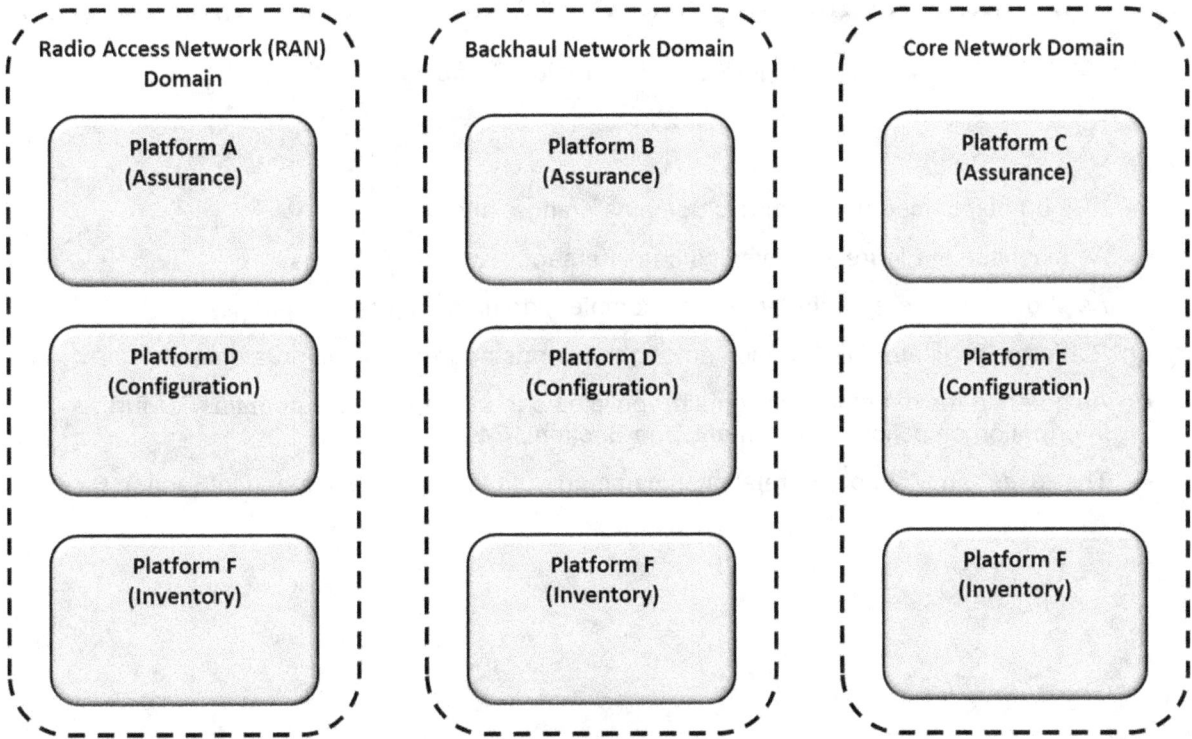

Figure 24. Network Management Example of Domains and Platforms

Figure 25 shows several overlapping domains. Each thing (black circles in the diagram) is in exactly three domains (one for assurance, one for configuration and one for security). In the figure, domains of the same type (e.g., assurance) do not overlap. However, it is possible for domains of the same type to overlap. This may be needed to support resiliency via redundancy.

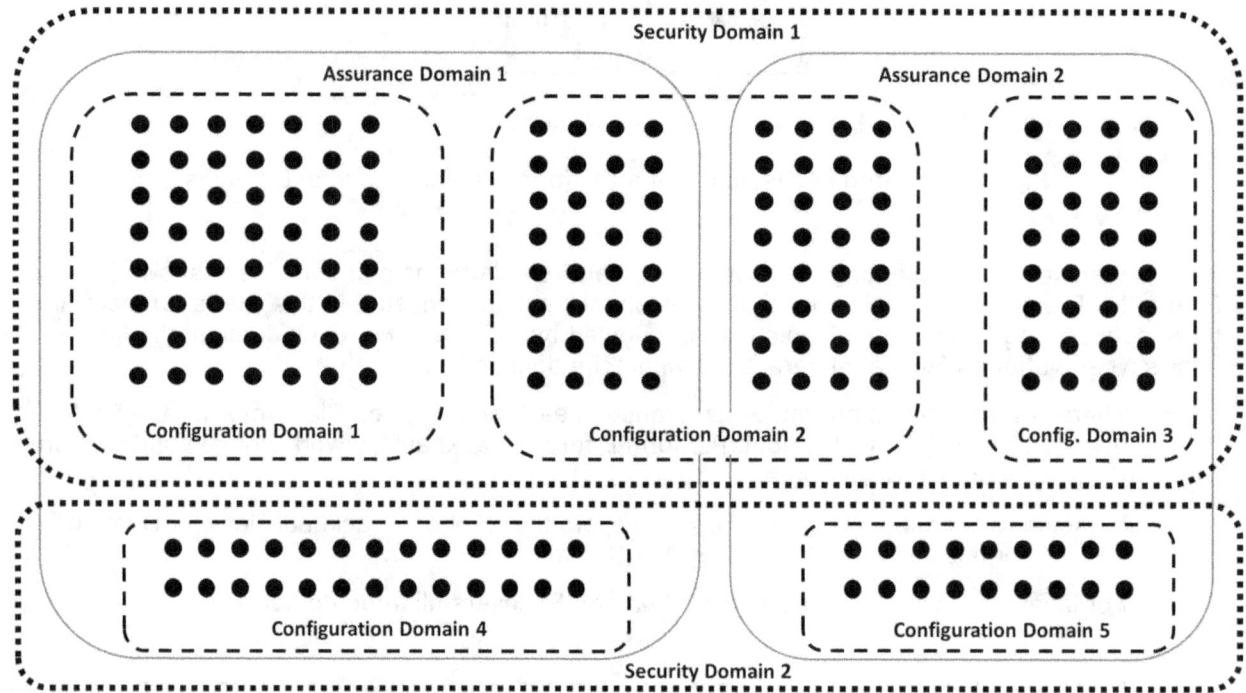

Figure 25. Overlapping Domains

6.2.5 Object Model

Figure 26 is an object model that relates domains, things, and platforms.

- As exhibited in Figure 25, domains can intersect.
- As shown in several of the previous examples, domains aggregate things.
- Platforms facilitate collaboration among the things aggregated within a domain.
- As noted in the definition of "domain," policies can be applied to a domain. For further information on policy management, see Section 12.2.4.
- The "uses" and "supports" relationships among platforms are explained in Section 6.4.

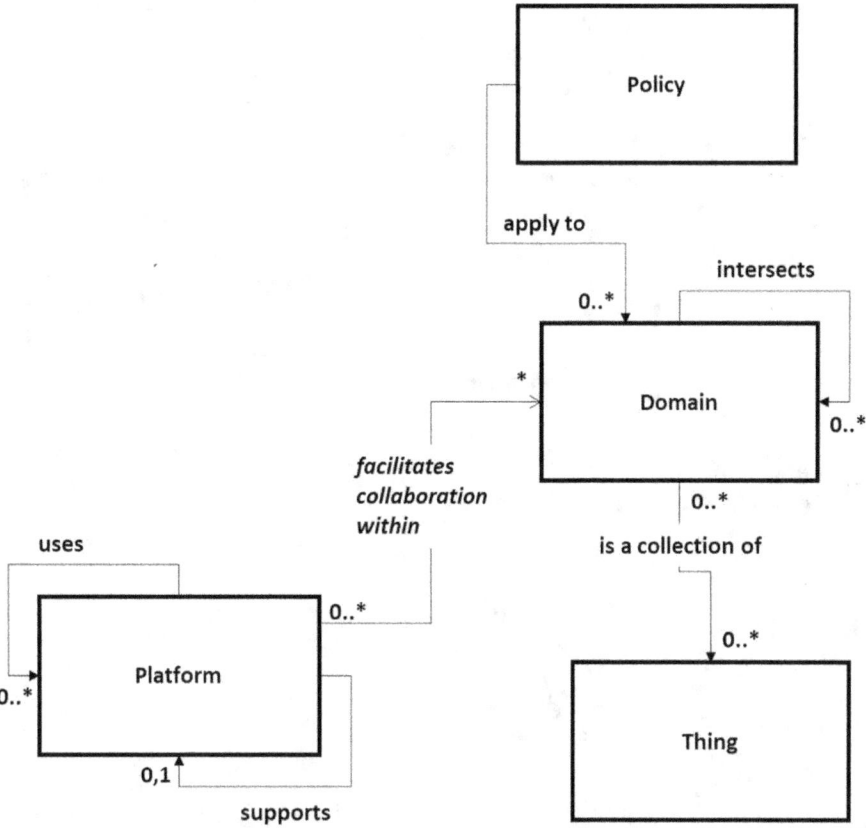

Figure 26. Object Model Relating Platforms, Domains, and Things

6.3 Platform Structure

6.3.1 External View

A platform is a thing and as such inherits the general structure of a thing (as defined in Figure 14). Figure 27 is a specialization of the general thing structure as applied to platforms. The only difference is that the Management interface is split into two types of interfaces.

- Capabilities Management – an interface (or interfaces) to manage the external capabilities offered by the platform. Capabilities management is focused on consumers of a platform.

- Platform Management – an interface (or interfaces) to manage the platform environment and native capabilities. Platform management is also used to control access rights to capabilities management, i.e., set access rights for consumers of capabilities management. Capabilities management, in turn, is used to set access rights for consumers of the platform's externally offered capabilities. This separation is in keeping with security requirement "Sc_R5: Assign Minimum Privileges" in Section 11.8.1.

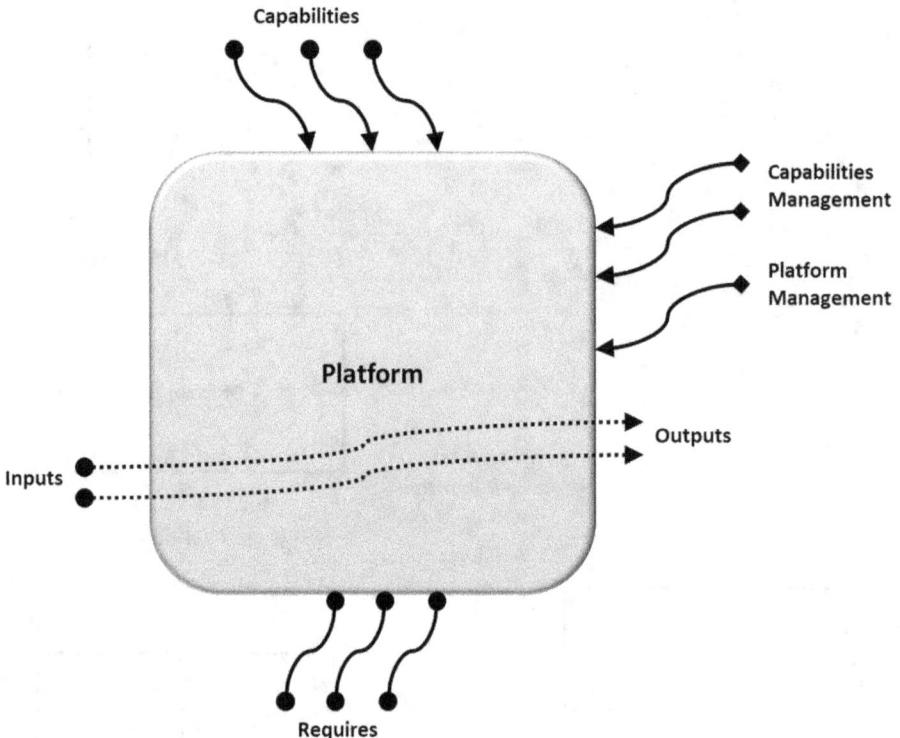

Figure 27. External View of a Platform

The separation between capabilities and platform management is mainly motivated by security concerns. Capabilities management is offered to external consumers of a platform while platform management is offered to entities representing the owner (or perhaps caretaker) of a platform.

6.3.2 Internal View

An example internal view of a platform is shown in Figure 28. The things that provide the native capabilities of the platform are shown in the box at the bottom of the diagram (Broker, Security and Capacity Management). It is possible for some of the native capabilities to be offered external to the platform, but their main purpose is to support the other things in the platform (A, B, C and D in this example).

If a given non-native thing proves to be generally useful, the platform owner could decide to recast the thing as a native capability of the platform. If the non-native thing comes from a third party, then the platform owner will need to negotiate with the third party concerning a licensing agreement.

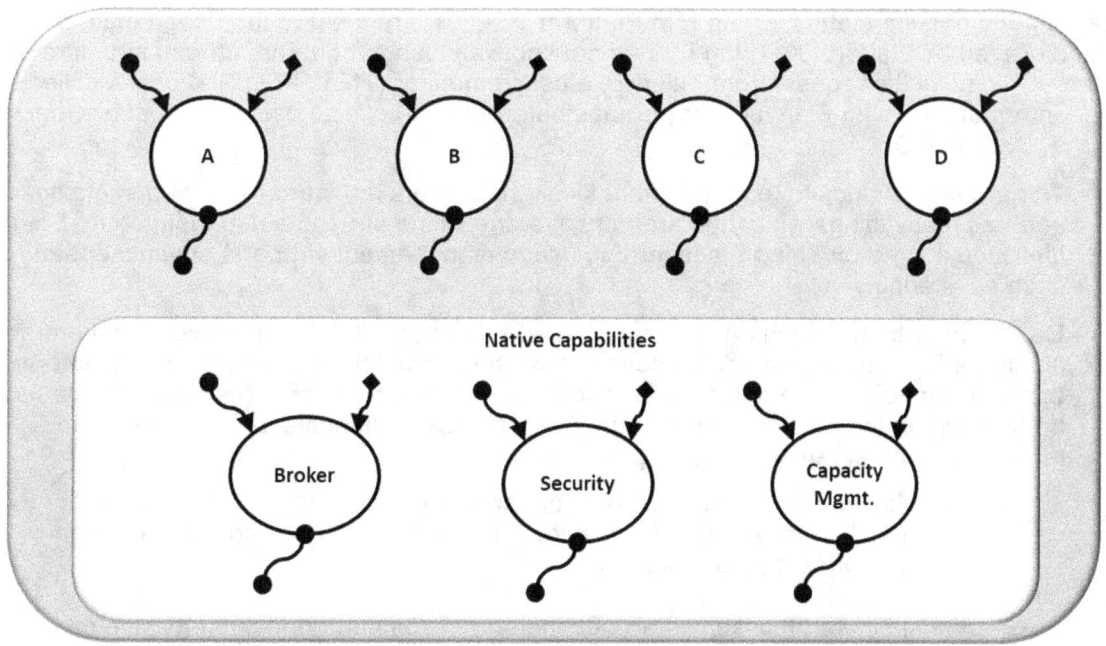

Figure 28. Internal View of a Platform

Figure 29 depicts a usage (accounting) management example.

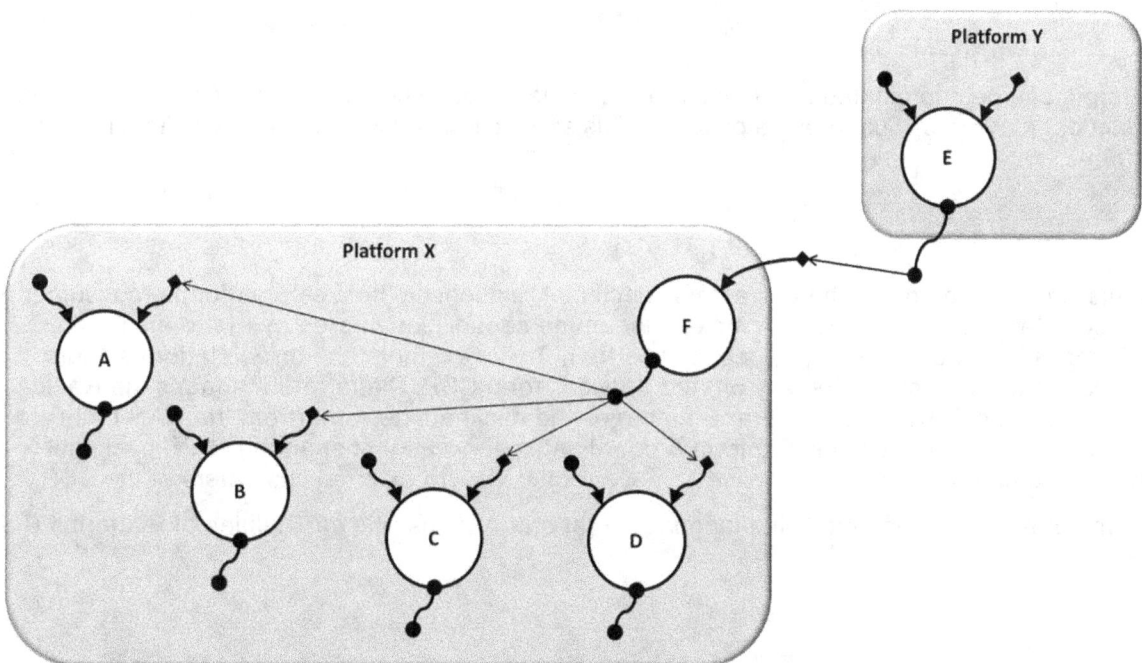

Figure 29. Usage Management Example

Platform X monitors the amount of money in wireless-equipped parking meters, and Platform Y is an accounting system for the local municipality. When it wants to collect usage information concerning the parking meters, Thing E in Platform Y sends a request to the usage management interface offered by Platform X. Thing E does not know anything about the internal structure of Platform X. To fulfill the request from Thing E, a usage monitor (Thing F) in Platform X collects the needed information. Thing F, in turn (or perhaps beforehand), collects using information from Things A, B, C, and D.

- Thing B is a composite (e.g., payment kiosk that covers an entire block of parking spaces) and has many things within the area of coverage which are subject to monitoring. So, the interface offered by Thing B concerning usage management supports advanced features such as filtering.

- On the other hand, Things A, C, and D are atomic in that they each serve as a meter for a single parking space. It is recommended that the usage interface offered by the internal things in Platform X (Things A, B, C, and D) be based on a subset (perhaps "profile" is a better term) of the usage interface offered by Thing F to things external to Platform X. This leads to a general requirement for platforms:

  - **Pf_R1**: Regarding a specific type of capability (e.g., usage or inventory), the things within a platform should offer a subset (or profile) of the associated external interface offered by the platform.

While the example in Figure 29 assumes an automated environment, one can envision other situations. For example, Platform X could be a warehouse with parts for various household appliances, where the area of interest is inventory management. Assume Thing F, in this scenario, is an inventory manager (a person – not an application). Further, Thing B is a person that oversees some portion of the warehouse. Platform Y could be an appliance repair company and Thing E could be an employee of Platform Y who wants to determine if Platform X has in stock a list of needed parts.

6.4   Platform Relationships

Platforms can be coordinated to provide more complex capabilities beyond that which any of the constituent platforms could provide by itself. This subsection covers ways for coordinating platforms.

6.4.1   Hierarchical

In a hierarchical approach, there is a one-directional relationship between platforms (consumer and producer). In Figure 30, Platform A makes use of the capabilities offered by Platforms B and C. Platforms B and C do not use any capabilities from A. For example, the three platforms might manage the network and externally offered services for a CSP. Platform B manages the Radio Access Network (RAN), and Platform C manages the backhaul network (from the RAN to the core network) and the core network. Platform A coordinates services that span the RAN, backhaul network and core network, and provides an abstracted view to external customers of the CSP.

In terms of an information modeling language, Platform A "uses" the capabilities of Platforms B and C.

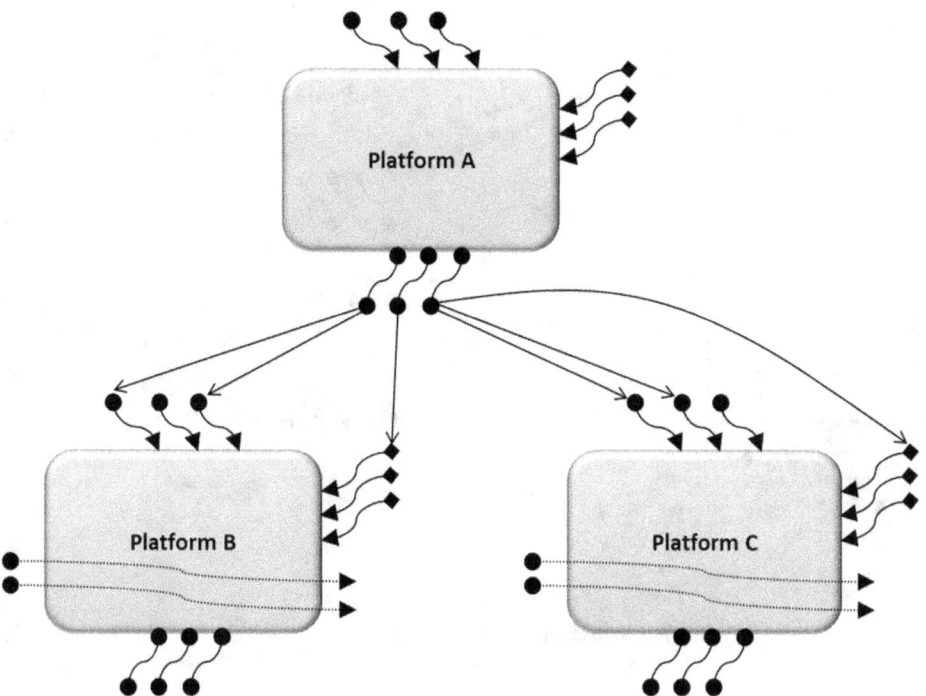

Figure 30. Example Hierarchical Relationship Among Platforms

Figure 31 is a continuation and expansion of the previous example, with a focus on Platform B and the platforms that it uses. Platform B manages Cell Tower Platforms X, Y and Z, and Things D, E, and F.

The cell tower platforms are mostly hardware (e.g., the tower itself, cell antennae, power supply, equipment to transcode the cell signals and place them onto the backhaul network). So, platforms are not just software entities.

Further, Platform B may also manage things directly (D, E, and F in this case). For Things D, E and F could be cell tower repair units (people, trucks, etc.). So, not everything needs to be within the confines of a platform.

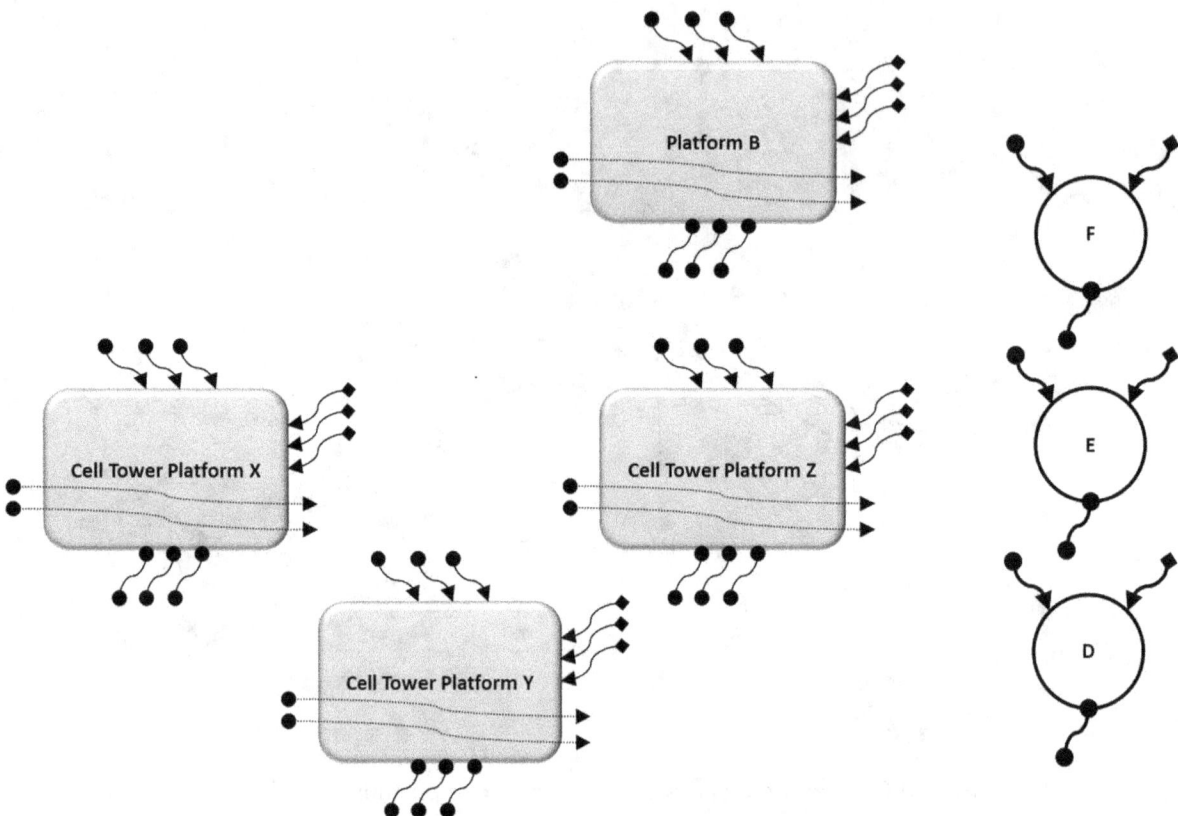

Figure 31. Radio Access Network (RAN) Example

6.4.2 Peer-to-Peer

Two platforms are said to be "peer-to-peer" (or just "peers") if they use each other's capabilities. In Figure 32, Platform B makes use of the capabilities of Platform C and vice versa. For example, Platforms B and C could be B2B gateways between two companies.

In terms of the information modeling language in Figure 26, Platform B "uses" the capabilities of Platform C and vice versa.

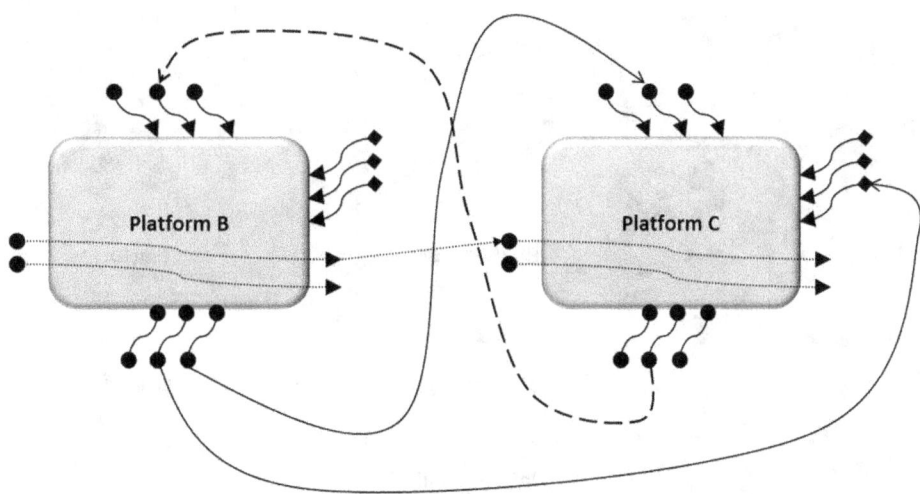

Figure 32. Example Peer-to-Peer Relationship Between Platforms

6.4.3 Hosting

Hosting is another form of platform relationship. In this arrangement, one platform (the host) supports several other platforms in its environment. In Figure 33, Platform Z serves as a host for Platforms A, B, and C. Platform Z could be a commercial cloud platform that provides basic storage, compute and network, and has no knowledge of the capabilities provided by Platforms A, B and C. Platforms A, B and C could be as described in the example associated with Figure 30.

In terms of information modeling language in Figure 26, Platform Z "supports" Platforms A, B, and C.

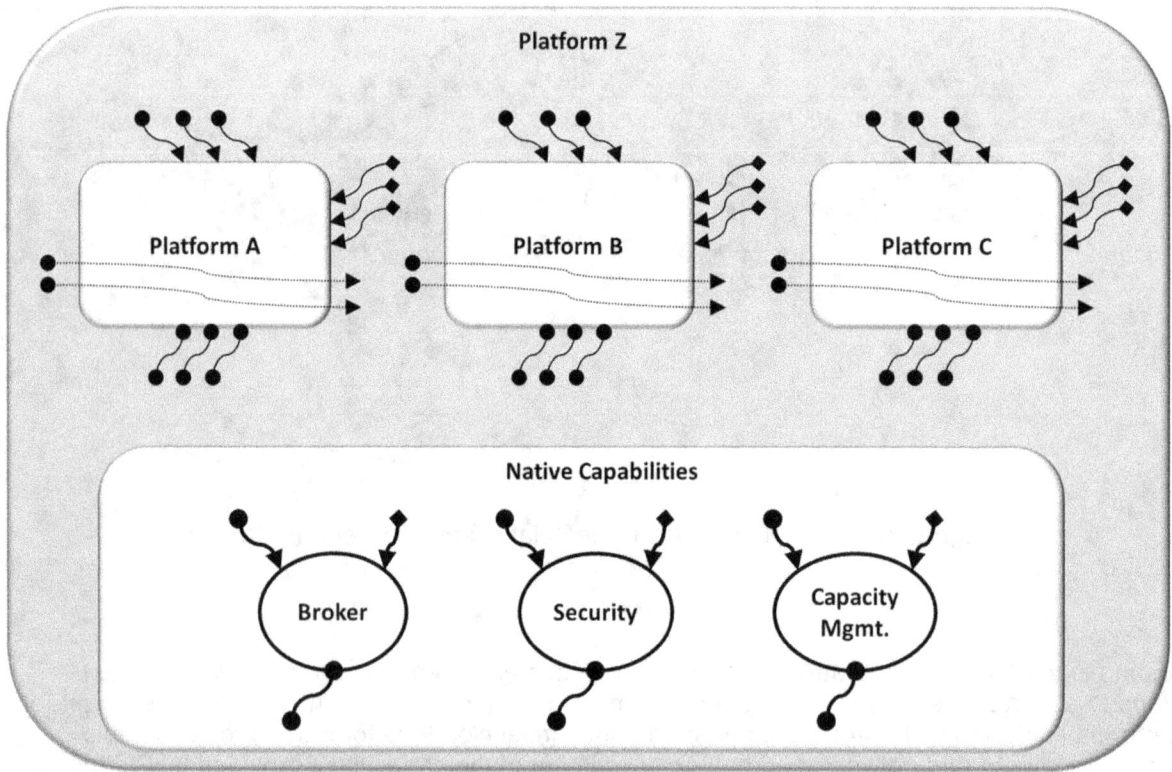

Figure 33. Example of a Platform Hosting Several Other Platforms

6.4.4 Anti-layering

While the need for a hierarchy of platforms is recognized (as noted in Section 6.4.1), it recommended that platforms and things in general **not** be put into layers. The use of layering is a common mistake in the management of things, leading to several significant problems:

- Defining a classification scheme is always difficult and can lead to more discussion about where to place something than it's worth. It is better to describe the characteristics of a thing in detail and group things, as needed, based on common characteristics.

- In digital environments, layers usually imply associated information models and interfaces (e.g., inventory management, catalog management, configuration). This can lead to unnecessary replication of information models and interfaces, where the only difference is the name of the layer being extensively inserted in various information model and interface artifacts while being otherwise the same. One generic interface and associated operations will do (in most cases) for a given management area such as inventory. It is inefficient and disadvantageous to have a different inventory interface for each layer.

- In the case of a model-driven approach (see Section 7.2), it is helpful (perhaps necessary) to use common patterns across all things in a given ecosystem. So, the creation of separate patterns per classification layer (where, as noted, the differences per layer are superficial) is effectively an anti-pattern. Rather, it is recommended to base the interactions among things on open interfaces. A key point here is that classification/layering focuses on strict relationships among things rather than the exposed capabilities of each thing.

For the reasons given above, the following recommendation is stated:

Pf_R2: It is recommended not to classify platforms into layers but rather focus on the capabilities offered by each platform.

The lack of layering does not prevent deep dependency relationships among things. Figure 34 shows a collection of related platforms, without the use of layering. The arrows in the figure show dependency (usage) relationships among the platforms. Further, it is assumed the platforms are within a given organization (e.g., a CSP, Smart Grid provider or any company that has a significant infrastructure upon which more advanced capabilities are composed and then sold to customers).

- The platforms at the bottom of the figure are focused on the infrastructure (they either directly encompass the infrastructure itself or are an abstraction that represents the infrastructure, e.g., an object model). For these platforms, the level of abstraction is low. These platforms tend to have a focus on a single domain, e.g., geographic, technology, legal or some combination of the previous restrictions.

- Moving up, the platforms take more of a functional or capability view, have a higher level (not layer) of abstraction, potentially coordinate among several domains and make extensive use of composition and aggregation.

- Eventually, the platforms at the top are customer-facing and take a commercial viewpoint (e.g., pricing, billing, contracts, and customer relationship management).

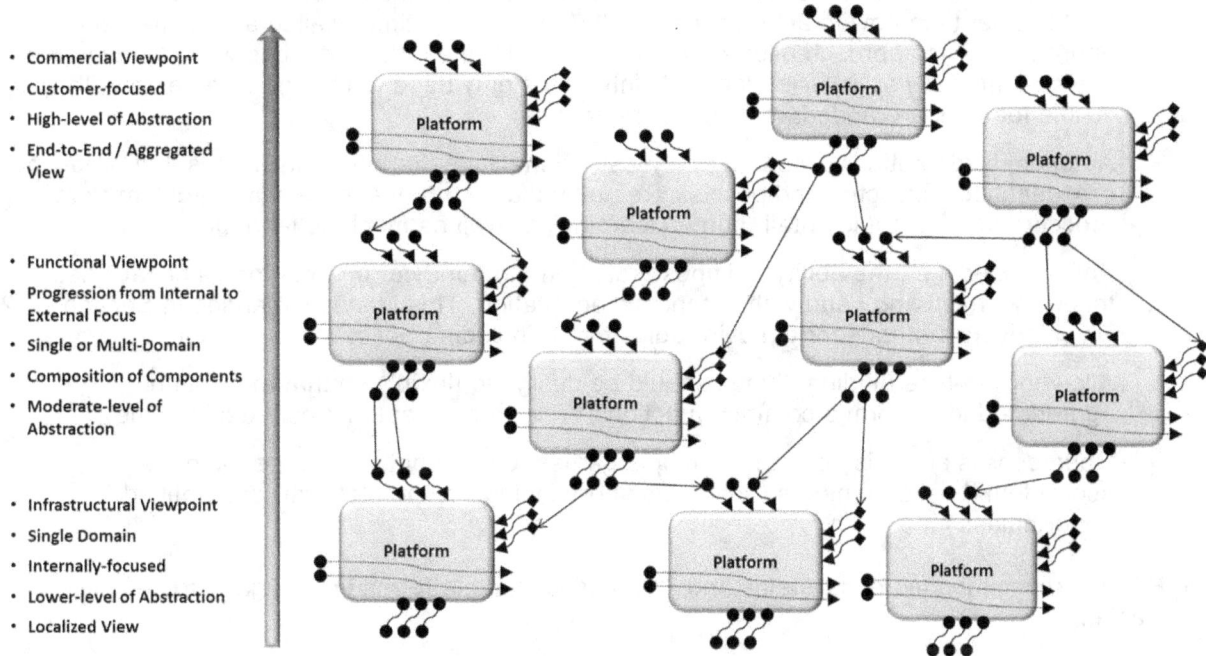

Figure 34. Platform Layering

Some platform models are less hierarchal. Consider, for example, a platform that matches people looking for rides with people willing to provide rides with their personal automobiles, or a platform that matches people looking for somewhere to stay during a trip with others willing to rent out part or all of their home or rental property. These platform models tend to be flatter.

6.5   Characteristics of an Antifragile Platform

In his book *Antifragile: Things That Gain from Disorder* [15], Nassim Nicholas Taleb defines the concept of "antifragility." As Taleb points out, the opposite of fragile is not "robust" but rather "antifragile." "Robust" or "resilient" means that something can resist and recover from shocks, volatility, randomness, and instability, while "antifragile" means that something gets stronger because of such stressors.

For an ecosystem and associated platforms to be antifragile, the following characteristics are required:

- Component-based: this is directly related to the open ecosystem requirement (see the last bullet item in this list). The things within a platform must follow a common architecture (as described in Section 5.1).

- Contract-based: it is critical that each thing in an ecosystem have a well-defined contract (guaranteed level of service) concerning its offered capabilities. Without well-defined contracts, a multi-party ecosystem will not work.

- Catalog-driven: things and their offered capabilities must be advertised in a catalog. This allows for component designers to more easily make use of the components of others. While each platform needs some catalog information to instantiate components, a comprehensive catalog of components is also needed (having descriptions of components that can be used in many different types of platforms).

- Outcome-based interfaces: the consumer of an interface shall specify the desired end-result rather than how to achieve the result. (This is sometimes called an intent-based approach.) This approach allows the internals of the platform to change while keeping the external interface as-is. The platform's interfaces only need to change when externally visible features are added, modified or removed.

- Autonomic adaptation, based on analytics and machine learning: this means that problems are identified, corrected and policies are put in place to prevent the same problem from reoccurring. This could entail "human learning" as well as machine learning.

- Policy-based, i.e., the ability to impose rules on the behavior of a platform's capabilities: this works hand and hand with autonomic adaptation. This idea is expanded in Section 12.2 which covers methods for behavior adjustment (including policy management).

- Allow for run-time binding: things should be designed flexibly so that they can be aggregated to perform a common function at run-time (or at least post-design-time).

- Open ecosystem: this allows for multiple parties to contribute components to the ecosystem, based on needs (perceived shortcomings of the platform) or identified opportunities for growth.

Pf_R3: It is recommended ecosystems and their associated platforms be designed to be antifragile.

7 Classification of Things based on Exposed Characteristics and Functions

7.1 Overview

As noted in Sections 5.2 and 5.3, it is essential to use a common set of interfaces to facilitate the composition, aggregation, and management of things in an ecosystem consisting of one or more platforms. In this section, an analysis of interface needs for components is presented. The identified needs are based on the type of characteristics exhibited and functions offered by a component. The focus is on management functions and not core capabilities since core capabilities vary greatly depending on the type of thing. The goal is for things to use common interfaces in support of common characteristics and management functions. In addition to facilitating composition and aggregation, this also simplifies the task of managing things.

The ideas in the section are based on TM Forum document *IG1174 Model-Driven Design of Management Interfaces for ODA Components* [16].

7.2 Model-driven Approach to Interface Generation for Types of Things

In this book, a model-driven approach is taken for the definition of management interfaces. The approach is summarized in Figure 35 and explained below.

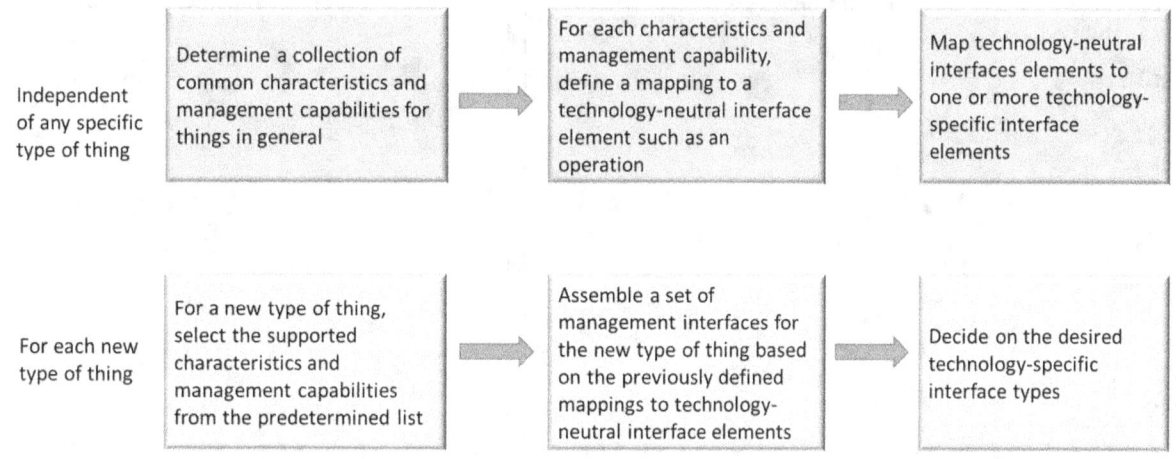

Figure 35. Model-driven Approach to Interface Design for Things

Top of Figure 35: Define a general interface model that can be applied to various types of things.

- The first step is to define a collection of characteristics and management capabilities, independent of any specific type of thing (a non-exhaustive set of such items is provided in Section 7.3).

- For each characteristic and capability, define the necessary interface support (i.e., required operations, notifications, and data model). The interface support is first defined in a technology-neutral manner and then mapped to one or more specific technologies. There are several reasons for the multi-step interface approach, i.e., several different technology-specific interfaces may be needed and interface technologies change over time. With the approach taken here, the technology-neutral interfaces can remain relatively stable while the interface technology changes.

Bottom of Figure 35: Apply the general interface model to a particular type of thing.

- When defining a new type of thing, consult a predefined list of characteristics and management capabilities to determine what applies to the new type of thing.

- Based on input (i.e., the selected subset of characteristics and management capabilities that apply to the new type of thing), automatically assemble the management interface for the new type of thing. This will be a technology-neutral interface.

- Decide on one or more specific interface technologies and map from the technology-neutral interfaces to the selected technology-specific interfaces.

Figure 36 shows the inputs to and outputs from the process of determining a management interface (or interfaces) for a new type of thing. From a predefined list, the designer checks-off the characteristics and management capabilities that apply to the type under consideration. In some cases, further information may need to be supplied for a given characteristic or management capability, e.g., the data model associated with an exposed internal view for a type of thing may be required input (see the details in Section 7.3.1). The designer also needs to indicate the desired interface technologies. With this information, the process can be automated to generate management interface specifications.

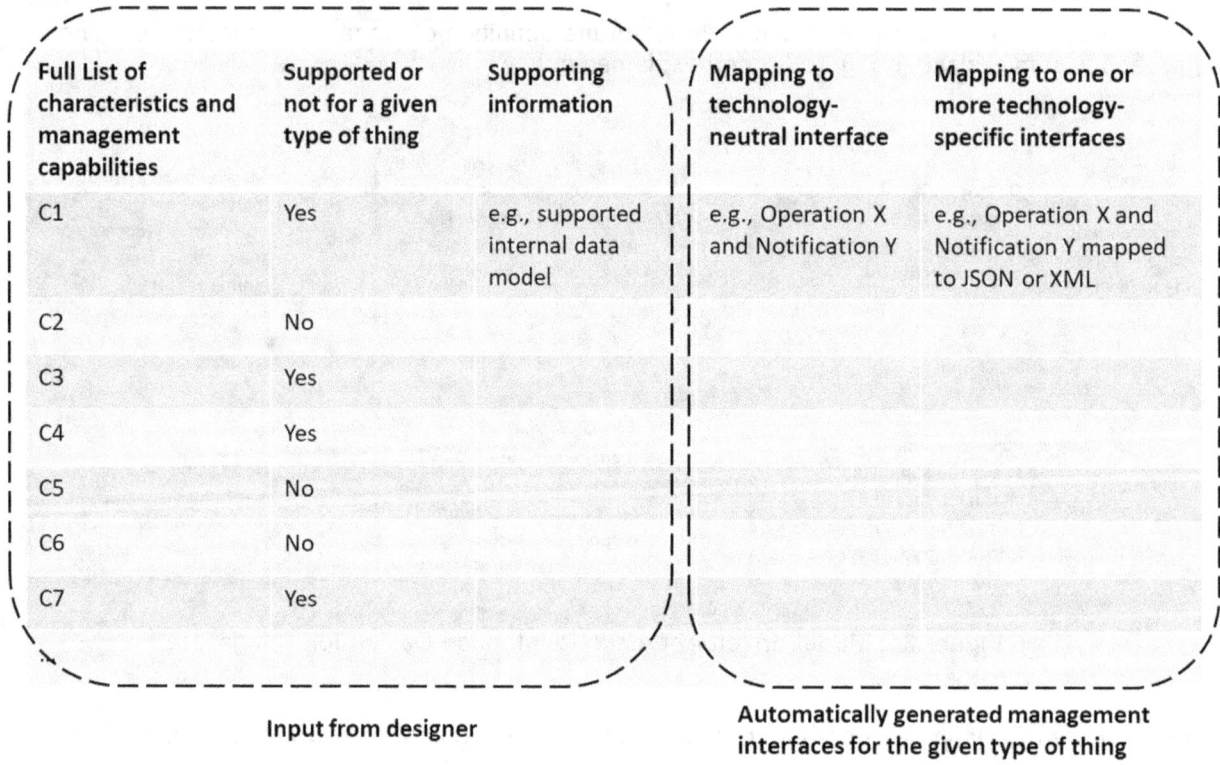

Full List of characteristics and management capabilities	Supported or not for a given type of thing	Supporting information	Mapping to technology-neutral interface	Mapping to one or more technology-specific interfaces
C1	Yes	e.g., supported internal data model	e.g., Operation X and Notification Y	e.g., Operation X and Notification Y mapped to JSON or XML
C2	No			
C3	Yes			
C4	Yes			
C5	No			
C6	No			
C7	Yes			

Input from designer   **Automatically generated management interfaces for the given type of thing**

Figure 36. Mapping from Characteristics and Functions to Exposed Interfaces

For example, if capability C2 in Figure 36 is "inventory retrieval with filtering based on attribute value matching," then the implication is that every type of thing that has capability C2 shall have the same technology-neutral interface for expressing such a capability. To see the value of this, consider a platform with multiple component (thing) suppliers each of whom have a different way of expressing capability C2, and then consider that C2 is only one out of many capabilities.

7.3   Characteristics and Management Functions

This section contains a non-exhaustive list of characteristics and management functions that can be exhibited by a given type of thing. As noted previously, the goal here is to have each thing (component) in a platform expose the same capability in the same way. The alternative is a difficult integration effort for the platform owner or caretaker.

7.3.1   Internal View and Control

For the benefit of its consumers, some things can provide an abstracted view of their internals and optionally, some level of control over the internal representation. In this document, it is assumed that exposure of an internal view is done via an object-oriented model. However, other options are possible, e.g., a list of attributes or tables.

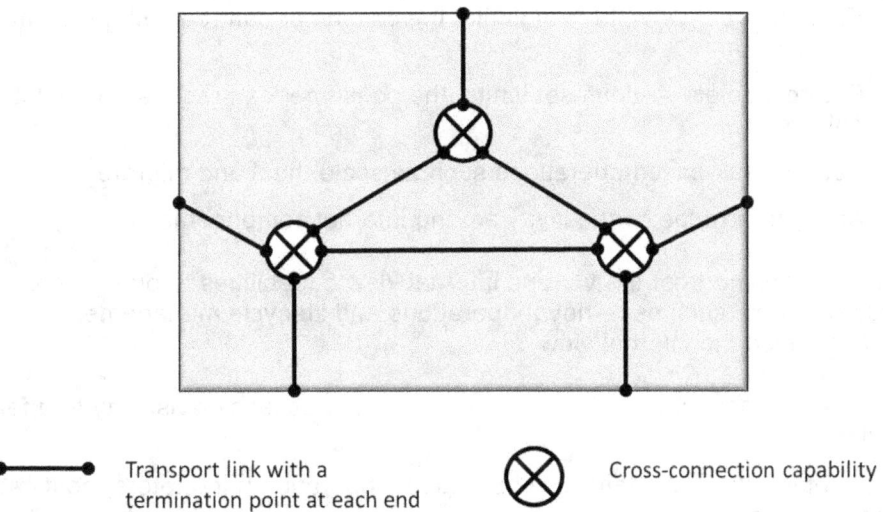

Figure 37. Virtual Private Network (VPN) with Exposed Internal View

Figure 37 depicts a carrier Ethernet Virtual Private Network (VPN) that exposes an abstracted view of its internals (cross-connections, transport links, and termination points). The consumer of the VPN could be given the ability to request the creation of additional cross-connections, transport links, and termination points. The termination points on the boundary are the Input-Output ports. The Capabilities, Management, and Requires interfaces are not shown in the figure.

As noted, the internal view of a thing is for the benefit of the consumer. It is not intended to reveal the constituent components for a thing. In the VPN example, the constituent components might be virtualized carrier Ethernet switches, virtualized firewalls and virtual tributaries within an optical transport. These details are not of interest to the consumer and thus are not exposed.

The characteristic of providing an internal view is a prerequisite for several of the other characteristics and functions that are described in the following subsections.

For things that expose an internal view, this is typically done via an object model. Depending on the type of thing, its consumers will be afforded different levels of visibility and control over the internal objects. The following list of exposed capabilities for a thing is divided into two basic cases, i.e., no consumer control, but with an exposed internal view, and consumer control):

- No consumer control:
  - Static – once an instance of a thing is created, the internal objects are fixed. In this case, the consumer is only given a view of the internal objects but no ability to make any changes.
  - Mutable – the thing itself may create, modify and delete internals objects. The consumer will get change notifications but has no control over the internal objects.
- Consumer control (the items below are not mutually exclusive and can be combined, depending on the type of thing and its internal model):
  - Externally configurable – at least some of the internal objects can be modified based on consumer requests.
  - External create – within set limits, the consumer can request the creation of internal objects.
  - External delete – within set limits, the consumer can request the deletion of internal objects.
  - Various task-based operations such as scale, heal and migrate.
  - Ability to arrange connectivity among internal components.

Table 3 provides a mapping from the various internal view capabilities to one or more technology-neutral interface elements such as retrieval operations and lifecycle management operations for the objects that comprise the internal view.

Interface Element – an aspect of an interface that provides access or visibility to a feature (as defined in Section 2.1).

- Examples of interface elements are operations, operation parameters, notifications, and notification parameters.
- The features of a thing are exposed by interface elements.

Table 3. Mapping of Internal View Capabilities to Technology-neutral Interface Elements

Characteristic or Capability	Technology-neutral Interface Elements as Presented to Consumer
Static	Operation to retrieve all internal objects (no filtering) Operation to retrieve by Id.
Mutable	Operation to retrieve all internal objects (no filtering) Operation to retrieve by Id. If there a large number of internal objects, a retrieval operation with filtering may be needed. Ability to send object creation, modification and deletion notifications.
Externally configurable	Operation to modify an internal object
External create	Operation to create an internal object

Characteristic or Capability	Technology-neutral Interface Elements as Presented to Consumer
External delete	Operation to delete an Internal object
Various task-based operations such as scale (increase or decrease capacity), heal (repair) and migrate (move to another location)	Typically, one API operation per task. However, tasks should follow a common format.
Ability to arrange relationships among internal components	This can be supported via a complex operation parameter (essentially a graph) that describes, in detail, how the internal objects of a thing are to be related.

7.3.2 Input-Output Flows

As described in Section 5.1, some things have the ability to transform flows.

The possible characteristics and capabilities of a thing that supports input-output flows are as follows:

- Static boundary (i.e., externally facing) ports – ports are visible to consumers but unchanging

- Configurable boundary ports – can be modified by consumers, e.g., increase capacity

- Ability to create or delete boundary ports upon request

- Ability to create and arrange internal flows upon request (this assumes that the associated type of thing supports the appropriate Internal View and Control characteristics)

- Ability to arrange external flows among things upon request. This capability would be supported, for example, by an agent that manages connectivity among a set of things.

The flows (streams) can be digital information, analog information, sound waves, electricity, water, etcetera (basically anything that can be routed or transformed).

Table 4. Mapping of Input-Output Flow Capabilities to Technology-neutral Interface Elements

Characteristic or Capability	Technology-neutral API as Presented to a Consumer of a Component
Static boundary ports	Operation to retrieve information about the boundary input-output ports of a thing
Configurable boundary ports	Operation to configure boundary ports, within the limits of the specification for the type of thing
Ability to add or delete boundary ports	Operation to create and delete boundary ports, within the limits of the specification for the type of thing
Ability to create and arrange internal flows	Operation to modify, create and delete internal objects related to the transformation of flows. This is a subset of the "Ability to arrange relationships among internal components" capability in Table 3.
Ability to arrange external connectivity among things	This requires the "Configure boundary ports" and "Ability to add or delete boundary port" capabilities and could possibly require the "Ability to arrange internal flows" to match external flow requirements.

7.3.3 Configuration

The capabilities covered in the previous two sections are special cases of configuration management.

The possible capabilities of a thing that supports configuration management are as follows:

- Static configuration – a thing's configuration does not change after it is created. The consumer is given a view of the configuration but cannot make any changes.

- Mutable configuration – a thing's configuration can change after it is created (via internal processes). Consumers can view but not request changes to the thing's configuration.

- Changeable configuration – a thing's configuration can be changed via external requests by consumers. Allowed changes can range from attribute value changes to creating, modifying and deleting internal objects and boundary objects such as ports.

Table 5 provides a mapping between the configuration capabilities noted in the list above and several technology-neutral operations.

Table 5. Mapping of Configuration to Technology-neutral Interface Elements

Characteristic or Capability	Technology-neutral API as Presented to a Consumer of a Component
Static configuration	Operation to retrieve the configuration of a thing
Mutable configuration	Operation to retrieve the configuration of a thing Ability to send configuration change notifications, including attribute value change notifications, object creation notifications and object deletion notification.
Changeable configuration	For things that expose capabilities, the thing needs to offer operations to create, modify or delete objects (internal or on the boundary). Operation to modify attribute values on the thing itself

7.3.4 Filtering

Filtering pertains to retrieval operations where there are many things that can be retrieved and the consumer may only want a subset. For example, the need for filtering presents itself in things that provide an internal view with many objects. Some use cases that necessitate filtering are listed below:

- With respect to Retrieval – may be needed if a thing uses many objects to represent its configuration and a consumer of the thing is only interested in a particular subset of those objects.

- With respect to Configuration – may be needed if the same operation (e.g., modify or delete) can be applied to many internal objects.

Table 6. Mapping of the Filtering Capabilities to Technology-neutral Interface Elements

Characteristic or Capability	Technology-neutral API as Presented to a Consumer of a Component
With respect to Retrieval	This can be handled with a filtering attribute in a retrieval request
With respect to Configuration	This can be handled with a filtering attribute in modification and deletion requests.

7.3.5 Metric Measurement

Most, if not all things, will have metrics related to their externally exposed interfaces. Some example metrics include the following: number of times a given operation is called, number of times a given operation succeeds or fails.

Further, some things that can provide metric measurements on their internal models. The idea is that the thing can collect and report on internal measurements, e.g., performance, usage, and security.

A thing may support some or all of the following capabilities related to the measurement and processing of metrics:

- Thresholds
- Support for actions to be taken when a threshold is crossed. This is a subset of policy management.
- Measurement Jobs
- On-demand retrieval of measured metrics.

The sole purpose of some things is to collect measurements and status information on other things. In the telecommunications industry, such things are called "probes." More generally, a **Probe** is a thing that is inserted into an ecosystem of things for the purpose of status monitoring or collecting data about the things in the ecosystem.

Further details on metrics can be found in Section 12.6.

Table 7. Mapping of the Metric Capabilities to Technology-neutral Interface Elements

Characteristic or Capability	Technology-neutral API as Presented to a Consumer of a Component
Thresholds	Operation to create, modify and delete thresholds Notifications when thresholds are crossed or cleared
Measurement Jobs	Operation to create, modify and delete management jobs
On-demand retrieval of measured parameters	Operation to retrieve a current measurement for a particular metric as applied to a given thing

7.3.6 Policy-enabled

As described in Section 12.2.4, there are two basic types of policy that a thing may support, i.e., event-driven and intent-based.

- In the event-driven case, predetermined conditions and associated actions are defined. When an event meets a condition (for a given thing or set of things), one or more actions are to be executed.

- In the outcome-driven case, the desired state for a thing is stipulated. The thing is expected to do whatever it needs to maintain the desired state. Cell homeostasis (the tendency of a cell to continue to function properly and efficiently by interacting with both inner and outer stimuli) is an example of an outcome-based policy. In this case, the policy is set by nature.

The term "rule" is used for both event-driven and outcome-driven policies, but the type of rule is different for each case. For event-driven policies, the rule states that "if a given condition is met, then do this." For outcome-driven policies, the rule declares (for example) that the component should maintain a given state or configuration.

Table 8. Mapping of the Policy-enabled Capabilities to Technology-neutral Interface Elements

Characteristic or Capability	Technology-neutral API as Presented to a Consumer of a Component
Outcome-driven policy	Operation to apply and un-apply policy rules Operation to retrieve currently applied rules
Event-driven policy	Operation to apply and un-apply policy rules Operation to retrieve currently applied rules Ability to make external requests or take actions mandated by a given policy rule when the conditions of the rule are met

In terms of implementation, rules can be created and stored in a specialized thing (e.g., a policy manager) and applied to things as needed.

The determination of rule conflicts may be done by a specialized thing (e.g., a policy manager). The goal is to detect rule conflicts before such rules are applied to a thing.

Some additional capabilities that could be offered by a thing or possible an agent that handles policy management for a collection of things:

- Policy traceability, i.e., given the current state of a thing what policies and events led to that state. This implies the need for a policy log (including records of policy versions that were active at different times).

- "What if" analysis of policy, i.e., given the current state of a thing what would be the expected (predicted) effect of applying a given set of policies.

7.3.7 Root Cause Problem Analysis (RCPA)

As described more fully in Section 12.7, root cause problem analysis is the process of identifying the root source (or sources) of a problem in an ecosystem of things. The capability of root cause problem analysis would typically be supported by a thing that serves as an agent for other things. A thing that supports root cause problem analysis may have some or all of the following capabilities:

- Ability to send a notification of a new problem, and whether it is attempting a solution or not. In the case that the thing is not attempting to solve the problem, this should be seen as passing responsibility for problem resolution to another thing.

- Ability to send progress reports on the status of a problem
    - This could include an indication of resolution.
    - This could entail an indication that the thing could not resolve the problem. This is needed for closed-loop control (passing ownership of the problem from an inner control loop to a wider external control loop).

- Ability to a close a problem upon request

- Ability to accept external input on an existing problem

- Ability to record and report on problem and symptom relationships
    - As RCPA is being performed symptoms and lesser (downstream) problems will be correlated with more fundamental problems until a root cause is found.

Ability to transfer ownership of a problem.

Table 9 provides a mapping of the above capabilities to technology-neutral interface elements. In general, interfaces specifically designed for RCPA do not yet exist.

Table 9. Mapping of the RCPA Capabilities to Technology-neutral Interface Elements

Characteristic or Capability	Technology-neutral API as Presented to a Consumer of a Component
Ability to send a notification of a problem	Problem report (as opposed to an alarm) with an indication of whether the component is attempting a solution or not
Ability to send progress reports on the status of the problem	Progress notification on an existing problem
Ability to a close problem upon request	"Close problem" operation
Ability to accept external input on an existing problem	This could entail an interaction consisting of several message exchanges.
Ability to record and report on problem and symptom relationships	An information structure is needed to show the various problem correlations As problem correlations are updates, notifications can be sent to interested parties. Alternately, interested parties can request the current correlation graph for a given problem.
Ability to transfer ownership of a problem	This can be recorded in a trouble ticket or problem entity (with a reference to the owner).

7.3.8 Discovery of Capabilities

For things to use the capabilities offered by a given thing, it is necessary to know what the given thing has to offer. This process is known as "discovery" (see Section 11.4). The capabilities offered by a thing are expressed via contracts (see Section 12.3).

With regard to discovery, a thing may offer some or all of the following capabilities to its potential consumers:

- Ability of a thing to return its type and associated specification upon request

    o This is more likely to be supported by a catalog manager on behalf of other things.

    o An instance of a thing (especially software components) may be able to return the name of its type if asked. The details of the type (i.e., the associated specification) can be obtained from a catalog manager.

- Ability of a thing to return its exposed capabilities upon request

    o This is needed when the specification allows for optional capabilities in an instance of a component type. Components instance would have this information, but such information could also be consolidated in an inventory manager.

- Ability of a thing to return its domain of coverage (i.e., the region over which a thing has control) upon request

    o For more details on domains, see Section 6.2.

- Ability to publish (e.g., to a catalog or inventory manager) any or all of the information listed in the previous bullet items.

- Ability of a thing to allow consumers to modify, add or remove its exposed capabilities. This includes modification of the domain of coverage for a thing.

    o For example, during a security breach, it may be necessary to shut-down some or all of the offered capabilities of a given thing.

Table 10. Mapping of the Discovery Capabilities to Technology-neutral Interface Elements

Characteristic or Capability	Technology-neutral API as Presented to a Consumer of a Component
Ability to return its type and associated specification	For the specification of a type, this is essentially a catalog retrieval request (most likely not supported by the thing itself). Some things may be able to return their type when asked.
Ability to return its exposed capabilities upon request	This is a get operation on the thing in question. The response would entail different information from a typical inventory retrieval.
Ability of a thing to return its domain of coverage	This is a get operation concerning the domains or regions covered by a given thing.
Ability to publish	In this case, the thing informs another thing of its specification, capabilities and domain boundaries. This allows other things to search for what they need rather than making requests to many different things.
Ability of a thing to allow consumers to modify its exposed capabilities and domain of coverage	Configuration operation to modify, add or remove capabilities. "Modify" includes the case of temporarily shutting-down a capability (possibly to be resumed later). Configuration operation to change the domain of coverage

7.3.9 Factory

As defined in Section 2.1, a factory is a thing that has the ability create instances of things (of one or more types). A factory (thing) requires the following capabilities:

- Support for discovery (see the abilities listed in Section 7.3.8)
  - o For example, a factory should have the ability to respond to requests for the list of types for which the factory can create instances.
- Ability to create, activate and initially configure instances of things
  - o Intent-based – driven by a desired outcome as defined by the characteristics and features requested by a consumer.
  - o Detail-based – allows a consumer to provide some details concerning the deployment of a component.

See Section 12.4 for further details on intent-based and detailed-based interfaces.

Table 11. Mapping of the Factory Capabilities to Technology-neutral Interface Elements

Characteristic or Capability	Technology-neutral API as Presented to a Consumer of a Component
Support for discovery	See Table 10
Ability to create, activate and initially configure instances of things	Operation to create and initially configure instances of the types supported by the given factory. One option would be to combine a factory with a configuration manager for modifications after a thing is created.

There are several aspects of "thing creation" by a factory that will affect the interface, e.g.,

- Is the requested thing created immediately or does its creation take some time and thus needs to be tracked? In the latter case, a mechanism is needed to track the progress of the creation request. See Section 11.9.3 concerning tasks and orders.

- Is it required to keep a record of a thing's creation? This is the case for many types of things (even for things that can be created immediately). See Section 11.1 concerning billing and accounting.

- Can a factory only create instances of one type of thing or can it be customized to create instances of several different types of things? Even in the former case, there may be multiple ways of deploying instances which can change over time (see Section 11.5 concerning deployment scenarios). In the latter case, a template could be used to support creation of the new type of thing (see Section 12.8 concerning templates).

7.3.10 Factory Value-Chains

In the previous section, the standard interfaces that need to be offered by a factory were discussed. However, this is only part of the story. Factories typically require capabilities from other things (often other factories). This can and usually does lead to a value-chain of dependencies. For example, consider the situation shown in Figure 38.

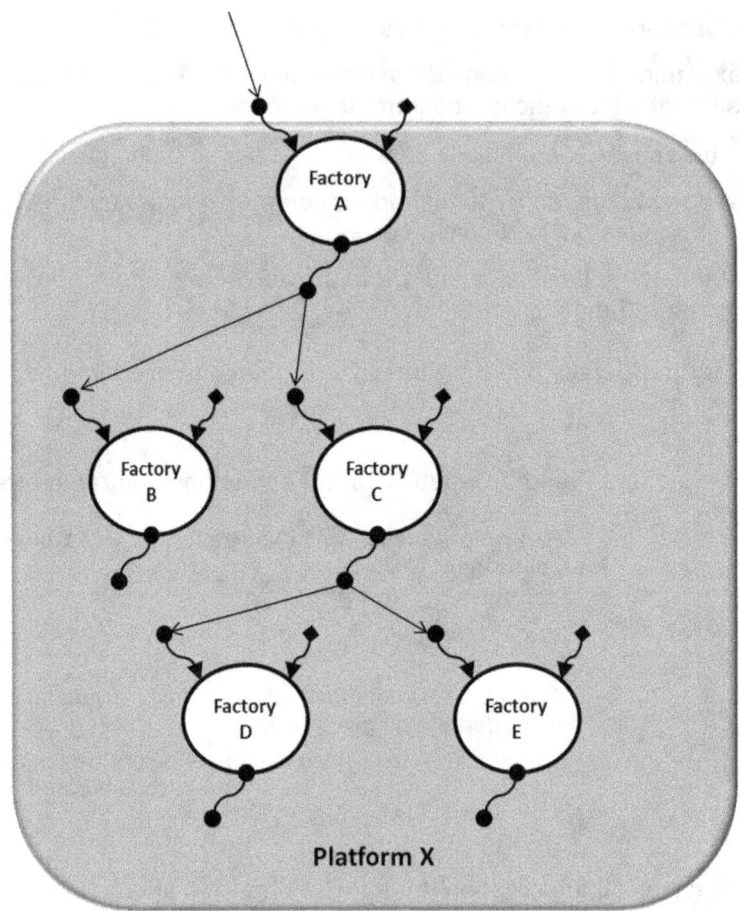

Figure 38. Factory Value-Chain

In Figure 38, Platform X supports a supply chain for an auto manufacturer.

Factory A is an auto manufacturing plant. Factory A requests parts and materials from Factory B (tires) and Factory C (sheet metal), using an ordering interface. The ordered parts arrive via a loading dock at Factory A. The loading dock is an Input interface (using the terminology of this document).

Factory C, in turn, requires materials from Factory D (steel ingots) and Factory E (sheet metal rollers and associated parts). Again, the material would be requested via an ordering interface.

In order to reduce unnecessary complexity, it is recommended that the same ordering interface be used by all the factories that are supported by Platform X.

7.3.11 Distributor

A distributor is similar to a factory in that it fulfills requests for instances of things. The difference is that a distributor does not do the actual creation of the instances.

Distributor – a thing that can distribute (but not create) instances of one or more types of things.

A candy vending machine is an example of a distributor.

A supermarket is a hybrid factory/distributor. Some items are prepared (created) in the supermarket (e.g., sandwiches) and other items (e.g., packaged goods) are simply distributed.

The distributor in Figure 39 is a convenience store. Factory A supplies packaged goods. Factory B supplies magazines and newspapers. Factory C supplies sandwiches and other perishable food items. The interfaces between the convenience store and the factories are realized by a combination of humans, delivery trucks and cell phones (for the orders). Some aspects of the interface can be automated, e.g., the convenience store manager could send order requests to the factories via an inventory application (perhaps running on a laptop or tablet).

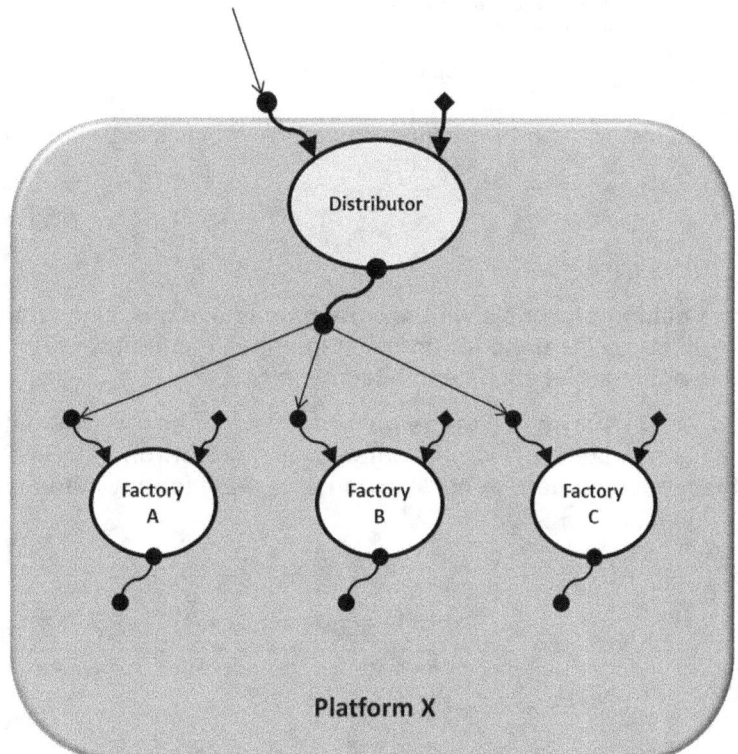

Figure 39. Distributor for Several Factories

The interfaces offered by a distributor to its consumers would be similar to the factory interfaces listed in Table 11:

- Distributors need to support the discovery of its capabilities (catalog of things) by consumers.

- Distributors need to support order requests for given things which may or may not be in-stock. For example, an auto dealer (distributor) has cars on their lot and can also order cars to fit a customer's needs. The order could be to another distributor (for an already existing car) or to a factory which would then build a new car with the specific options requested by the customer.

7.3.12 Agent

Agents were discussed in Section 2. A factory is a type of agent (as depicted in Figure 4). Other types of agents are possible, e.g., agents that cover areas such as performance management, root cause problem analysis, data analytics or connectivity management. Agents require some or all of the following capabilities:

- Support for discovery ((see the abilities listed in Section 7.3.8))

- Capabilities specific to the aspects of a thing being covered, e.g., root cause problem analysis.

Table 12. Mapping of the Agent Capabilities to Technology-neutral Interface Elements

Characteristic or Capability	Technology-neutral API as Presented to a Consumer of a Component
Support for discovery	See Table 10
Capabilities specific to the function being covered	The required operations will need to be considered on a case by case basis.

7.4 Example Platform with Factories, Agents, and Things

This section contains a platform example with several agents and the things handled by the agents. The goal is to illustrate the need for common interface elements in support of the various characteristics and management functions exhibited by things.

The following example entails only a few of the possible types of agents and only two types of things handled by the agents, i.e., VPNs and Content Delivery Networks (CDNs). The concepts, however, can be extended to the more general situation of a platform with many different types of agents and associated things.

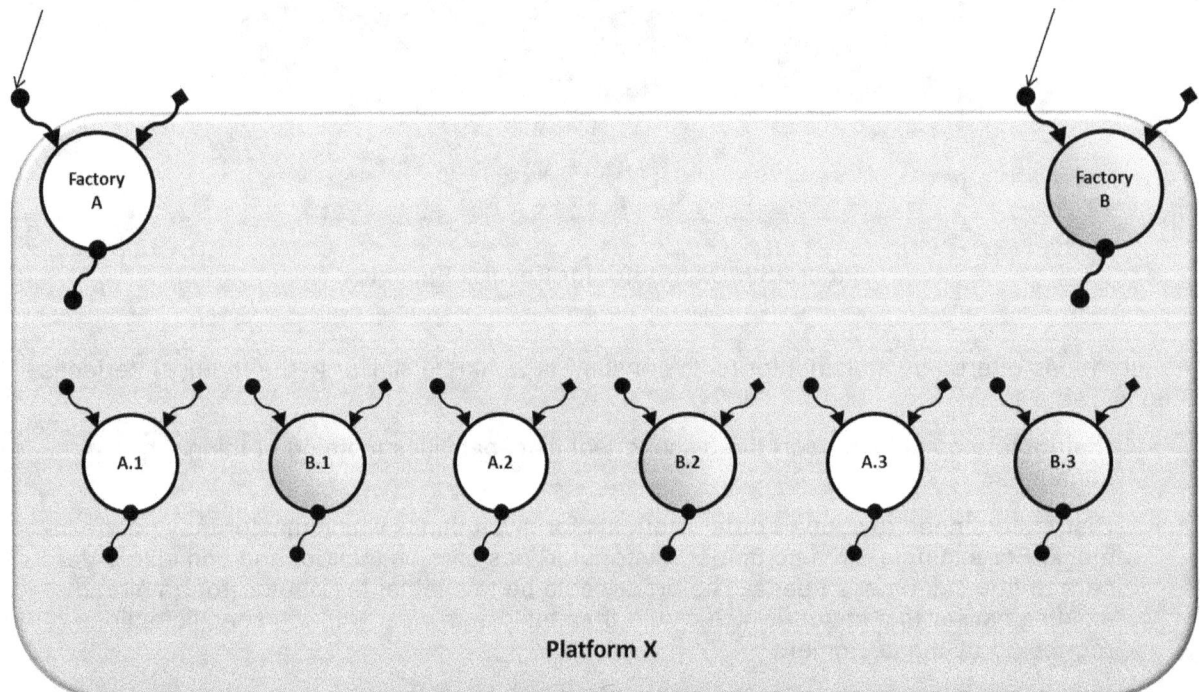

Figure 40. Platform with Factories

Figure 40 depicts a platform with one instance of two different types of factories. Factory A is able to create instances of the VPN type and Factory B is able to create instances of the CDN type. In response to requests from consumers external to Platform X, Factory A has created several VPNs, i.e., A.1, A.2, and A.3. Similarly, Factory B has created several CDNs, i.e., B.1, B.2, and B.3. For the example at hand, assume that the factories play no role in the lifecycle management of the things that they create.

While not shown in the example, it is possible for a factory to produce instances of several different types. This is true for software factories and is also possible for factories that produce physical things, e.g., cars, wood furniture, and laptop computers.

Figure 41 extends Figure 40 with the addition of several agents that handle various aspects of lifecycle management for the VPN and CDN instances.

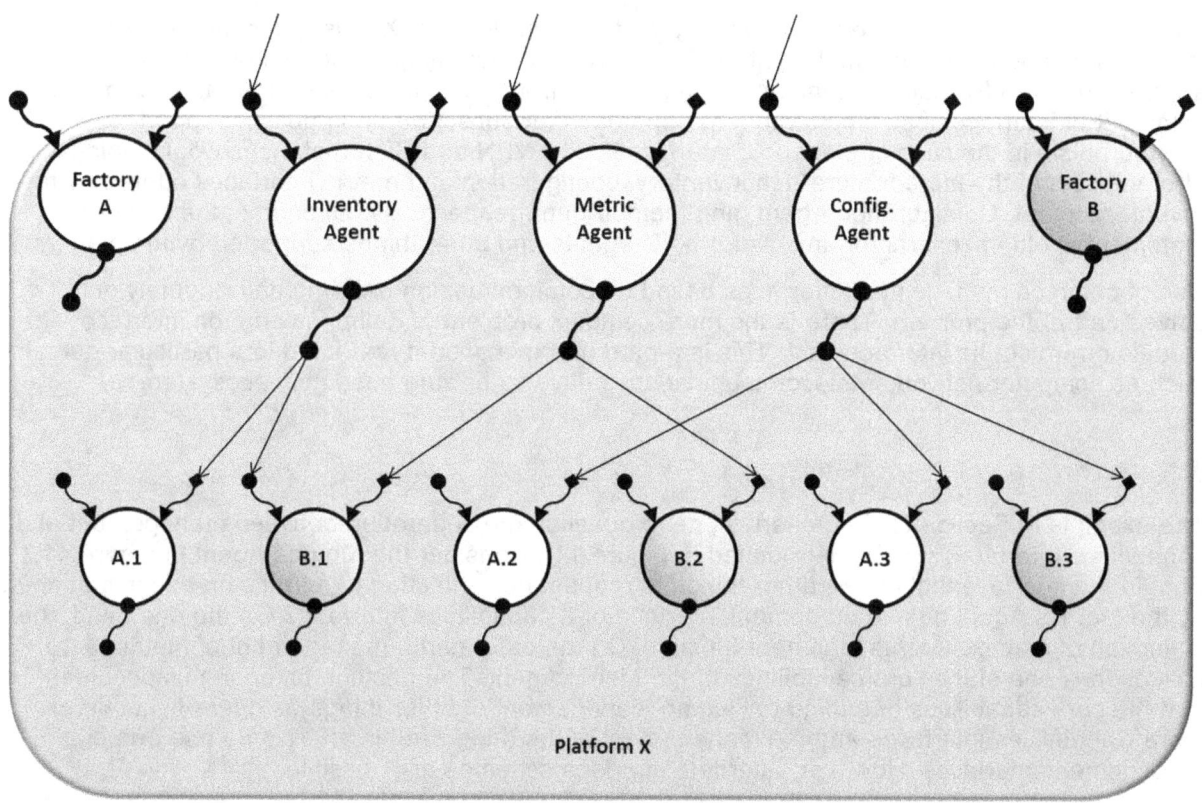

Figure 41. Platform with Factories and Agents

The Inventory Agent keeps track of the VPN and CDN instances, their external ports and their internal objects. Recall from the example in Figure 37 where the VPN had internal transport links, internal ports and cross connections (all of which need to be tracked by an inventory agent). The Inventory Agent could become aware of the VPN and CDN instances via object creation notifications from the factories. Alternately, the Inventory Agent could poll the factories on a regular basis concerning the instances they have created. In any event, information about the ever-changing internal object configurations would come from each VPN and CDN instance. Further, external consumers of the platform can make requests of the Inventory Agent concerning VPN and CDN instances. The interface offered by the Inventory Agent to external consumers is likely to be full-featured with support for filtering. The inventory interfaces offered by the VPN and CDN instances can be less feature-rich.

The Configuration Agent handles changes to the VPN and CDN instances. The changes can be requested by external entities or the Configuration Agent can decide on required changes to the instances that it handles based in its own internal policies. The VPN and CDN instances may also make changes to their configurations, within the boundaries of their defined behavior. In all cases, configuration changes are reported to and then stored by the Inventory Agent.

The Metric Agent takes care of measurement collection and reporting for the VPN and CDN instances. It relies on the Inventory Agent for an accurate view of the VPN and CDN instances and their configuration. Some of the required measurements will be statically mandated in the specification of the VPN and CDN types. The collection of such measurements will be initiated when a given instance of a VPN or CDN is created. Other measurements can be requested by an external consumer via the external interface offered by the Metric Agent. For example, if a given VPN is experiencing problems, an external consumer (perhaps a specialized problem resolution entity) may request additional measurements on the given VPN.

To limit the complexity of integration among the things in Platform X, it is recommended that the inventory, configuration and metric interfaces offered by each thing in the platform (factories, agents, and the VPN and CDN instances) be derived from a common set of interfaces using the same set of interface design patterns (e.g., approach for subscribe and publish, support for polymorphism in the case of electronic interfaces). The VPN and CDN instances would typically offer subsets of the more feature-rich inventory, configuration and metric interfaces offered by the Inventory Agent, Configuration Agent, and Metric Agent, respectively. Of course, the above statements hold in general for any platform, its agents and other things supported by the platform.

Use of common management interfaces based on common design patterns unfortunately only solves part of the problem. There is the more complex problem of defining common interface models on which the interfaces act. This is a hard problem even if restricted to a particular domain such as computer networks, telecommunications networks or auto-assembly ecosystems.

7.5   Alternative External Views of a Thing

The example in Section 7.4 might leave one to question the separation between management and capabilities interfaces (as first introduced in Figure 14). Consider the Metrics Agent in Figure 41. Should the interface that allows other things to request the collection of metrics on things managed by the Metrics Agent be a management interface or a capabilities interface? On the one hand, the collection of metrics is a management function. On the other hand, management of metric collection is one of the core capabilities of the Metric Agent. The position taken in this document is that the core capabilities of a thing (including management of other things) is offered via one or more Capabilities interfaces and the management of the thing itself is offered via one or more Management interfaces. However, alternate interface schemes are possible.

Figure 42 depicts an alternate interface scheme from the one described in Section 5.1. This scheme is driven by security concerns and focused on things that reside in platforms.

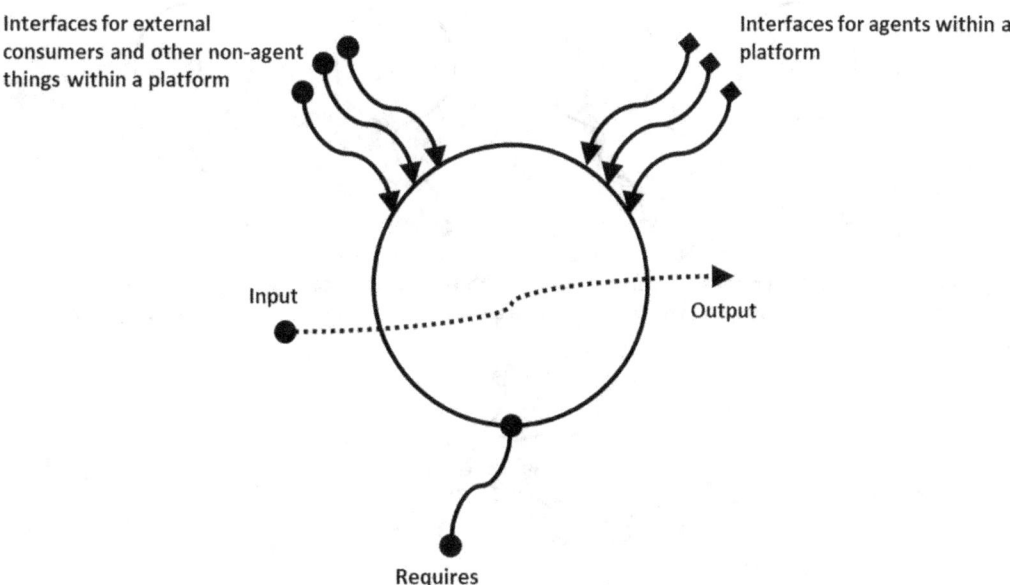

Figure 42. Alternate External View of a Thing

The interfaces on the right of the diagram in Figure 42 are reserved for things with higher security rights (e.g., agents). These interfaces could include the core capabilities of the thing, management of the thing and in the case of agents, capabilities to manage other things subtending from the agent.

The interfaces on the left of the diagram are reserved for consumers of the thing (typically with lower and more focused security rights). These interfaces could include core capabilities of the thing and even limited access to some management functions.

Further, there is no reason for this to be binary (i.e., separation based on consumers and agents). There could be more than two security levels that provide access to the management and core capabilities of a thing. In this case, the thing (playing the role of provider) simply offers a set of interfaces (combination of management and core capabilities). Access to the interface functions is regulated by pair-wise contracts between the provider and each consumer (see Section 12.3 for more details on contracts).

An example of a contract-based approach is depicted in Figure 43. Thing Z plays a provider role to Things A, B, C and D. Access to the functions offered by Thing Z is via a set of interfaces (not necessarily divided along the lines of management and core capabilities). Each of the consumers (A, B, C, and D) have separate contracts (agreements) with the owner/caretaker of Thing Z concerning their level of access to the functions provided by Thing Z.

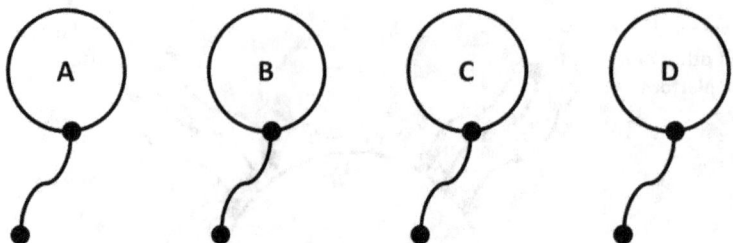

Things A, B, C and D each have a separate contract with Thing Z. Each contract has an associated access level for the consumption of functions (core capabilities and management) offered by Thing Z.

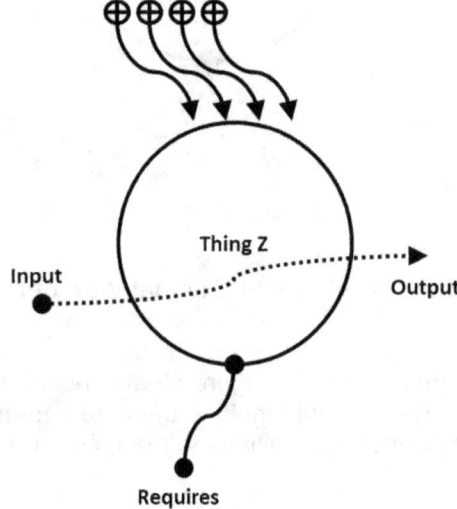

Figure 43. Contract-based Access to a Thing

8 Viewpoints

A thing can be represented from several viewpoints.

- The **Commercial Viewpoint** concerns the transfer of ownership and has information such as price, warranty and delivery charges.

- The **Capability Viewpoint** concerns the uses of a thing (functional characteristics) and how well it can provide its capabilities (non-functional characteristics).

- The **Environmental Viewpoint** describes the expected or acceptable environment for a thing. In general, the environmental viewpoint states what a thing requires of other things in order to provide its capabilities. This is basically a statement of dependencies.

- The **Composition Viewpoint** gives some information about how a thing can be used to create more complex structures.

There is some overlap among the viewpoints, e.g., minimum compressive strength (listed under the capability viewpoint) is also important in the composition viewpoint regarding stacking of bricks. When such overlaps occur, one can simply list the characteristic under several viewpoints.

Figure 44 shows several viewpoints of a brick:

- The commercial viewpoint of a brick includes items such as price, warranty and delivery options.

- Regarding the capability viewpoint of a brick, there are standards that specify functional and non-functional characteristics for bricks, e.g., see ASTM C62, *Standard Specification for Building Brick* [17].

- The environment viewpoint of a brick concerns the expected environment, e.g., temperature range or moisture constraints.

- The composition viewpoint describes how the brick can be used to compose more complex structures, e.g., the exterior of a house or paving for a patio.

Commercial Viewpoint

Price: $.60/brick or $100/250 bricks
Warranty: 20 years
Delivery:
    $20 / 250 bricks
    Free for orders of 10000 or more bricks

Capability Viewpoint

Functional characteristics:
    Can be used as a sidewalk paver
    Can be used in home construction
    Not for use in fireplaces
Non-functional characteristics: e.g.,
    Minimum Compressive Strength: 3000 PSI
    Maximum Water Absorption (5 hour boiling): 17%
    Grade: Severe Weathering
    Minimum Weight: 5.3 lbs.
    Length: 8 inches; Width: 3.75 inches; Height: 2.25 inches
    Color: Red
    Material: Clay

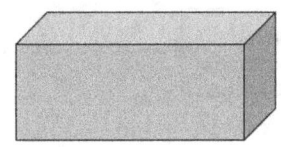

Composition Viewpoint

As a paver:
    Recommended spacing ...
    Recommended fill between bricks ...
    Recommended base layer below bricks ...
In home building:
    Recommended types of mortar

Environmental Viewpoint

Requires:
    Temperature Range: -50 F to 150 F

Figure 44. The Life of a Brick

Figure 45 applies the viewpoint model to a virtualized (software-based) firewall for a communications network. The firewall is represented using the general structure of a thing (from Figure 14).

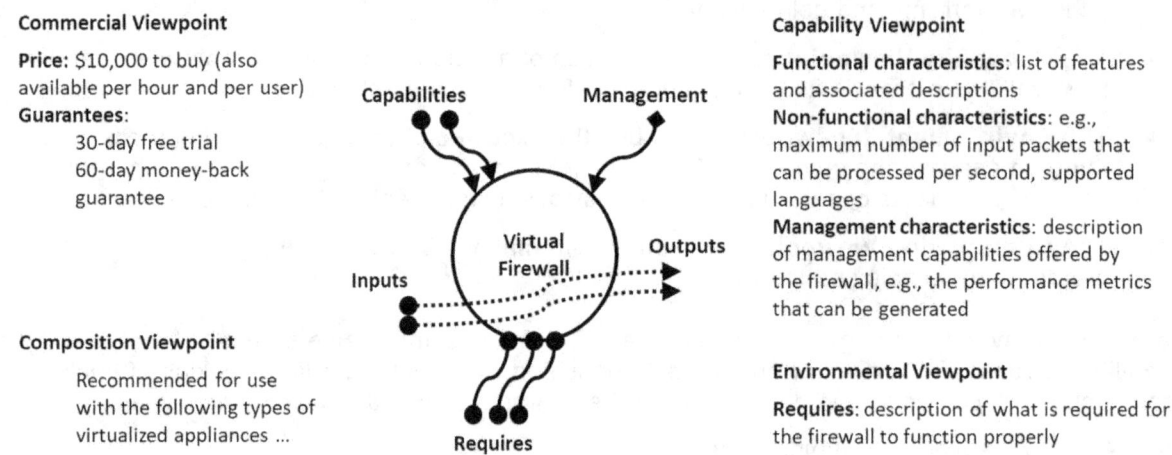

Commercial Viewpoint

Price: $10,000 to buy (also available per hour and per user)
Guarantees:
    30-day free trial
    60-day money-back guarantee

Composition Viewpoint

    Recommended for use with the following types of virtualized appliances ...

Capability Viewpoint

Functional characteristics: list of features and associated descriptions
Non-functional characteristics: e.g., maximum number of input packets that can be processed per second, supported languages
Management characteristics: description of management capabilities offered by the firewall, e.g., the performance metrics that can be generated

Environmental Viewpoint

Requires: description of what is required for the firewall to function properly

Figure 45. Viewpoints of a Virtual Firewall

The viewpoint model presented here is not meant to be prescriptive (just an example). Other viewpoint models are possible, e.g., see *Reference Model of Open Distributed Processing (RM-ODP)* [18] [19] [20].

The point is that a thing can be viewed from multiple viewpoints and each viewpoint has different information associated with it, but there is only one thing being represented. The reader is strongly cautioned against treating each viewpoint as a separate thing. This leads to multiple representations for each thing which in turn, can lead to the layering issues stated in Section 6.4.4. A better solution is to present different external views of a thing based on a need to know.

Figure 46 depicts the specification of a thing and its associated viewpoints. Thing Specification has general information about a type of thing, e.g., the name of the type and a description. The Thing Specification contains a specification for each of the four viewpoints. Together all five specifications describe a type of thing.

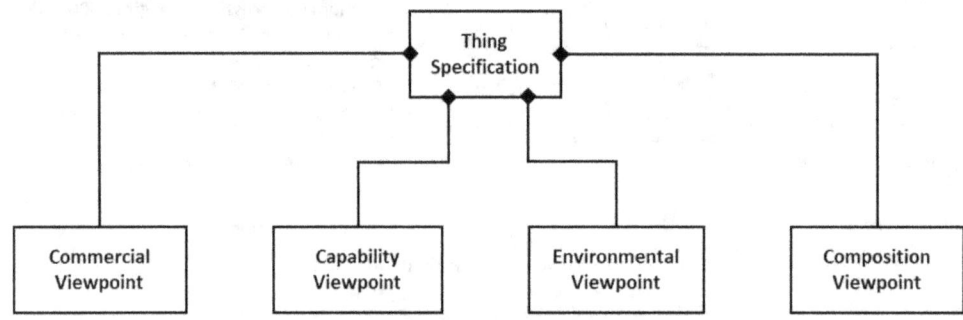

Figure 46. Dividing the Specification of a Thing into Viewpoints

9 Information Model Summary

This section provides a summary of the information fragments presented in previous sections and several topics to be covered in later sections, i.e., Contracts (Section 12.3), Templates (Section 12.8) and Policy (Section12.2.4).

The information model is shown in Figure 47. This is a summary of only some of the information model elements presented in this document. A complete information model would require a very large and complex diagram (best suited for viewing and editing via a formal information modeling tool).

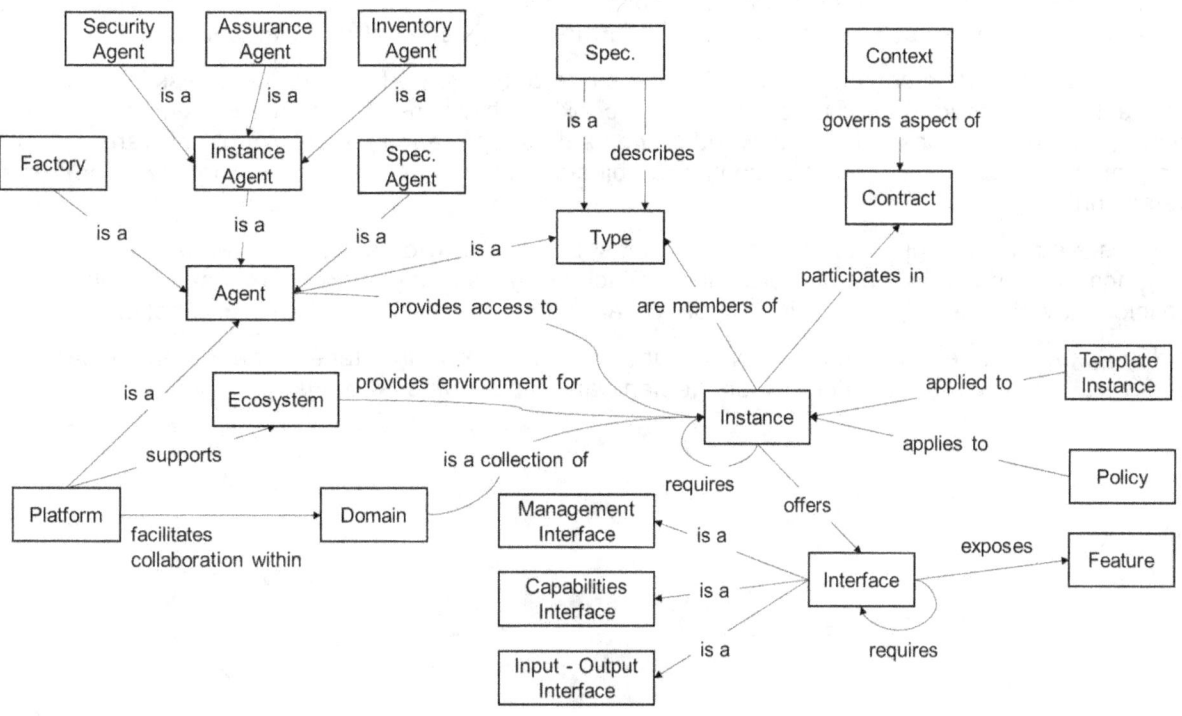

Figure 47. Information Model Summary

In the upper-left of the diagram is the agent object. An agent provides access to a collection of instances. As shown in the diagram, an agent can be specialized, e.g.,

- A factory (agent) creates instances of things.

- An inventory agent manages information about a collection of instances, and a specification agent (such as a catalog) manages information about types of things.

A platform is sort of a super-agent in that it can handle multiple agent functions for a collection of things. For example, Platform X in Figure 41 provides two factories and several agents that handle inventory, metrics, and configuration for the things supported by the platform.

- The boundary of a platform (i.e., the set of things handled by a platform) is defined by one or more domains.

- One or more platforms may be used to support the environment underlying an ecosystem. However, as noted in Section 6.1, it is not necessary for an ecosystem to be supported by platforms.

As shown in the bottom-right of the diagram, things offer interfaces. Interfaces, in turn, can be classified as being management, capabilities (core function of the thing) and input-output (non-message based, e.g., a video stream). The interface classification is explained further in Section 5.1.

- The externally visible characteristics and capabilities of a thing (i.e., features) are exposed via interfaces.

- A platform (being a type of thing) also offers interfaces. The management interfaces for platforms are further divided into capabilities management and platform management, as described in Section 6.3.1.

An agreement among two or more things is called a contract. A contract can be divided into smaller units knows as contexts. See Section 12.3 for further details on contracts and contexts.

Templates are used in conjunction with interface operations to perform the same task in a similar or exact way on several things. For example, a cookie cutter is used to create cookies of the same shape, a carpenter uses a jig to cut wood in the same shape, and in the realm of software, templates can be used to create or configure objects in the same way. See Section 12.8 for further details on templates.

Policies are rules assigned to one or more things. Policies provide a way to externally modify or enhance the behavior of one or more things. Since domains and platforms are types of things, policies may also be applied to either. Policy management is discussed further in Section 12.2.4.

A thing exposes it features (characteristics and capabilities) via interfaces. The interfaces can be of several kinds: core capabilities, management, and input-output streams.

10 Healthcare Applications Ecosystem Example

The section uses a healthcare applications ecosystem to further illustrate and tie together several of the key concepts from previous sections in this document. In this example, the suppliers of the healthcare applications (web-based software) are part of an ecosystem. The ecosystem provides governance (including business and technical rules), a common platform, marketing, and a brokering capability to match consumers with healthcare application providers. It is possible that some (or all) of the app suppliers are also included in the ecosystem governance.

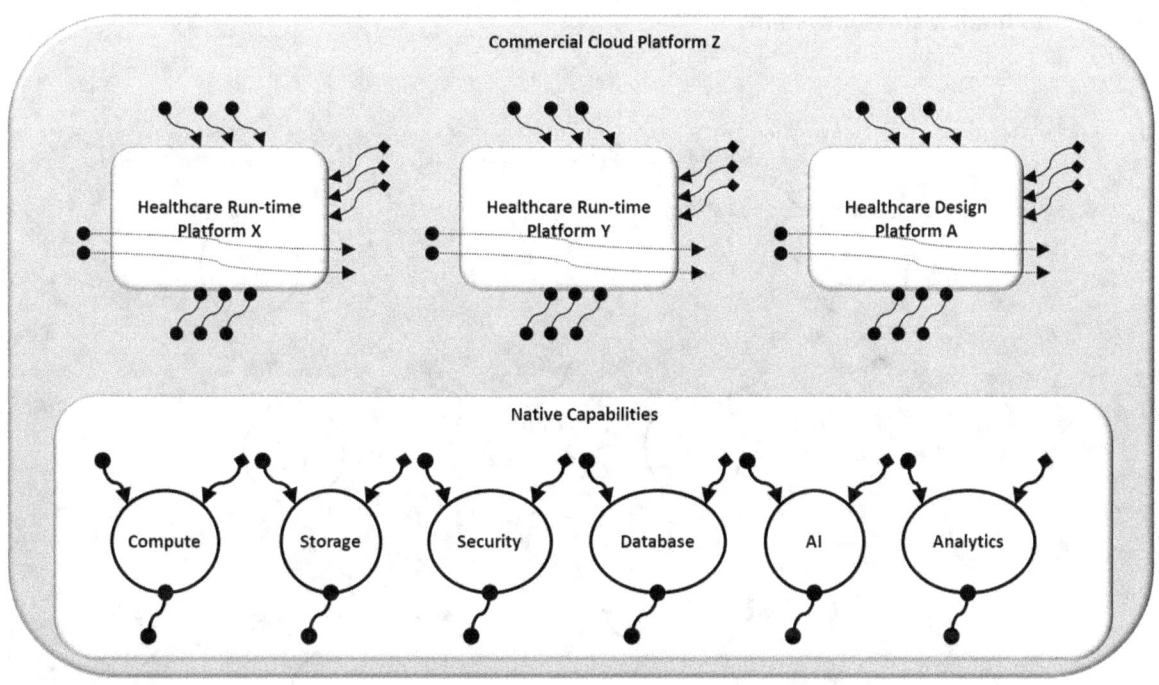

Figure 48. Healthcare Applications Platforms supported by a Commercial Cloud Platform

Figure 48 shows the platforms that support the healthcare applications ecosystem. In particular, there are two instances of the healthcare run-time platform (Platforms X and Y) and one instance of the healthcare design platform (Platform A), all three of which are supported by Commercial Cloud Platform Z.

- The commercial cloud platform provides common functions such as compute, storage, security, database, Artificial Intelligence (AI) support and analytics. Assume the ecosystem governance team has decided there is no reason to replicate such capabilities on the healthcare-specific platforms (i.e., Platforms X, Y, and A).

- When the healthcare apps are serving consumers (such as patients and healthcare providers), they are being supported by a run-time platform which in turn, builds upon the commercial cloud platform. Several instances of the healthcare run-time platform may be needed, e.g., to support geographically distributed consumers or for resiliency purposes.

- The healthcare design platform is used by the suppliers of healthcare apps who are part of the ecosystem. The healthcare design platform supports the design of new apps and the subsequent deployment of new (or updated) apps to the healthcare run-time environment (in this case, Platforms X and Y).

When a concept for a new type of app is identified by a supplier, it enters the Inventing phase. At this point, the supplier may not want to reveal the concept to the other suppliers in the healthcare ecosystem. Once the supplier of the new app type has sufficiently protected its idea (e.g., via a pending patent), the supplier may reveal the app to the other suppliers in the ecosystem and start to use the healthcare design platform to plan for and then build the new app type (noting that the new app type may make use of other app types that are already in the ecosystem). Alternately, the healthcare design platform could allow a supplier to start the design of their app without revealing the app to other app suppliers. In any event, once the new app type is ready for use by consumers, it is deployed into a healthcare run-time environment and put into the Operating phase. The consumers could be external end-users, other apps within the healthcare ecosystem or even apps outside of the healthcare ecosystem.

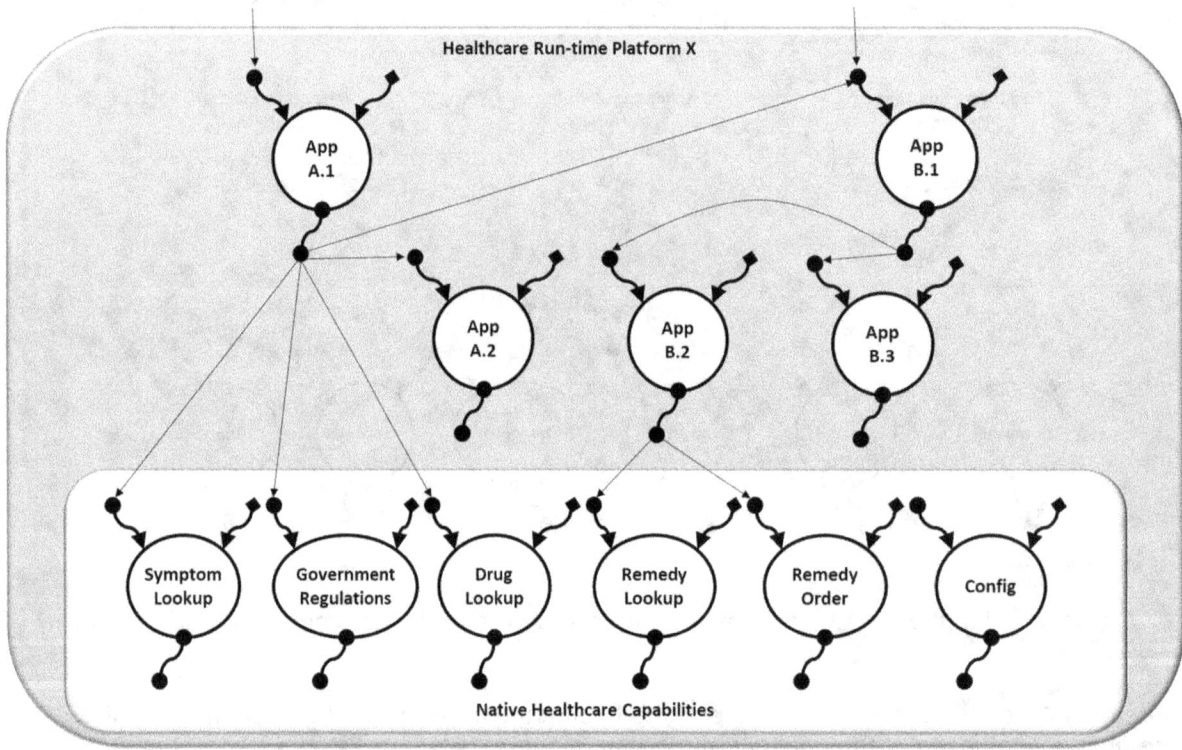

Figure 49. Application Interactions in a Run-time Platform

Figure 49 depicts an expanded view of Platform X in Figure 48. (Platform Y is assumed to have a similar structure to Platform X.) The applications in Figure 49 (Apps A.1, A.2, B.1, B.2, and B.3) are all in the Operating phase. The arrows show usage relationships, e.g., App A.1 is making use of App A.2 and App B.1, and the Symptom Lookup, Government Regulations and Drug Lookup things from the Native Healthcare Capabilities part of Platform X.

- The Native Healthcare Capabilities are supplied by the ecosystem and are generally useful things for the apps in the healthcare application ecosystem. The idea here is to put redundant (and non-competitive) functionality into the Native Healthcare Capabilities and thus, help the healthcare app suppliers to focus their efforts.

- The Config thing is essentially an agent that provides a common way to configure the various apps that reside in the run-time platform. For this example, it is assumed there is an ecosystem agreement that all healthcare apps support configuration via the Config agent which is why the Config agent is shown as being a Native Healthcare Capability. It is important to have a common configuration interface between the Config agent and the other apps residing on Platform X.

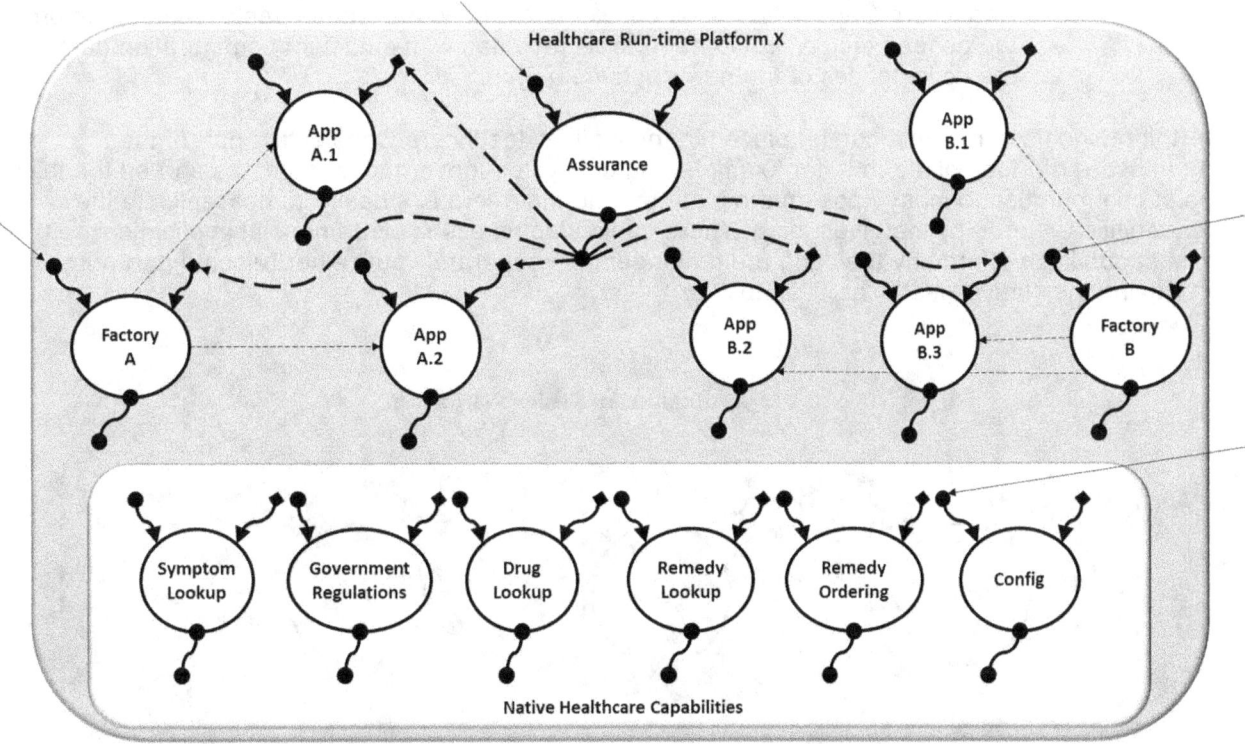

Figure 50. Management in a Run-time Platform

Figure 50 provides an expanded view of Platform X from Figure 48, with a focus on management aspects.

- The Assurance agent handles assurance issues (e.g., root cause problem analysis) for some of the apps running on Platform X.

    o   If it is agreed that the Assurance agent is to handle assurance aspects for all the apps on Platform X, the Assurance agent could then be moved and recast as a Native Healthcare Capability.

    o   The management interactions are shown with thick dashed lines from the Requires interface on the Assurance agent to the Management interfaces on the various apps. As with configuration, it is important to use the same assurance interface between the Assurance agent and the other apps that it manages.

- Factory A has created Apps A.1 and A.2 (the act of creation is depicted with the thin dashed lines). Similarly, Factory B has created Apps B.1, B.2, and B.3.

    o   In this example, the Assurance agent handles assurance aspects for other agents (including factories).

    o   Factories A and B offer capabilities to consumers external to Platform X (depicted with the thin lines extending from Factories A and B to the outside of Platform X). This is a Capabilities interface (and not Management) since the creation of things (app instances in this case) is a core capability of a factory.

- o The implication of having several factories is that the app types are sufficiently different that a common factory is not possible or easy to create, or it may be that different suppliers insist on each having their own factory. If a single factory was possible and desired by the ecosystem governance team, it would become a Native Healthcare Capability. In this case, when a new app type is deployed in a platform, the generic factory would need to be provided with sufficient configuration data to create instances of the new app type.

A thing, such as an agent, can be placed in the Native Healthcare Capabilities part of the healthcare run-time platform if, for example, the ecosystem governance team has agreed the thing is of common use to many apps on the platform and that there is a desire to not replicate the capabilities offered by the given thing. There could also be associated financial implications, e.g., the capabilities offered by the thing are no longer sold separately but rather become part of the fee for using the Native Healthcare Capabilities.

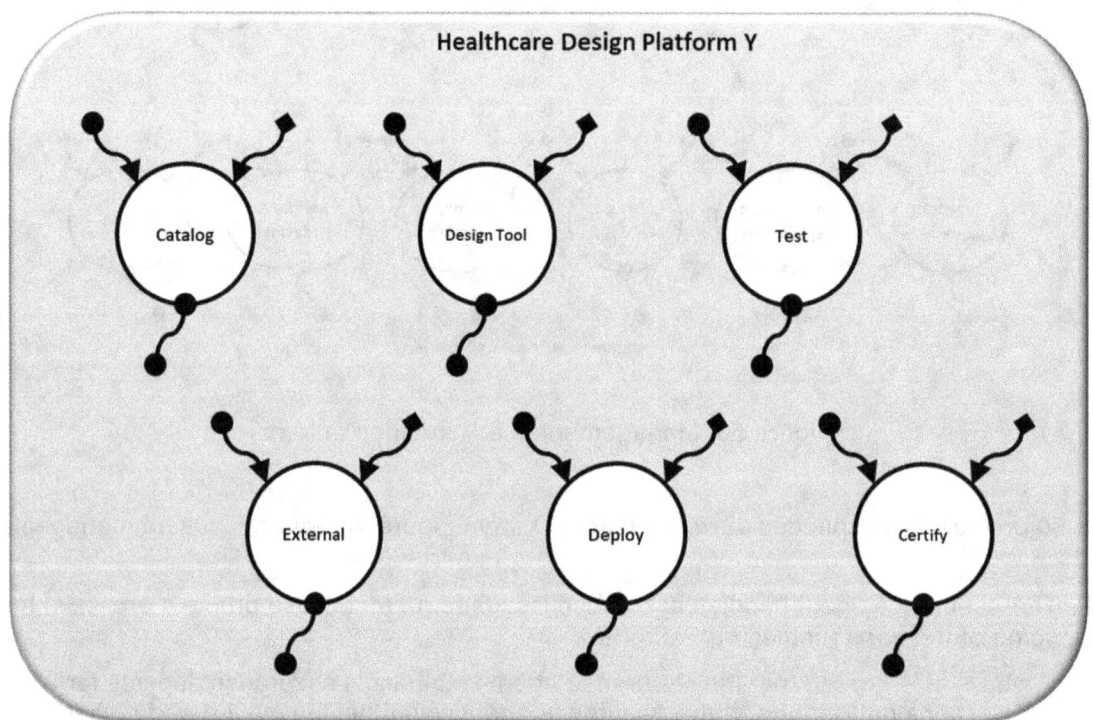

Figure 51. Design Platform for Healthcare Apps

Figure 51 provides an expanded view of Platform Y from Figure 48.

- (Design Tool) The healthcare design platform is used by app developers to design new types of apps while (possibly) making use of existing apps (via composition and aggregation), the native healthcare capabilities and the capabilities of the underlying cloud platform.

- (External) If healthcare-related capabilities are required outside of the ecosystem, access to such capabilities is coordinated by the External agent. This is just one option. Another option is to allow the healthcare apps in the ecosystem to directly access external capabilities.

- (Test) The healthcare design platform supports a test environment for new types of apps.

- (Deploy) Once the app designer thinks the app is ready for use by consumers, the healthcare design platform will assist in deploying the app type to one or more healthcare run-time platforms.

- (Catalog) App types and their current phase are listed in the Catalog. Listing in the catalog can start from as early as the Inventing phase and continue until the app type has reached the Retiring phase.

- (Certify) In some cases, the ecosystem may require certification of new app types before they can be deployed in a healthcare run-time platform. If so, the certification process (including various tests) can be automated in the healthcare design platform. This is depicted as the Certify thing in Figure 51.

11 Concepts concerning Management Areas

This section contains descriptions of concepts concerning the management of things. Section 12 covers general patterns that apply across several of the management areas defined in this section.

The subsections of this section are listed in alphabetical order and can be read in any order the reader desires. However, as noted in the introduction to this book, there are many cross-references among the subsections in this section and Section 12.

For a more comprehensive list of management areas (albeit focused on telecommunications) see ITU-T Recommendation M.3400 [21]. The set of concepts in this section were chosen because they are generally applicable to many industries.

11.1 Billing

11.1.1 Terminology

Figure 52 depicts a sketch of a billing process. The process starts with consumer and provider (or their agents) agreeing upon terms for usage or sale of a thing or set of things. Such an agreement is called a contract (see Section 12.3 for more details on contracts). The contract covers pricing, method of payment, guarantees and compensation when guarantees are not met, expectations and requirements on the consumer and provider, and other details concerning the usage or sale of things, e.g., licensing and copyright issues. Once the contract is agreed, the consumer can start to use the thing or collection of things covered by the contract. Measurements are collected in support of usage-based charging to ensure that contract guarantees are being upheld. Contract violations may have charging implications, e.g., refunds. Next, the charging process determines the cost based on input from the accounting process. Finally, the payments (or settlement) process handles the exchange of compensation.

In this book, the term "billing" is used to cover the entire process described above. In other contexts, "billing" has a more focused definition, e.g., "the preparing or sending out of bills or invoices."

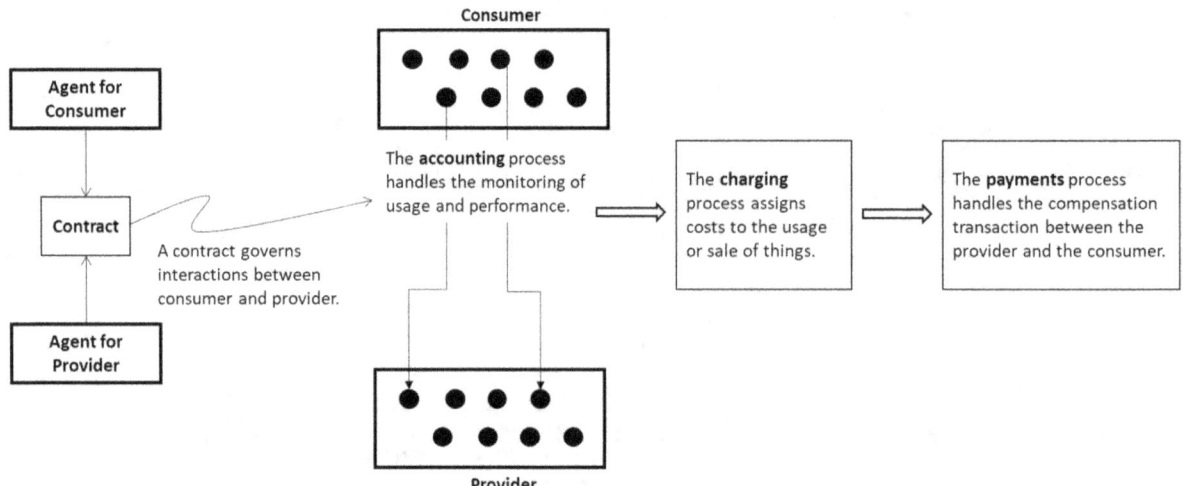

Figure 52. Sketch of Billing Processes

The following definitions are relative to a given contract between a consumer and a provider (or between their agents):

Accounting – the process of tracking the usage and performance of a thing or set of things.

- Performance measurements are tracked regarding contract guarantees. There is another aspect of performance tracking related to assurance which is out of scope for the accounting process.

Billing – the process that governs the usage or sale of a thing or set of things between a provider and consumer.

- As defined in this book, contract management (only the compensation aspect), accounting, charging and settlement are all part of the billing process.

Charging (or Rating) – the process of determining a price for the sale or usage of a thing or a collection of things.

Payments (or Settlement) – the process that covers the compensation transaction between the provider and the consumer of a thing or collection of things.

The following recommendations are offered:

- **BI_R1**: Contracts (with regard to billing) shall be intent-based, with a focus on what is to be provided and for how much but not on how the contract is to be fulfilled.
    - This approach allows for the internal implementation of a thing to change without affecting the external interfaces it offers to other things. See Section 12.4 for more on intent-based approaches.
- **BI_R2**: A given accounting approach shall support various charging methods. In other words, an accounting approach shall not limit the possible charging methods.
    - It is true, however, that the charging process may impose requirements on the accounting process.
- **BI_R3**: A given charging approach shall support various payment methods. In other words, a charging approach shall not limit the possible payment methods.

The general idea of the above requirements is to enforce weak adhesion (or coupling) among the processes within billing, i.e., accounting, charging and payments.

11.1.2 Accounting

Accounting entails the measurement of usage and performance characteristics related to the usage or sale of a thing or set of things. Even in the case where a thing is sold, there may still need to be accounting, e.g., after a new car is sold, various guarantees depend on mileage (tracked by the car itself) and the car owner having routine maintenance performed on the car such as engine oil changes.

Table 13 lists some accounting measurements that are needed in support of charging.

Table 13. Accounting Categories and Examples

Category of Measurement Capability	Description	Examples
One-time (transfer of ownership)	Ownership of a thing is transferred from one entity to another There can be guarantees associated with the transaction and this may require accounting.	Buying food at a supermarket Buying a car Buying a house or condominium Buying a meal at a restaurant
Time (duration)	Based on the duration that a capability is provided	Parking meter Various consulting services, e.g., legal services on a per hourly basis Stay at a hotel Car rental
Usage (unlimited)	Usage is not restricted, but may still be monitored and recorded for security or consumer behavior analysis	Health club membership Some phone plans (e.g., unlimited calls and text within a given country)
Usage (discrete)	Based on the type of capability and how many times the capability is used There is usually a time limit applied, e.g., per usage fee for entry into a museum but access is limited to one day.	City tram/shuttle bus with a fixed rate per ride Entry into a museum Movie rental Entry to a for-fee park, e.g., a beach entry fee
Usage (continuous or volume)	Based on how much of a thing is used	Various utilities such as electricity, gas and water (one could argue that this example fits under One-time (transfer of ownership)

Quiz for the reader – classify the following:

- "All You Can Eat" buffet at a restaurant

- Leasing a parking space at a train station (you keep the spot for as long as you continue to pay but cannot leave the spot to your heirs)

- Barter, e.g., trading several lessons in Calculus for several car washes

- Having routine service done on your car, or a specific set of repairs

- Currency exchange

- Taking a loan from a bank

- Leasing a car and then buying it when the lease expires.

Some of the above items fit into several accounting measurement categories, e.g., the "All You Can Eat" buffet has elements of One-time and Usage (discrete). The Time category is also possible in the sense that a customer cannot continue to eat after normal closing time and cannot resume the next day. Perhaps more important than the accounting category is a determination of what exactly needs to be tracked for proper charging, which leads to the following subsection.

11.1.3 Charging (or Rating)

Charging entails the application of a price to the sale or usage of a thing. Charging often relies on a mixture of accounting measurements as can be seen in Table 14.

Table 14. Charging Examples – Requirements on Accounting

Example	Charging	Required Accounting
Magazine – paper subscription	First month free, and then a fixed monthly rate for 3 years	Track duration in terms of the number of issues sent to the consumer
Magazine – online	Download a maximum of any combination of 15 past issues or new issues for the duration of one-year	Track duration of the contract Track number of downloaded issues
Cell phone service plan	Flat rate for • 5 GB high-speed data access at speeds based on 4G LTE, and with data speeds reduced after the 5 GB allowance is used • Unlimited domestic calls, texts, and images in messages	Track data usage Keep voice call records (perhaps to satisfy a legal requirement) Track international calls (based on destination and duration of the call)
Buying food at supermarket	Some items are charged per weight, e.g., produce Other items are charged per quantity, e.g., toothbrushes	One-time measurement (at the cash register) of quantity or volume depending on the type of thing
Car rental	Charge based on the duration of the rental (in number of days) Charge for gasoline if the tank is not full when the car is returned	Track days of use Record gasoline level in the tank (at beginning and end of car rental)
Ride on city metro	Flat rate charge that depends on zones crossings	Track where the consumer enters and leaves metro to determine the number of zones crossed for a given ride
Residential electricity usage (with "net metering" see [28])	Charging is based on kilowatt-hour (kWh) used by the consumer minus the electricity produced by the consumer (e.g., via solar panels) and put back onto the grid	Track consumer usage of electricity from the utility company Track consumer production of electricity that is put back on the grid

11.1.4 Payments (or Settlement)

Various payment arrangements are shown in Table 15. The charging and payment approaches should be separate. A given charging approach should not assume or force the use of a particular payment approach.

The table is divided into two basic approaches for payments, i.e., pre-paid and post-paid.

Table 15. Types of Payments

Type of Payment	Description	Examples
Pre-paid		
Lump-sum	Payment is in the form of a lump-sum or several lump-sums over time (with no schedule)	Gift card (some types of which can be replenished)
Auto-refill	Consumer makes an agreement with a provider to have money automatically withdrawn from, for example, their checking or savings account This can be based on a given condition, or on regular time intervals.	Payment for highway and bridge tolls (auto-refill by a fixed amount whenever unused pre-paid funds go below a set threshold, e.g., auto-refill by $25 whenever the pre-paid amount goes below $10) Pre-paid auto insurance on a quarterly basis
Post-paid		
Immediate	Payment is made at the time of transaction concerning a sale or lease	This is typical of transfer of ownership (especially for less expensive purchases such as food and clothing)
Regular intervals	Payment is made at regular intervals after capabilities are provided	Utilities Internet service Health insurance
Deferred	Typically, as an incentive to purchase, expected payment is delayed for a time period. Once the deferral period is over, payment can be immediate or over regular intervals.	New car purchase (e.g., no payments for 6 months, followed by regular payments for 3 years) Various house remodeling work, e.g., a new kitchen or bathroom

11.2 Capacity Management

For a thing to operate properly as defined in a contract, it typically needs to use the capabilities of other things. In this book, the process of ensuring that a thing has access to required capabilities (in a suitable amount) from other things is known as **capacity management**. In other words, the job of capacity management is to ensure the matching of capabilities and needs among things. Capacity management has been well studied and documented in the IT industry, see ITIL Capacity Management [33].

11.2.1 Terminology

The following terms are related to capacity management.

Capacity – the ability to provide a given set of capabilities at a given level of service.

- The above definition attempts to distinguish "capacity" from "capability" where capacity adds the concepts "how much" and "how well".

- A typical dictionary definition of capacity is "the power or ability to hold, receive, absorb or accommodate something." There is also an implication of "maximum" attached to such definitions, e.g., "the capacity of a food container is 4 liters."

Load Balance – to distribute a workload among several similar things (each with the ability to fulfill, satisfy or process the given type of workload).

Scaling – increase (or decrease) the capacity of a thing.

- **Scale-up** (vertical scaling) – an approach for increasing the capacity of a thing by increasing the capability of the things directly supporting a given thing.

  - o The above definition is a generalization of "scale-up" from the computer industry where the thing being scaled-up is a software application and there is but one thing directly supporting the application (a computer or virtual machine). In this case, the supporting computer or virtual machine has its capacity increased which, in turn, increases the capability of the software application.

- **Scale-down** (vertical scaling) – the opposite of scale-up.

- **Scale-out** (horizontal scaling) – an approach for increasing the capacity of a thing by increasing the number of things that directly support a given thing.

  - o The above definition is also a generalization from the computer industry. In this case, the thing being scaled-out is a software application. The software application's capacity is increased by adding more computers or virtual machines in support of the application.

- **Scale-in** (horizontal scaling) – the opposite of scale-out.

11.2.2 Concepts

11.2.2.1 Internal and External Capacity Demands on a Thing

Figure 53 shows several things (on the left) sending requests to Thing X. The requests effectively make capacity demands on Thing X. For example, if Thing X is an elevator, then it will need electricity to arrive at the various floors to collect passengers (the things on the left). It will also need an air supply for its passengers. Further, Thing X may have internal capacity demands, e.g., electricity to operate the onboard processors. So, from the perspective of Thing X, its capacity needs (internal and external) are electricity and air. From the perspective of the person managing the building, he or she needs an elevator with a given capacity to transport passengers among the floors of the building at a given speed. For example, the requirement could be for an elevator to transport a maximum weight of 1500 kilogram at a speed of 20 meters/second.

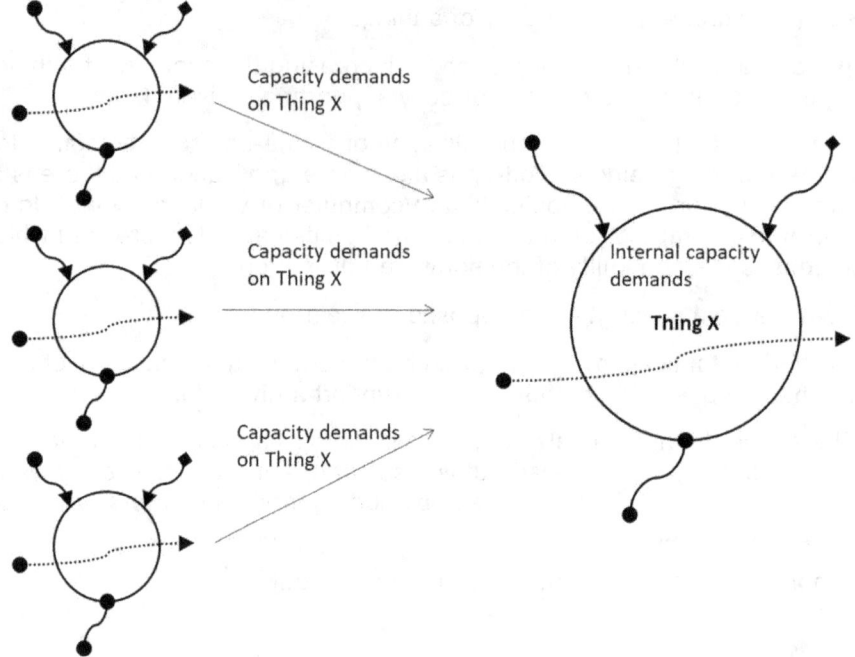

Figure 53. External and Internal Capacity Demands on a Thing

11.2.2.2   Load Balancing

A common technique to distribute demand (not necessarily evenly) over several suppliers is known as load balancing.

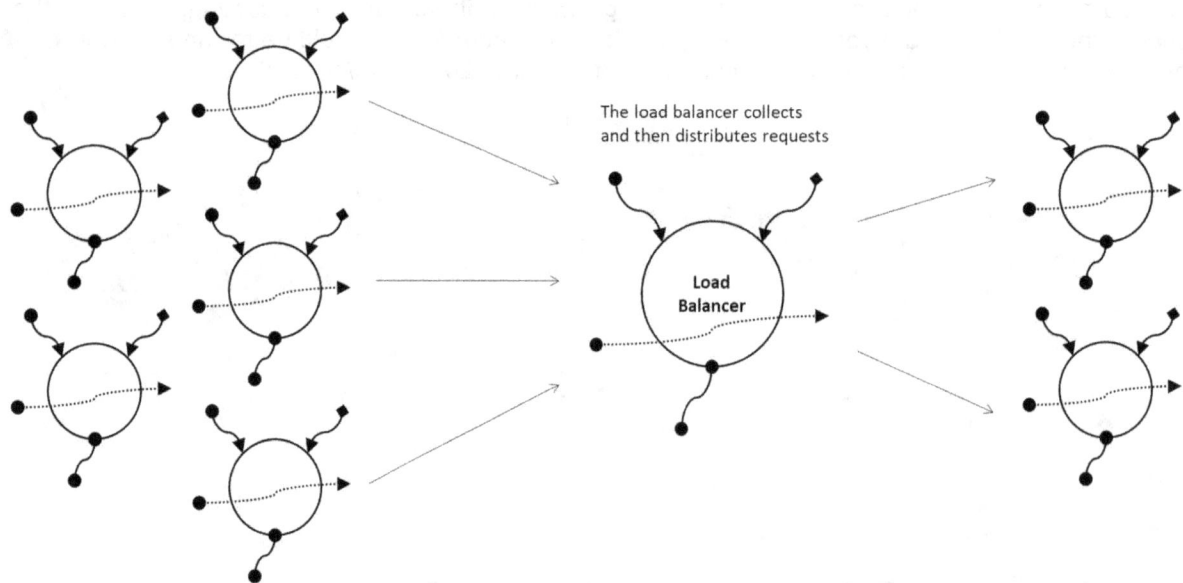

Figure 54. Load-balancing Among Several Things

Figure 54 depicts several things (on the left) making requests for the same capability (e.g., access to an authentication service) which is offered by the two things on the right. The load balancer in the middle of the diagram makes sure the requests are evenly distributed among the things on the right. Load balancing aims to optimize resource use, maximize throughput, minimize response time, and avoid the overloading of any single thing (among a set of things that provide the same capabilities).

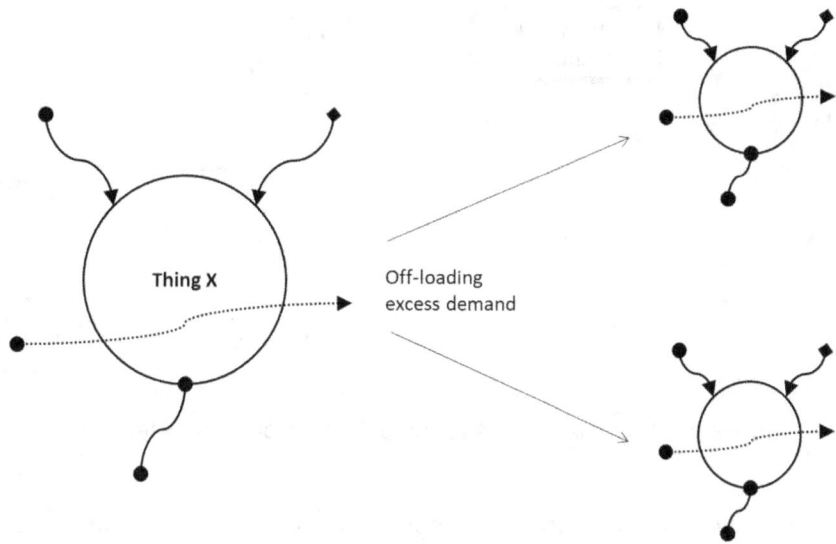

Figure 55. Off-loading Excess Demand

When possible, it is good practice **not** to build a thing to handle the maximum load (on its own) since this leads to additional and unnecessary cost. In Figure 55, Thing X is designed to function at something less than the expected maximum demand (say 70%). When Thing X hits its maximum capacity, it off-loads work to other things (shown on the right of the figure). An example of this would be a business that has an internal private cloud that uses one or more external public clouds when extra capacity is needed. Another example is a business that hires temporary workers to meet higher than usual demands during peak times of the year. [Note: the above example only applies when the load is variable. If the projected load is only in one of two states (zero and a constant) there is no benefit in designing at less than maximum expected demand.]

11.3 Catalog and Inventory Management

11.3.1 Terminology

Inventory and catalog management entail the tracking of information about things and relationships among things. The difference is that inventory management concerns instances of things and catalog management concerns types of things.

Catalog management is the process that tracks, updates, analyzes and provides search capabilities to access types of things.

Inventory management is the process that tracks, updates, analyzes and provides search capabilities to access instances of things.

11.3.2 Concepts

Figure 56 depicts the various dimensions/aspects of inventory management:

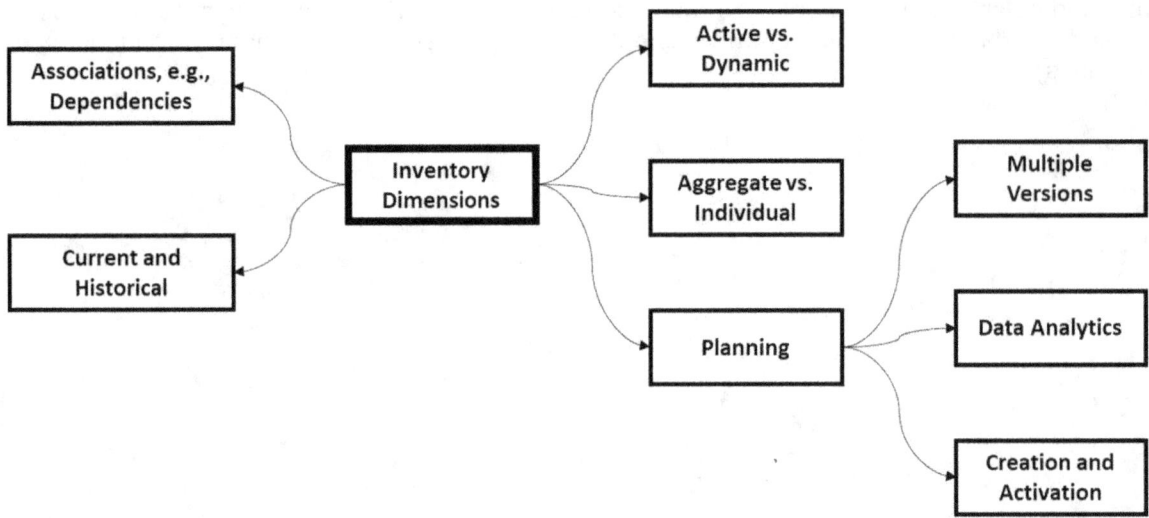

Figure 56. Dimensions / Aspects of Inventory Management

- Associations – inventory management in some cases requires the tracking of relationships among things (in addition to tracking things in isolation). For example, an inventory system that tracks IT assets will need to track each asset (e.g., laptop computer) as well as associations to other entities (e.g., to whom the laptop is assigned, what department owns the laptop, warranty/contract).

- Current and Historical – inventory management does not necessarily cover only the current state. In some cases, historical inventory may be needed, e.g., to track trends, to diagnose problems in cases where the current inventory (including associations among inventory items) has changed since the problem originally occurred, legal/regulatory requirements.

- Active versus Dynamic – in some cases, the relationships among things are determined on-demand and as needed (this is called dynamic inventory) and in other cases, the relationships are actively updated (this is called active inventory). In both cases, the inventory changes. In the active case, inventory relationships are recorded and kept current. In the dynamic case, inventory relationships are constructed as needed.

  o The inventory of artwork in a museum is most likely handled via an active inventory approach. New artwork is immediately recorded along with any related information such as location in the museum and owner (if the artwork is on loan).

  o The relationship between software applications and the supporting compute and storage facilities in a commercial cloud environment is something that changes dynamically and may not typically be recorded. However, if there is a problem with a software application instance, it may be necessary to determine (on-demand) the supporting compute and storage facilities.

- Aggregate versus Individual – for some scenarios, each individual thing needs to be inventoried (e.g., artwork, employees, cars) and in other scenarios, it is sufficient to only kept track of a collection of (typically similar) things. As an example of aggregate inventory, consider processors in a server farm. It may be sufficient to keep track of the number of operational (i.e., not broken) processors but not the individual processors.

- Planning / Future – planning for the future state of inventory is also needed in many cases. The planning may be based on an analysis of past demand trends (data analytics) and on existing orders for things. For more complex scenarios (such as telecommunications networks), it may even be necessary to have multiple plans for future inventories at different times. The various inventory plans are handed-off to a creation and activation process which, in turn, delivers the required things in the required time frame.

Figure 57 shows the dimensions/aspects of catalog management:

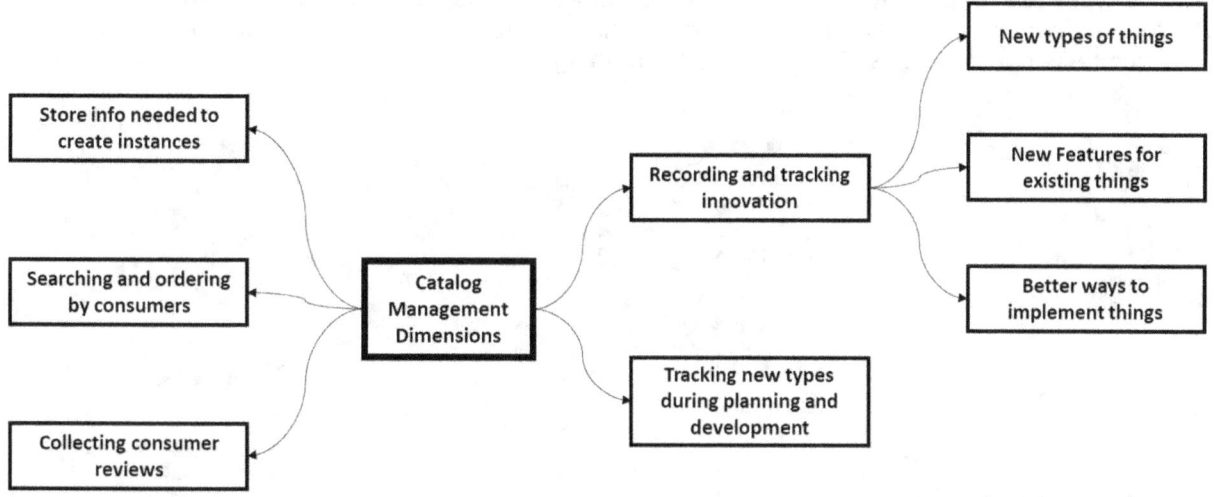

Figure 57. Dimensions / Aspects of Catalog Management

- A catalog can be used to record and track new innovations. This can be for new types of things, new features/capabilities for existing types of things or better ways to implement existing types of things.

    o For example, some large companies have "suggestion boxes" for new ideas. The suggestion box is basically an innovation catalog which the company can use to inspire new products, product features or to better implement existing products.

- During the planning and development phase for a new type of thing or an update (revision) of an existing type of thing, the associated catalog is updated to reflect the status of the type (e.g., expected availability date), description, supported features and deployment requirements.

- During the operating phase for a type of thing, a catalog serves several purposes:

    o A catalog can be used to store the instructions for creating and deploying instances. This is particularly relevant for software applications.

    o A catalog is used by consumers to decide what type of thing satisfies their needs.

    o With the advent of online catalogs, it is now possible to accept consumer reviews of things and present the reviews to prospective buyers. Some online catalogs go even further and allow consumers to ask questions about a given catalog item and for other consumers or the supplier of the thing to answer the questions.

11.3.3 Examples

Consider a time before the advent of electronic catalogs. An apparel company designs a new type of woman's jacket. The new jacket is advertised in a paper catalog and can be ordered via postal mail, phone call or going in person to one of the store locations of the apparel company. Once a jacket is ordered, the apparel company checks their inventory to see if they have an existing jacket of the correct measurements and color. If so, the jacket is delivered to the customer. If not, a new jacket is created to fulfill the order.

Figure 58 shows an automated process that starts with the design of a new type of thing (the Type Design and Catalog Management Platform on the right). Once designed, the new type is onboarded onto Platforms A and B which can, upon request, create instances of the new type. Assume Platforms A and B are physical factories with people and machinery. As new instances of various types are created by Platforms A and B, they are transported by truck or airplane to Platform C (basically a warehouse). Platform C has an automated inventory application and can fulfill requests concerning its current inventory of things.

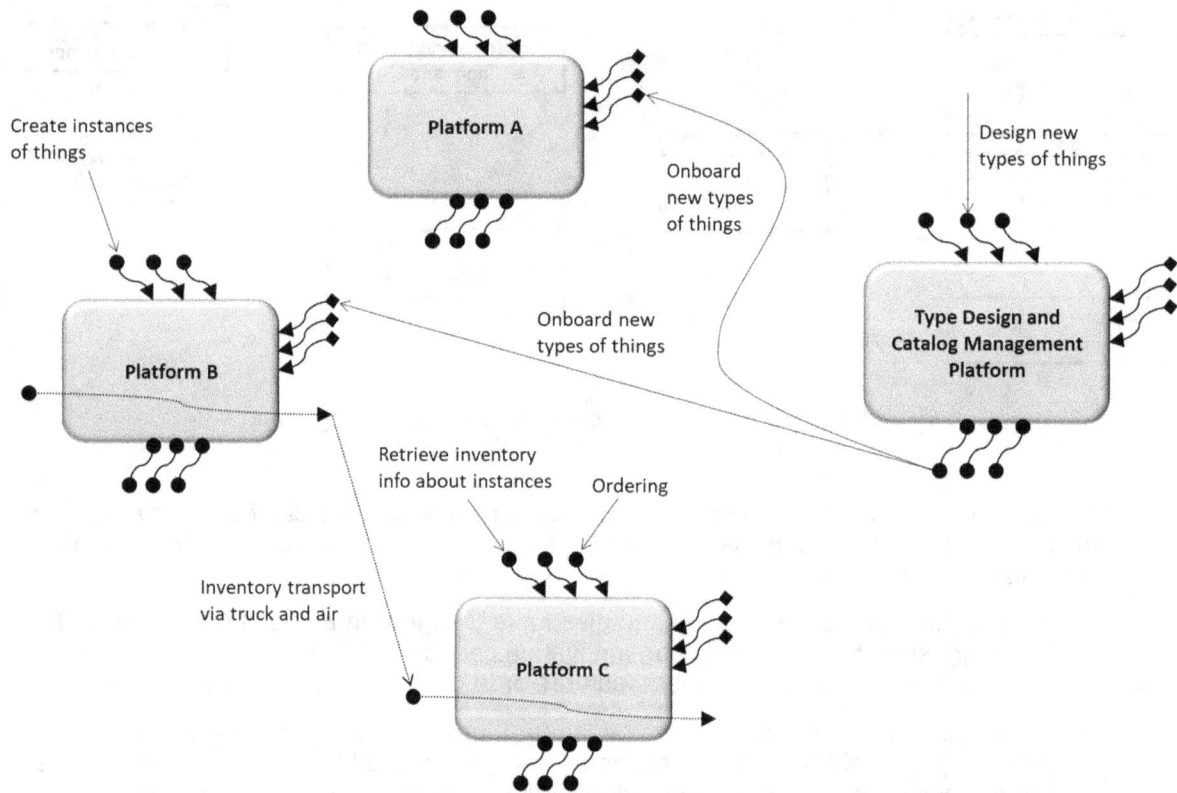

Figure 58. Type Design, Type Onboarding, Instance Activation, and Instance Inventory

Figure 59 provides further insight into the relationship between a type of thing and the associated instances. Assume that all three platforms are within a single organization (e.g., a sporting goods company).

- Using the web interface to the Externally Facing Ordering Platform, a customer orders a pair of trekking poles.

- The Externally Facing Ordering Platform checks with the Inventory Platform to see if there are any existing instances of the given type of trekking pole in the warehouse.

  o If there are available instances of the required type of trekking pole, then the trekking poles are assigned to the order and arrangements are made to mail the items to the customer.

  o If there are not any existing instances of trekking poles of the required type, the Activation and Configuration Platform (a factory for trekking poles and other hiking equipment) is asked to create two trekking poles of the type chosen by the customer. Once the items are ready, they will be sent to the customer.

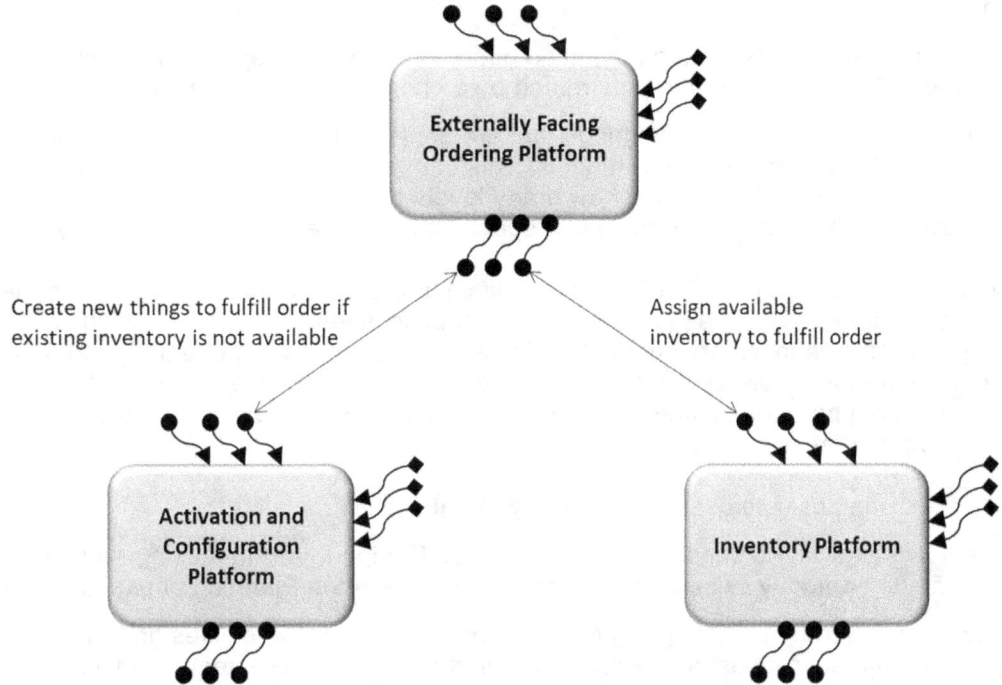

Figure 59. Ordering, Inventory and Creation

In the above example, either existing instances of a given type can be allocated to fulfill an order, or if appropriate instances do not exist, new items of the required type can be created (if inventory is depleted). For some businesses and the types of things for which they sell or lease, the only option is to offer existing instances to consumers. This would be the case for the hotel, real estate (focusing on the resale of existing homes), apartment rental and used car businesses. One could classify these as existing inventory-based businesses. For other businesses, all sales are based on the creation of new instances of types (with typically no instance inventory), e.g., custom-made clothing such as suits, airplanes, personalized items such as bank checks and address labels, and dental braces. However, these businesses do have an inventory of components (e.g., clothing material, airplane parts, blank paper, and dental brace components) but not of the final consumer product.

11.3.4 Requirements

The following requirement is in keeping with the anti-layering admonitions in Section 6.4.4.

Iv_R1: It is recommended that one inventory retrieval and update methodology be used for all types of things.

It is possible to define generic inventory retrieval operations that can be applied to instances of any type of thing. The following is a partial list of generic inventory retrieval operations:

- Get by Identifiers (Ids) – retrieve instances of things by supplying their Ids. For this operation and those that follow, "retrieve" means to get the data structure for the thing. The response shall include the characteristics of the thing and associations to other things.

- Get by Characteristics Filter – retrieve all instances whose characteristics match a given filter.

- Get by Type – retrieve all instances of a given type. This can be further constrained by a characteristic filter.

- Get by Graph – this is a more advanced query where a subgraph of the inventory graph is selected. This can be further constrained by a characteristic or type filter.

- Get by Containment – retrieve things that are contained within a thing. This only works for hierarchal (containment-based) models. This can be further constrained by a characteristic filter or by a scope filter (stating how many levels down the retrieval shall proceed from a top-level thing). This type of query is a special case of the Get by Graph query.

Inventory update is less common and a bit more difficult to explain. Inventory update is the opposite of inventory retrieval, i.e., inventory retrieval pulls inventory information while, in contrast, inventory update pushes inventory information. Inventory update allows one thing to tell another about planned inventory. However, there is no expectation that the receiving thing needs to perform, or make happen, the planned inventory changes. This is what makes inventory update different from configuration (see Section 7.3.3).

Figure 60 shows one possible usage of inventory update:

- The flow starts with a consumer of the Instance Design Platform making requests to design new things or modify existing things. The things are in the Planning phase at this point.

- Upon request from its manager (perhaps a human), the Instance Design Platform sends an inventory update request to the Inventory Platform. The update request includes a collection of planned changes that the Instance Design Platform had been storing internally while awaiting instructions to proceed.

- The Inventory Platform validates the request and sends an acknowledgment to the Instance Design Platform. The key point here is that the inventory update request is not a "create and activate" request (or "provisioning" request, to use the TM Forum term). It is just a way for the Instance Design Platform to convey an inventory plan to the Inventory Platform.

- The Inventory Platform now starts the process of moving the planned things to the Operating phase. This will entail several requests to the Activation and Configuration Platform and the factories within.

- When the Inventory Platform is done with the creation and activation process, it could send an inventory update notification to the Instance Design Platform, or some other discovery method could be used (see Section 11.4 on Discovery).

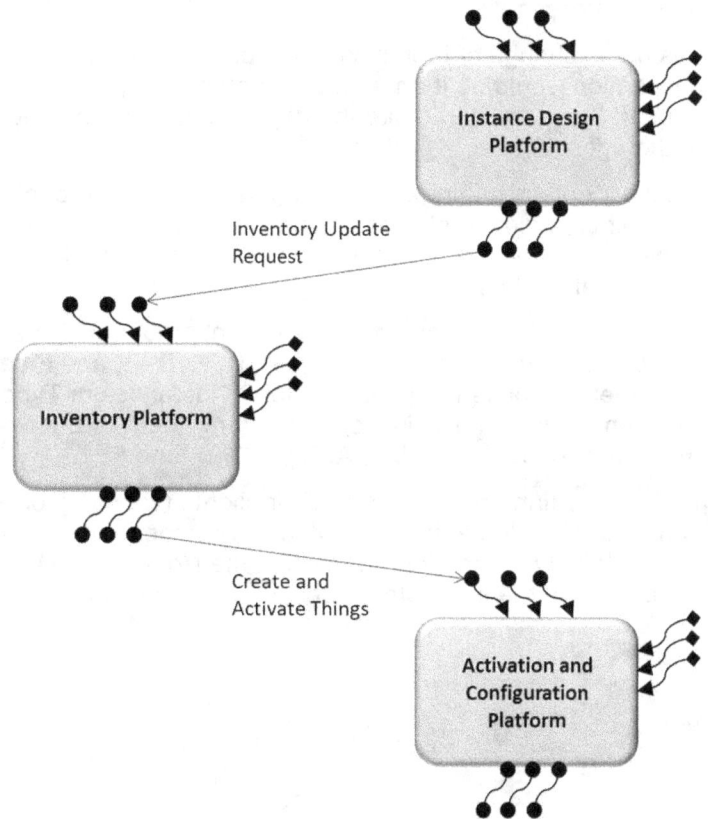

Figure 60. Inventory Update with Subsequent Creation and Activation

Catalog management also has type retrieval needs, but such needs are much less than that of inventory since there are many more instances than types. For software-based things (e.g., Virtualized Network Functions as described in the example associated with Figure 64), it is not just a matter of adding a type specification to a catalog. The actual mechanism (e.g., factory) to create instances of the software also needs to be made available. These two items (loading specification to a catalog and deploying a factory) is part of an onboarding process for a new type.

In keeping with the anti-layering admonitions in Section 6.4.4, the following requirement is stated:

Cat_R1: It is recommended that one catalog methodology be used for all types of things.

Standards bodies and fora in the telecommunications industry are, for the most part, not following the above requirement, and have defined separate (but almost the same) information models and interfaces for catalog management based on layering. The layers are based on a product/service/resource classification scheme. This approach leads to unnecessary replication and associated maintenance of multiple information models and interfaces that effectively provide the same thing.

11.4 Discovery

For a thing to make use of the capabilities of another, it must first discover (become aware of) the other thing and its exposed capabilities. Discovery is also needed at the type level to design compositions and aggregations of things.

Discovery – the process of things becoming aware of each other, including information about interfaces and associated addresses.

Discovery usually entails the exchange of identification information so that the things can find each other and interact. An exception would be if an agent tells other things that it now provides access to instances of a new type of thing and can make the capabilities of such things available when requested. In the case, the agent acts as a broker.

In its simplest form, discovery entails a thing announcing itself directly to another, e.g., someone introducing himself or herself to someone else at a conference while giving the other person a business card. The business card could also provide a brief description of the holder's capabilities, e.g., CPA – specializing in estates planning.

When many things (e.g., managers) are interested in the creation of new instances of a given type, a notification method can be used. In Figure 61, Things A, B, C, D, E, and F have subscribed to receive notifications from Agent X concerning the creation of instances of Type Y. The figure depicts a creation notification (concerning Thing Z) going from Agent X to a Notification Distributor and then to the previously subscribed things, i.e., A, B, C, D, E, and F.

This could be as simple as a law firm announcing to their clients (via email or postal mail) that they have a new patent attorney, or it could be an automated environment in a communications network where Thing Z is a newly installed carrier Ethernet switch, the Notification Distributor is a commercial notification server and the interested (subscribed) things are systems that manage various aspects of Thing Z.

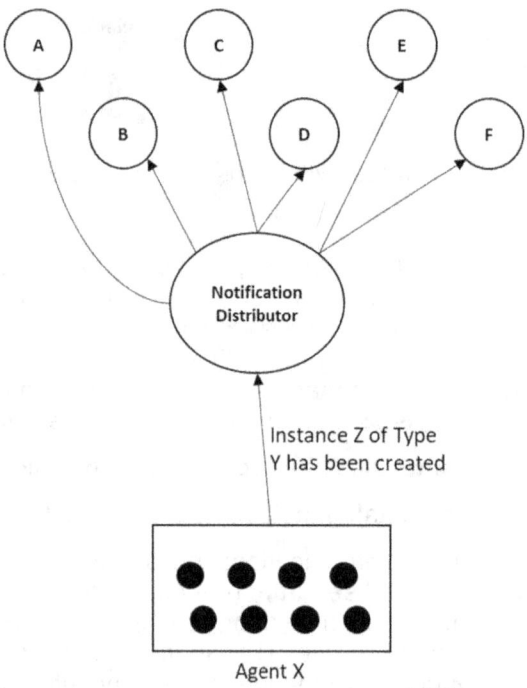

Figure 61. Discovery via Notifications

If the thing being discovered is comprised of many other things (either via composition or aggregation), the notification approach is problematic since the notifications subscribers will be inundated with a storm of notifications and left with the complex task of reassembling the relationships among the constituent things. In such cases, it is better to announce the composition or aggregation via a notification and then let the notification subscribers decide on whether to retrieve the constituent things via an inventory request. Figure 62 shows an example of inventory retrieval after a composition has already been discovered (in this case, Thing Z). For example, Thing B might ask Agent X to retrieve all the things (and associated characteristics) that comprise Thing Z.

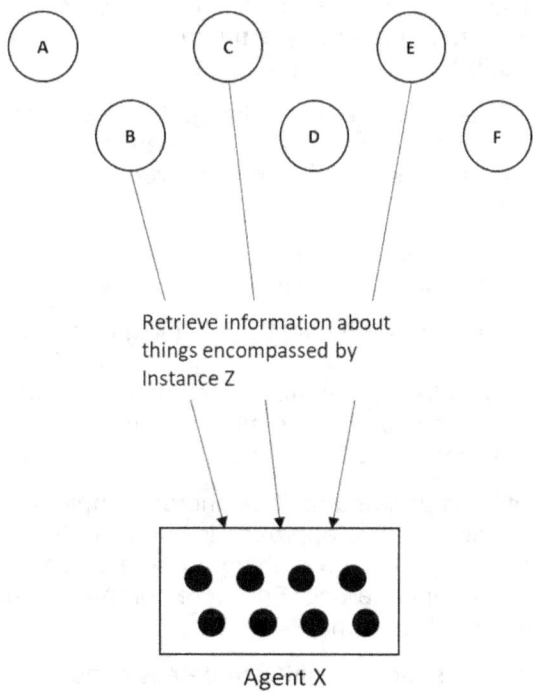

Figure 62. Discovery via Retrieval

There are several possible variations to the discovery through retrieval approach:

- If there are many subscribers, there will be many retrievals of a potentially large amount of information with associated processing costs to compile the requested information repeatedly. This can be addressed by creating a file with information about the internal constituents (of the composite or aggregate) and their relationships, and then putting the file location in the initial creation notification. In this way, interested parties (B, C and D in the example) can retrieve the internal details of the composite or aggregate by downloading the associated file. The potential downside is that the internal structure of the composite or aggregate may change and so, the file may only be valid for a limited time.

- Yet another approach is for interested parties (B, C and D in the example) to send periodic inventory retrieval requests (to Agent X) concerning instances of given types of things. The requests can stipulate that only changes from a given time shall be provided (this feature is available in some commercial inventory systems). Notifications are not necessary for this approach. This approach can, more generally, be used to synchronize inventory between agents. The downside is that things may be created and deleted during the interval between inventory retrievals and possibly not visible to interested managers unless a record of deleted things is kept in inventory.

11.5 Factories and Deployment Scenarios

11.5.1 Overview

In Section 2.1, the concept of a factory was defined. This section goes into further detail concerning the necessary input it takes to design a factory for a type of thing and then create instances of the given type. The focus in this section is on manufactured things. For natural things (e.g., trees, vegetables and animals), the factory is nature itself which can in some cases be modified, e.g., Genetically Modified Organisms (GMOs).

In order to build (or organize) a factory for a type a thing, it is necessary to fully define the type, i.e., it is necessary to provide a detailed specification (as defined in Section 2.1). As shown in Figure 63, a concrete (implementable) specification for a type of thing can take several steps (possibly with some iterations):

- First, define an abstract specification for the type. At this point, the specification is focused on the consumer and not on the underlying dependencies (requirements).

  o For example, consider an architect's specification for a type of house. The specification serves at least two purposes: (1) to help the potential home-owner decide if they would like to purchase such a house and (2) as input to a civil engineer who will provide more detailed specifications for construction. The potential homeowner may be shown a simplified version of the architect's plans.

- The abstract specification is updated until a concrete (implementable and detailed) plan is achieved. In Figure 63, this iterative approach is shown in the second process block that points back to itself. For a simple type of thing, there may only be one step from an abstract specification to a concrete one. For more complex types (e.g., an automobile), there could be several steps/iterations.

- The finalized concrete type specification (with details concerning dependencies on other types) is used to build a factory to create instances of the desired type.

  o This is not a waterfall model. The factory design could very well start earlier (even during the definition of the abstract type).

  o The term "factory" is used very generally here. It does not necessarily need to be a physical plant that creates things. The factory could be a collection of people with detailed instructions for creating instances of a particular type of thing.

- Finally (bottom process block in Figure 63), a consumer of a given type of thing may be given choices (options) concerning a desired instance. The consumer's input and possibly the present state of the environment are used to customize the details of the desired instance.

  o A detailed plan for creating a particular instance of a type of thing is called a **Deployment Scenario**. The factory uses a deployment scenario to create an instance of the thing.

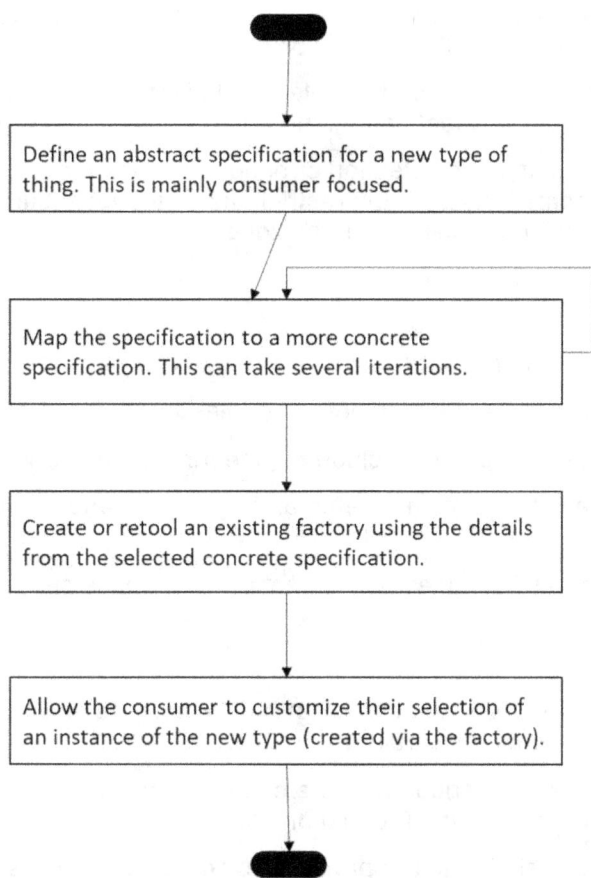

Figure 63. Process Flow for Type Specification and Instance Selection

As noted previously, a deployment scenario can be computed using the consumer's input (e.g., selection of features for a given instance of a type of thing) and the current environment. Another option is to have a static mapping between the consumer's input and a fixed set of possible deployment scenarios. While not recommended, yet another option is to directly present the deployment options to the consumer and let the consumer decide. This forces the consumer to understand the deployment details of a thing, see Section 12.4 concerning intent-based and detailed-based methods).

11.5.2 Examples

This section contains several examples that further illustrate the concepts of "factory", "specification" and "deployment scenario."

11.5.2.1 "Conventional" House

Abstract specification – architect's plans

- This could be a one-off plan, e.g., as requested by someone who owns a parcel of land and wants to build a house on the parcel.

- This could also be a plan for a home building company that wants to apply the plan many times over.

Concrete specification – architect plans with detailed engineering instructions and description of dependencies, e.g., requirements on the foundation.

Factory – the "house factory" is the team of people who build the house on site (carpenters, roofers, plumbers, electricians) plus tools and materials.

Deployment scenario – variations and selection of options by the home buyer (e.g., a downstairs bedroom versus a family room), plus possible restrictions by the local building authority (elevation above ground level which may be required in flood zones).

11.5.2.2 Modular House

Abstraction specification – set of rules for valid combinations of modules

- This implies the need to have a catalog of modules.

- The abstract specification should include engineering instructions for combining modules

Concrete specification – selection of components and desired arrangement for a given type of modular house.

- This specification should include requirements on the house site, e.g., requirements on the foundation.

Factories

- Module factory, e.g., a physical factory that builds modules and then ships them to the required location for house construction.

- Onsite assembly factory – various workers can know how to combine the modules and incorporate the modules into the foundation.

Deployment scenario – this is similar to the previous example. In both cases, it is recommended that the consumer (home buyer in this case) be shown an abstract, intent-based view of the available house designs and allowable customization rather than the details of how each type of house is built.

11.5.2.3 Cake

Abstract specification – recipe ingredients (including possible substitutions and optional items) and cooking instructions

Concrete specification – customized recipe by someone who plans to make the cake

- The customization could go beyond the possible substitutions and options in the original recipe. In this case, one could claim a new recipe has been specified. This is not necessarily inheritance, composition or aggregation. "Version" may be a better term. This can lead to multiple branches from the original recipe (not that anyone actually tracks such things).

Factory – the "cake factory" is the chef and the "tools" in his or her kitchen (including the mixer and oven). Alternately, the recipe could be used by a local bakery, supermarket bakery or industrial bakery that sells cakes to various retailers. In these cases, the factories are progressively more industrial, but the concept is the same.

Deployment scenario – depending on what entity is producing and selling the cake, consumer customization may be possible, e.g., a local bakery would likely be able and willing to put "Happy Birthday, Steve" on a cake or similar text for the occasion.

11.5.2.4 Automobile

Abstract specification – consumer-focused design, covering areas such as appearance to the driver (inside and out), performance, reliability, features such as a rear-view camera or sunroof.

- This could lead to the creation of a concept car which is used as input to the design of a production automobile.

Concrete specification – detailed engineering plans that fulfill the abstract design

Factory – could be a new factory or "retooling" of an existing factory.

- An automated software factory could be data-driven, with a general-purpose interpreter that alters the factory based on configuration data. The automobile factory equivalent would entail a transition from fixed automation (customized around a single type of thing and a specific task) to flexible manufacturing (ability for a factory or sub-factory to be quickly and easily re-purposed for different types of things or tasks).

Deployment scenario – based on customization by the car purchaser. This is based mostly on features as represented in the abstract design and not how the features are implemented. Automobile advertisements may use a combination of high-level features (e.g., climate control) and component details (e.g., a specific type of engine as opposed to the performance provided by the engine).

11.5.2.5 Software Component

Abstract specification – description based on features, i.e., what the software component does and not how. This allows the consumer of the component to select what it requires from among the features offered by the software component without needing to know how the features are implemented. This is an intent-based approach (see Section 12.4 for further details).

Concrete specification – detailed description of the component, including how it is to be managed and dependencies, e.g., required capabilities from other components.

Factory – software that is able to create instances of a given type of software component. The factory arranges for the required infrastructure in support of a software component instance, e.g., compute, storage and network connectivity. Software component factories can be classified as follows:

- Specialized for one type of component - this may make more sense for complex components.
- Generic factory that can create instances of many types of components.

Deployment scenario – based on input from the consumer (e.g., selected features for a given instance of a software component type) and the current state of the environment, the factory computes a deployment scenario for the software component instance. This includes allocation of infrastructure for the component, binding to external components (possibly creating required external components if they do not yet exist) and identification of sub-components that are required based on the consumer's feature selection. Concerning sub-components, the idea is that a software component may be comprised of sub-components, some of which are needed for a given feature and others are not. In some cases, the sub-components may map very closely to the externally exposed features but this is not necessarily the case. In any event, it is recommended that software components be defined to expose their capabilities via features (intent-based) and not on how they are constructed internally (i.e., sub-components and their interconnectivity).

11.5.2.6 Personal Computer (PC)

Abstract specification – general design for a given model of laptop PC, based mostly on features (e.g., processor speed, size of memory, disk memory, battery charge duration, add-on software).

- It is true that some of the features are tightly coupled to hardware components. Some PC suppliers do offer some support intent-based approach. For example, rather than focusing on the hardware specifications, some suppliers will state the PC's category, e.g., heavy-duty gaming, light-weight / travel (notebook), and special-purpose such as PC optimized for Computer Aided Design (CAD). Similarly, an intent-based approach can be taken for storage. For example, state how many photos can be stored or how many full-length movies can be stored (with some qualifications concerning the size of the photos and movies).

- Some features concern guarantees, e.g., 3-year coverage for replacement of failed parts and associated labor, excluding maintenance.

Concrete specification – detailed design of a PC model including internal components, and the arrangement and connectivity of those components.

- The concrete specification should include a mapping from the features (as exposed to the consumer) and the required internal components in support of the selected features.

Factory – various options are possible for building a PC instance, e.g.,

- The PC manufacturer could completely assemble the PC.

- The retailer could customize the PC before sale, e.g., replace Hard Disk Drive (HDD) with an Solid-State Drive (SSD).

- The consumer could also further customize the PC (after purchase), e.g., by upgrading internal components or adding external peripherals such as printers (this is aggregation rather than composition).

Deployment scenario – based on consumer input, the PC manufacturer or retailer can customize the PC instance.

11.5.3 Summary and Recommendations

The detailed/implementable specification for a type of thing allows for the design of an associated factory that can automate the creation of instances of the given type. The type specification, consumer input (e.g., requested features) and possibly the current state of the environment are inputs to the factory concerning the creation of an instance of a thing. Based on the input, the factory determines a deployment scenario for the requested thing and then creates the thing in the context of the identified environment.

The following recommendations apply to specifications, factories and deployment scenarios:

Spec_R1: Each type of thing shall have an abstract (intent-based) specification that describes **what** capabilities are provided by instances of the type.

- It is recognized that for some type of things the "what" may be closely related to the "how."

- There are several advantages of an intent-based approach:
  - The implementation can change while the manner of exposure of capabilities (i.e., interface) to consumers remains the same.
  - The consumer is not required to understand how a thing is implemented to use it.

Spec_R2: Each type of (manufactured) thing shall have a detailed specification (i.e., **how** instances of a type of thing are realized) that can be used as a basis for the design of an associated factory.

Spec_R3: Each instance of a (manufactured) thing shall be created based on a deployment scenario.

- The deployment scenario is generated by the associated factory based on the type specification, consumer input and possibly the current state or even the expected future state of the surrounding environment.

- Concerning the environmental aspect, an example would be a thing (say a video conference) where the connectivity is typically via a 4G cellular network but in a particular case, some of the conference participants areas only served by 2G or 3G. This may affect how the video conference instance is created.

11.6 License Management

11.6.1 Overview

The term "license" is used in two different ways. On one hand, there are licenses to practice medicine or law, do plumbing or electrical work, drive a car, go fishing, go hunting and practice engineering. There are two common themes for this type of license, i.e., ensuring a minimum standard of competence, skill or capability among a collection of things in an ecosystem (e.g., driving license, plumbing or electrician certification), and limiting or controlling the number of things that can legally perform some task. On the other hand, licenses are used to transfer rights concerning the use of intellectual property, e.g., music, photographs, patents, books and software. The former case concerns licensing that allows a thing "to do" something and the latter case concerns licensing "to use" something. The focus here is on the "to use" meaning of license (sometimes referred to as Product Usage Rights (PUR)).

11.6.2 Virtualization Example

In the "to use" meaning of licensing, there is an assumption that the intellectual property being licensed can be easily reproduced and therefore, easily stolen. The recent focus on virtualization in the telecommunications industry provides some insight into "to use" licensing. Telecommunications equipment (physical devices) such as IP routers, add-drop multiplexers and carrier Ethernet switches are sold or perhaps leased but not licensed. (It is recognized that the software residing on such physical devices may be independently licensed). Further, when these physical devices are virtualized, the virtualization software is, in fact, licensed.

In terms of background, ETSI and several other telecommunications standards organizations have taken on the task of defining what is called Network Functions Virtualization (NFV). The idea is to "virtualize" (with software) various network functions (e.g., firewalls, routers, load balancers and content delivery networks). The Virtualized Network Functions (VNFs) are ultimately supported by physical entities. However, the mapping between virtual and physical is not one-to-one and can change over time.

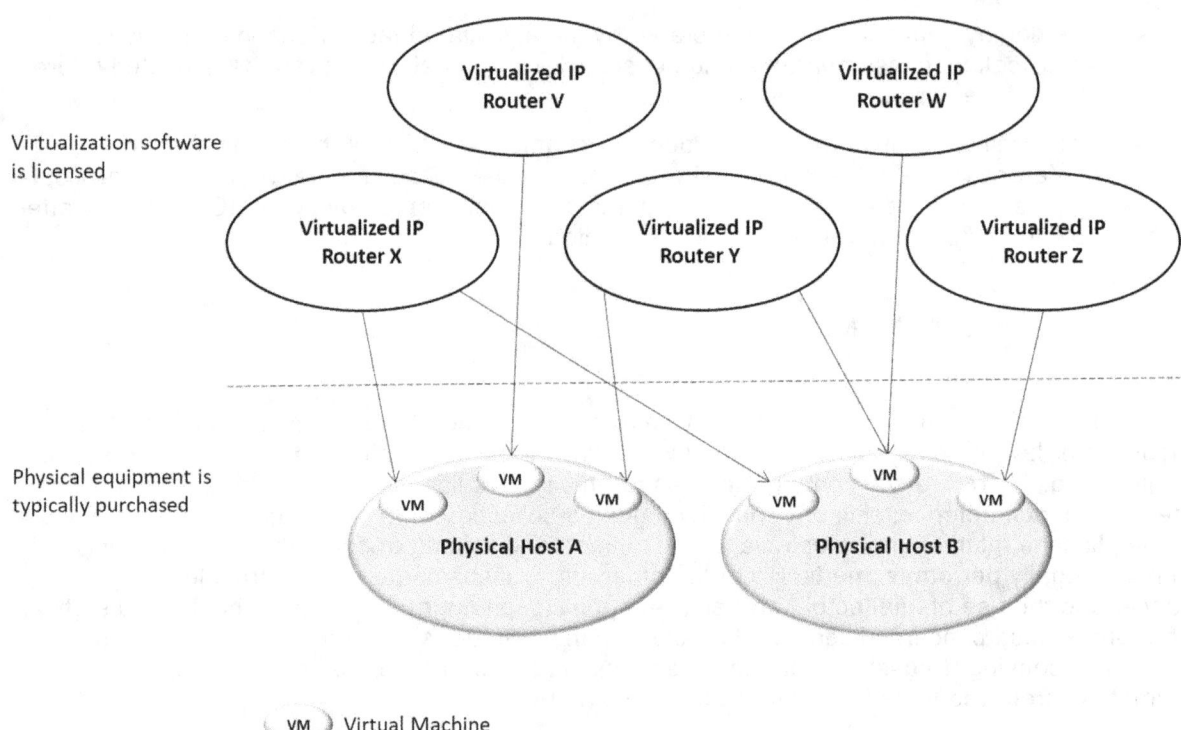

Figure 64. Virtualization Example

Figure 64 depicts several virtualized routers being supported by Virtual Machines (VM) on different hosts. Routers X and Y are using VMs on different physical hosts to ensure resiliency. For more details on NFV, see the ETSI standards [37] and [38].

11.6.3 License Dependencies

For "to use" licensing, it is critical to keep track of the licensing dependencies. For example, CSPs are very concerned that in their NFV environments the expiration of a license for one type of VNF will have a ripple effect and cause many VNFs to stop working because they all depend directly or indirectly on instances of the VNF type whose license has expired. This topic is further explored in the ETSI document *Report on License Management for NFV* [39] and the TM Forum document *IG1141 Procurement and Onboarding Suite* [40].

In fact, there have been outages (in wireless telecommunications networks) caused by license certificate expiration in relatively insignificant software. For example, there was a network affecting issue for an entire country when out-of-date licenses were used in conjunction with a software upgrade from a telecommunications equipment supplier. For the details of this event, see the article [42]. In order to protect against such events, some CSPs now require a licensing model that is not based on expiration but rather on a usage.

11.6.4 Terminology and Requirements

A **license** (in the "to use" sense) is an agreement by which the owner (known as the licensor) of a type of thing grants to another party (known as the licensee) some subset of the rights of the type of thing. Further, a **sub-license** is an agreement by which the licensee (known as the sub-licensor) grants to another party (known as the sub-licensee) some of the licensee's rights regarding a type of thing.

For the "to use" type of licensing, there are many aspects to consider, e.g., charging, right to use, right to modify, right to use in a derived or composite product, right to distribute, right to sub-license. Many of these aspects arise in software licensing (see the Wikipedia article on Software Licensing [41]).

To illustrate the complexity of the problem of license management, consider the situation depicted in Figure 65. Instances of Type X are composed of instances of Types A, B and C, plus instances of three home-grown types from the supplier of Type X. Instances of Types A, B and C, in turn, are composed of components from yet other suppliers. It is assumed Types A, B and C come from different suppliers.

- The supplier for Type A composes instances of Type A using three home-grown components, two external components with a yearly subscription fee, one component with a monthly subscription fee (payment due the 1st day of each month) and another component for which charges are based on usage. Instances of Type A are offered for use on a monthly subscription basis (payment due on the 15th day of each month).

- The supplier for Type B composes instances of Type B using 5 components that have been purchased at a flat rate, three components with a monthly subscription fee (payment due on the 15th day of each month) and two components with a yearly subscription fee. Instances of Type B are offered for use on a monthly subscription basis (payment due on the 1st day of each month).

- The supplier for Type C composes instances of Type C using three home-grown components, three components for which charges are based on usage, one component with a monthly subscription fee (payment due on the 1st day of each month) and one component with a monthly subscription fee (payment due on the 15th day of each month). Instances of Type C are offered for use on a yearly subscription basis (payment due on the 1st of January).

The supplier of Type X, in turn, offers instances of Type X on a monthly subscription basis (payment due on the 1st day of each month). If any of the licenses for Type A, B or C, or the components of Type A, B or C lapse, then instances of Type X will not be able to function properly, if at all.

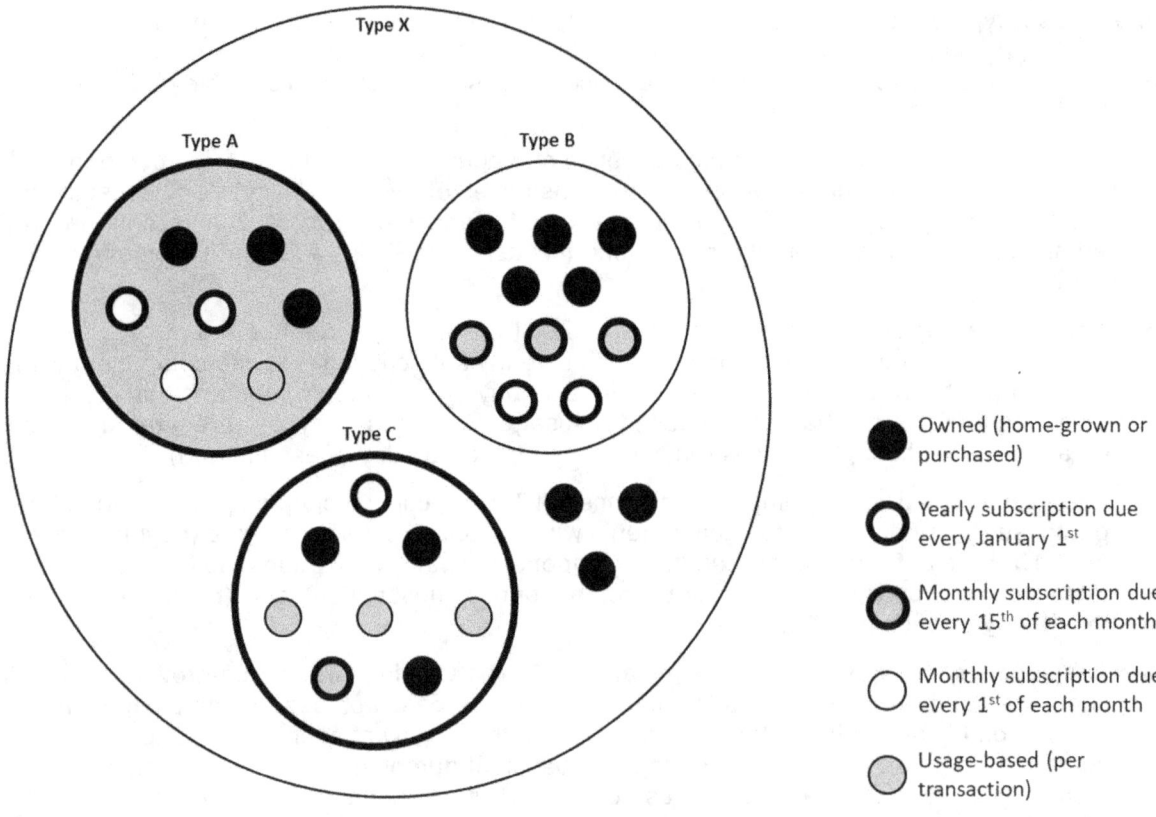

Figure 65. Licensing Impacts on Composition

For an ecosystem that allows and encourages composition and aggregation of components, the licensing problem can be staggering (as can be seen by the relatively simple example above). The following recommendations are made concerning the management of a multi-supplier ecosystem of things that allows for composition and aggregation (related to a single domain such as smart grid management):

- **Ls_R1**: It is recommended that a license management system be provided for the ecosystem. The license management system shall

    o   Keep a record of the license option(s) for each type of thing.

    o   Keep a record of the license expiration for each instance of each type of thing and be able to send warnings (notifications) as the expiration time approaches. This implies an understanding of how various types are composed which may be considered as proprietary information by a supplier. So, it is critical that the organization managing the ecosystem be seen as a trusted party by the component suppliers.

    o   Act as a license broker for the suppliers of components to the ecosystem, thereby providing one common way to purchase licenses within the ecosystem.

- **Ls_R2**: It is recommended that the ecosystem have an agreed set of licensing options.

    o   The rationale is to limit the number of different licensing options for suppliers of things to the ecosystem and thus, reduce the complexity of license management. Allowing each supplier to define its own licensing approach, with no guidance, will lead to immense complexity.

- **Ls_R3**: It is recommended that the ecosystem have an agreed set of formats for reporting usage information.

The above approach is not currently used in commercial cloud environments. However, such environments are open to suppliers of software components from many different domains. Thus, there is less commonality across the components which makes it harder to fulfill the requirements stated above.

Further, as noted, some organization require contracts that do not support license expiration. In such cases, requirement Ls_R1 does not apply.

11.7 Revenue Assurance

11.7.1 Terminology

The following definitions are taken from TM Forum document GB941D Revenue Assurance Revenue Leakage Framework and Examples R18.0.1 [47].

"**Revenue Leakage** – Relates to lost revenues where a chargeable event occurred which should have been billed to the customer or operator but was not, or was charged at a lower rate.

Cost Leakage – Relates to overpayment of costs for chargeable services to a third party

Revenue Opportunity – Relates to the situation where a business policy is in place to set pricing levels, but these are either set at negative or unintentionally low margin levels or the situation where a revenue assurance artificially limits the revenues that can be generated from a subscriber."

The following definition of "revenue assurance" is used in this document:

Revenue Assurance – the process of detecting and correcting revenue leakages, and proactively preventing future revenue leakages.

- The revenue leakage detection process is facilitated by continuous auditing.

11.7.2 Examples

The concept of detecting and healing revenue leakages is sometimes referred to as "revenue assurance." The term originated in the telecommunications industry, but the concept can be applied to many industries. Initial work on revenue assurance was done in the TM Forum, see [45], [46] and [47].

Examples of revenue leakages include

- unintentionally providing external consumers a higher level of service than purchased

- providing a service to an external consumer but failing to activate the associated billing

- marking things as being fully allocated and thus not available for use, but in fact, they are idle (stranded capabilities)

- installing new things but not recording the new thing in active inventory (stranded capabilities)

- provisioning more capacity than is needed for a thing or collection of things.

Figure 66 depicts an example of a top-down audit, intended to detect revenue leakages. It is assumed that all the platforms shown in the diagram belong to one organization. Thing W provides a capability to some external consumer (not shown in the diagram). The intent of the audit is to ensure that Thing W provides exactly what is guaranteed to the external consumer. This may entail tracing dependencies several steps away and possibly across several platforms. For example, in

Figure 66, the audit may entail dependency tracing within Platform A and into supporting platforms (i.e., Platforms B, C, D, E and F).

The audit should also make sure that proper billing has been activated.

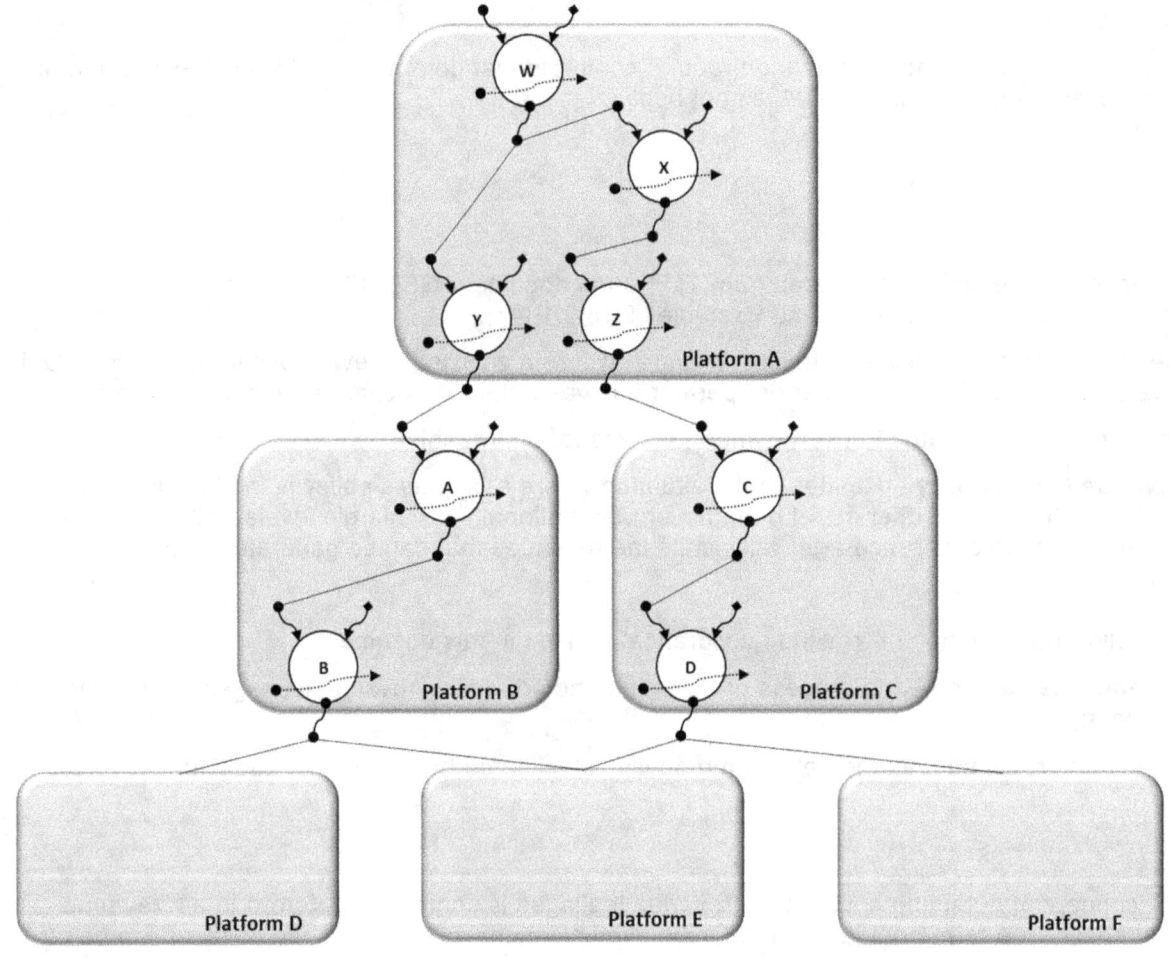

Figure 66. Top-down Audit

Audits are also recommended for internally-facing but high-value types of things. For example, perhaps Thing A in Figure 66 is an expensive item. A bottom-up audit can be done to make sure that Thing A is not stranded, i.e., idle but not properly listed as available for use. In this case, the bottom-up audit would determine that Thing A is in use and is at least partially supporting an external capability provided by Thing W.

Top-down audits may also be beneficial for things at the boundaries of platforms. For the example in Figure 66, top-down audits are recommended for Things A and C, and for the things at the boundaries of Platforms D, E and F (details not shown in the figure). The reason is that platforms are only expected to be aware of dependencies among internal things. For example, Platform B may think that Thing A is being used by Thing Z in Platform A (which is not the case). An audit of Platforms A and B would detect the issue.

Before a new type of thing is introduced into a platform (especially if it exposes capabilities at the boundary of a platform), there should be an audit plan. The plan may, at first, be partially or mostly manual, but the goal should be to automate the audit. Further, the audit should be followed by the correction of any discrepancies. Even better, the root cause of the discrepancies should be found and then corrected so that the same problem does not reoccur. See Section 12.7 concerning root cause problem analysis.

In some cases, the revenue leaks are due to fraud. However, that should not change the approach suggested here. The various audits should be designed to detect intentional (e.g., process design and information synchronization issues) and unintentional (i.e., fraud) revenue leaks.

11.7.3 Requirements

The preceding discussion is summarized (and extended) in the recommendations below.

"Externally-facing thing" refers to a thing in a platform that offers capabilities to an organization or entity outside of the jurisdiction of the platform.

"On the boundary of a platform" refers to things in a platform that offer capabilities to things outside of the platform. Externally-facing things are on the boundary of a platform but not the other way around.

Ra_R1: For each externally-facing type of thing, there shall be an audit plan to ensure that instances of the type provide what is agreed to the external consumer (no more and no less) and to make sure proper billing is established.

Ra_R2: For each high-value type of thing (regardless of whether it is on the boundary of a platform), there shall be an audit plan to ensure that instances of the type provide what is agreed to its consumers (no more and no less).

Ra_R3: For each type of thing whose instances are used at the boundary of a platform, there shall be an audit plan to ensure that instances of the type provide what is agreed to its consumers (no more and no less).

Ra_R4: For each externally-facing type of thing and for other types of things that have many underlying dependencies, there shall be a test to ensure that no underlying thing is stranded when instances of the given thing transitions to either the Operating – Deactivated state or the Retiring phase (as defined in Section 4.3).

Requirement Rca_R5 in Section 12.7.4 (concerning proactive prevention of problems) also applies here.

Perhaps not a requirement but certainly it is a goal to minimize the potential areas where there can be a revenue leak. Such areas can be determined via a continual auditing process. This goal is similar in concept to "Sc_R4: Minimize the Attack Surface" concerning security (see Section 11.8.1).

11.8 Security

Of all the topics covered in this book, the area of security is the most difficult since it is changing at the fastest rate. The reason being that malefactors continue to devise new methods of attack (especially in computer networks and the Internet).

11.8.1 Requirements

The following fundamental principles are often stated regarding information security, but since the scope of this book is wider, the principles have been modified to apply to any type of thing. It is assumed that the requirements pertain to things that may come under security attacks.

- **Sc_R1**: Confidentiality – information about a thing shall only be visible to things authorized to access it.

- **Sc_R2**: Integrity – changes to a thing (including by not limited to its information) shall only be possible by authorized things. All such changes shall be recorded in an immutable manner.

- **Sc_R3**: Availability – a thing shall be available for use only by its authorized consumers as agreed in the contract with each consumer.

The fundamental principles noted above are supported by a secondary (albeit important) set of requirements:

- **Sc_R4**: Minimize the Attack Surface – The attack surface of a thing shall be as small as possible while allowing for authorized consumers to use the thing (per the agreed contract with the thing).

  - For a building or a house, this would mean limited entry points while still allowing for authorized people to enter and in keeping with fire codes. For computer networks, this means fewer and more tightly controlled interfaces.

  - The attack surface for a thing is the collection of points (known as "attack vectors") where an unauthorized thing (known as an "attacker") can attempt to harm, modify or extract information from a thing. In term of the structure of a thing in Figure 14, the attack surface is the totality of all interfaces (Capabilities, Manage, Input / Output and Requires).

- **Sc_R5**: Assign Minimum Privileges – Relative to a given contract between producer and consumer, the consumer shall be given the minimum access rights that still allow for the contract to be fulfilled.

- **Sc_R6**: Assignment of Roles – Access to a thing shall be based on the role assigned to a consumer.

  - This is related to Sc_R5, and the two requirements imply that minimum access privileges should be assigned on a per (contract, context, role) basis.

  - The structure of a thing in Figure 14 already separates the interfaces into two categories: capabilities and management. The structure of a platform (in Figure 27) further divides the management aspect into capabilities management and platform management. These interface types can be further divided as needed (possibly for security reasons).

- **Sc_R7**: Defense in Depth (also known as the Castle Approach): The security defense for a thing shall entail multiple independent layers.

  - There is a tradeoff to be considered here. The number of defensive layers should be related to how much damage can be caused by unauthorized access to a given capability.

- **Sc_R8**: Record Activities – All access to a thing shall be recorded.

  - This should be done regardless of whether there is a current security breach or not. The activity record can be used to help determine the genesis of security breaches and to help prevent future breaches of a similar nature.

- **Sc_R9**: Run Tests – A thing shall be tested on a continual basis for security weaknesses and be improved to thwart discovered weaknesses. The tests shall cover potential security breaches as well as existing breaches.

  - It is not uncommon for breaches into the computer networks of companies to continue for long periods before being detected.

- **Sc_R10**: Plan for Recovery from Attacks – Each thing shall have a plan of recovery concerning security attacks.

11.8.2 General Security Strategy – Defense and Offense

The requirements in the previous section are all defensive in nature. This is true in general for most security approaches in computer networks (e.g., virus detection and removal, firewalls, passwords, access right management). Even for non-digital assets (e.g., homes, buildings, cars), the security approaches are mostly defensive.

While defensive approaches are needed, it is recommended that more emphasis be put on offensive approaches to security. The idea is to change the cost/benefit analysis of the attackers. This is hard to do for an individual or even an organization (such as a commercial enterprise). A combination of offensive technologies, laws and collaborations (perhaps facilitated by a government) are required to support an offensive approach to security.

Offensive approaches can be divided into punitive and reward-based (as discussed in the following subsections).

11.8.2.1 Traps and Active Tracking of Perpetrators

In terms of offensive security technologies, there are already existing approaches, e.g., honeypots. In the realm of computer networks, a honeypot offers what appears to be legitimate information or functionality but in fact is a trap to detect and possibly track security attacks. This is similar in principle to a law enforcement sting operation. Appropriate laws need to be put in place that set the legal boundaries for offensive security strategies such as honeypots.

Tracking the sale of stolen information (sometimes over the Internet) such as credit card numbers, personal identification information, health records and intellectual property is more detective work than technology-driven at this point.

A collaboration between law enforcement, potential victims and technology suppliers is critical. The recommended end-game is a web of security traps and tracking mechanisms designed to catch malefactors. This needs to be supported by associated criminal laws, law enforcement and multi-organizational cooperation (i.e., local and federal governments, businesses and academia).

11.8.2.2 Rewards

While traps and actively tracking of perpetrators fall into the punitive category, there are also positive approaches that reward those who report and fix security bugs in things.

In the area of software applications, there is something called a bug bounty program. Such programs are offered by software application producers to software hacking experts (something referred to as "researchers"). The researchers are given access to the software application (possibly but necessarily web-based) and financially rewarded for finding bugs (focus is on security bugs). In some cases, a solution to resolve the bug is also required. These programs encourage researchers to discover and fix bugs before the general public is aware of them, thereby preventing potential security breaches. This approach is somewhat like open source software development in that many eyes (from different organizations) have a vested interest in improving a given software product. For more information on bug bounty programs see the Wikipedia article on this topic [53].

11.8.3 Platform Security Strategies

Security strategy with respect to a platform can be divided into several aspects (as shown in Figure 67).

At the top of Figure 67 are the things that make use of the externally visible capabilities and management interfaces offered by the platform. The external things should not see the internal structure of the platform but rather, just the externally exposed interfaces.

At the bottom of Figure 67 are the native or core things. The platform owner or overseers, in the case of an open source platform, decide on what gets into the core. For the core, an open source approach is recommended because this implies many independent eyes need to examine a thing before it can be added to the platform as a core capability. See the Wikipedia article "Open-source software security" [54] for further insights into security in an open source environment.

In the middle of Figure 67 are the non-native things that are added to the platform by external entities (e.g., application developers). There are several approaches to security in this case.

- In one option, the platform infrastructure provider takes responsibility for the security of both the native and non-native things. This makes sense if the things within the platform are closely related and are intended as possible components in more complex things.

- In another option, the platform infrastructure provider may only take responsibility for the security of the infrastructure (native things) and leave security of the non-native things to the entities that place the non-native things in the infrastructure. This is, in fact, the approach taken by commercial cloud providers. In the figure, that would mean that security for A, B, C, D, E and F would be the responsibility of the entities placing these things within Platform XYZ. If A, B, C, D, E and F each use a different security scheme, aggregation (or composition) of these components may be complex or infeasible.

Regardless of the selected option, for the non-native components within a platform that have the potential to be aggregated or composed, it is recommended that they follow the same security scheme. Further, it is necessary that the security requirements for each type of non-native thing placed within the platform be documented in a catalog.

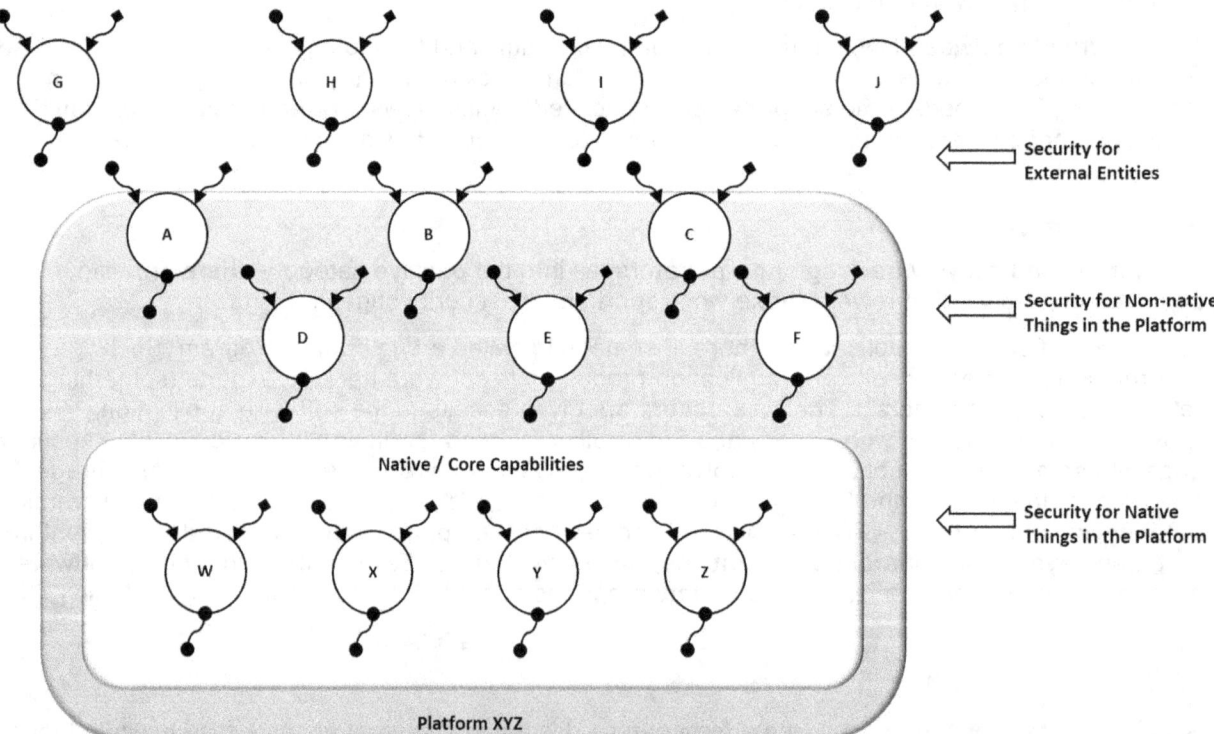

Figure 67. Security Aspects Relative to a Platform

Figure 68 shows a possible division of security responsibilities.

- The Commercial Cloud Platform takes responsibility for the security of the infrastructure, including the native capabilities.

- Each of the domain-specific platforms have their own security scheme for the things that they manage. For example, the Telecommunications Platform could be an open source platform which has its own native capabilities and allows for external entities to place their applications on the platform. The owner of the Telecommunications Platform could mandate the same security scheme for both native and non-native applications (within the Telecommunication Platform). A similar approach could be taken by the Smart City and Smart Grid Platforms.

If an application is needed in several of the domain-specific platforms, it could either be replicated in each domain-specific platform where it is required or be cast as a native capability of the commercial cloud platform. In such an arrangement, isolation is required. For example, the Smart City Platform (because of a malfunction or because of a security breach) could temporarily consume excessive resources from the underlying Commercial Cloud Platform to the point where the other domain-specific platforms are adversely affected. This implies a need to assign resource usage boundaries for each client of the Commercial Cloud Platform. Further, clients of the Commercial Cloud Platform that have clients (e.g., the domain-specific platforms) would need to set resource boundaries for their clients. It would be helpful to have threshold crossing notifications as the various boundaries are approached.

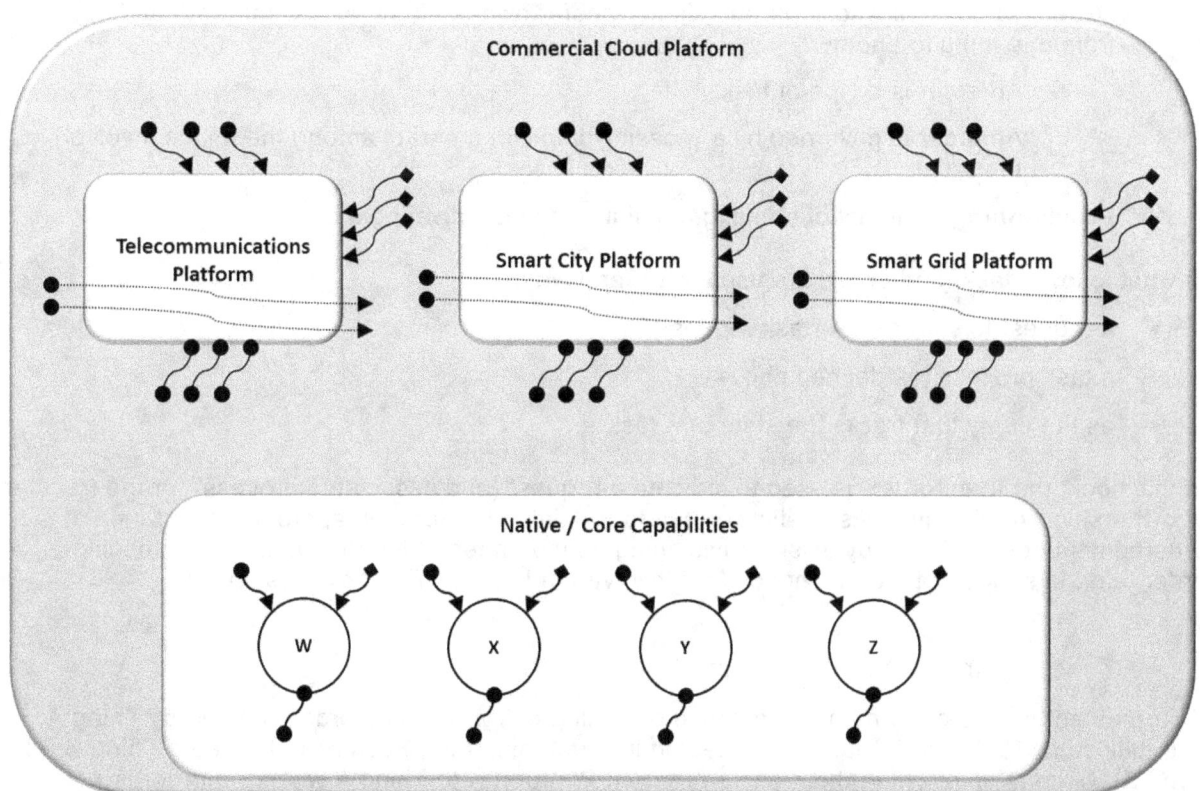

Figure 68. Division of Security Responsibilities

11.9 Transfer of Ownership or Control

11.9.1 Overview

This section is about the transfer of ownership or control between things. "Transfer of control" is weaker than "transfer of ownership." In the former case, ownership is retained by the leaser but the lessee is afforded some level of control over the thing, e.g., leasing a car. In what follows in this section, the phrase "transfer of ownership" is used to cover both cases, unless stated otherwise.

For some things, an order is used to transfer ownership, e.g., ordering a book online or ordering a car part from an auto supply store. In some cases, the order is for an existing thing and it is just a matter of transferring ownership. In other cases, the ordered thing first needs to be created, e.g., ordering a custom-made suit, and then ownership is transferred. The distinction is "sell from stock" versus "build to order."

For more complex things (e.g., a customized personal computer), there may also need to be configuration and activation before the thing is transferred for use to another owner.

For yet other things, no explicit or written order is needed to transfer ownership, e.g., buying food items at a local market. Even in these cases, it is usually possible to get a receipt which is sort of an order completion record. In yet other cases, there is not even a receipt, e.g., gifts.

Some basic terms:

- **Task** – a process within a thing that produces a result.

    o An externally offered capability of a thing is fulfilled by one or more tasks.

- **Order** – a process whose purpose is to transfer ownership or control for a set of things from one thing to another.

    o An order is a type of task.

    o An order is governed by a (possibly implicit) contract among the things involved in the order.

- **Provisioning** – the act of creating, configuring and activating a thing.

In what follows, task (and order) are used in several ways:

- a request to start a task (task request)

- a task process (as defined above)

- as the entity that tracks the state of a task.

In this book, the term "order" is used to indicate a request (and associated process) for the transfer of ownership. Provisioning is sometimes needed to fulfill an order if an appropriate instance of the ordered item does not already exist. Provisioning may be needed independent of any specific order, e.g., in support of internal needs (not involved in the transfer of ownership).

11.9.2 Ordering and Provisioning Example

Figure 69 entails the ordering of an instance of a thing of Type Z. The order is made by Thing A and fulfilled by Platform X. Platform X uses an internal thing (i.e., Factory Y) to create Thing B (of Type Z). Ownership of Thing B is transferred from Platform X to Thing A when the order is completed.

Some key points regarding the sequence shown in Figure 69:

- The Message Exchange Patterns (MEP) are either Request-Reply or One-way. (See Section 12.5 for further details concerning MEPs.) The state of the interaction between

Thing A and Platform X is kept in an Order object, and the state of the interaction between Platform X and Factory Y is kept in a Task object.

- Thing A sends messages to an external interface offered by Platform X. The external interface is supported by some internal thing within Platform X, e.g., an order management thing. So, to be precise, it is the order management thing that is interacting with Factory Y.

- Concerning the last step, i.e., "Thing A can now make requests of Thing B," this assumes that Thing B is a digital thing that is managed by a platform external to Thing A. If Thing B was a physical item (e.g., a photo album) the item would, of course, be delivered directly to Thing A.

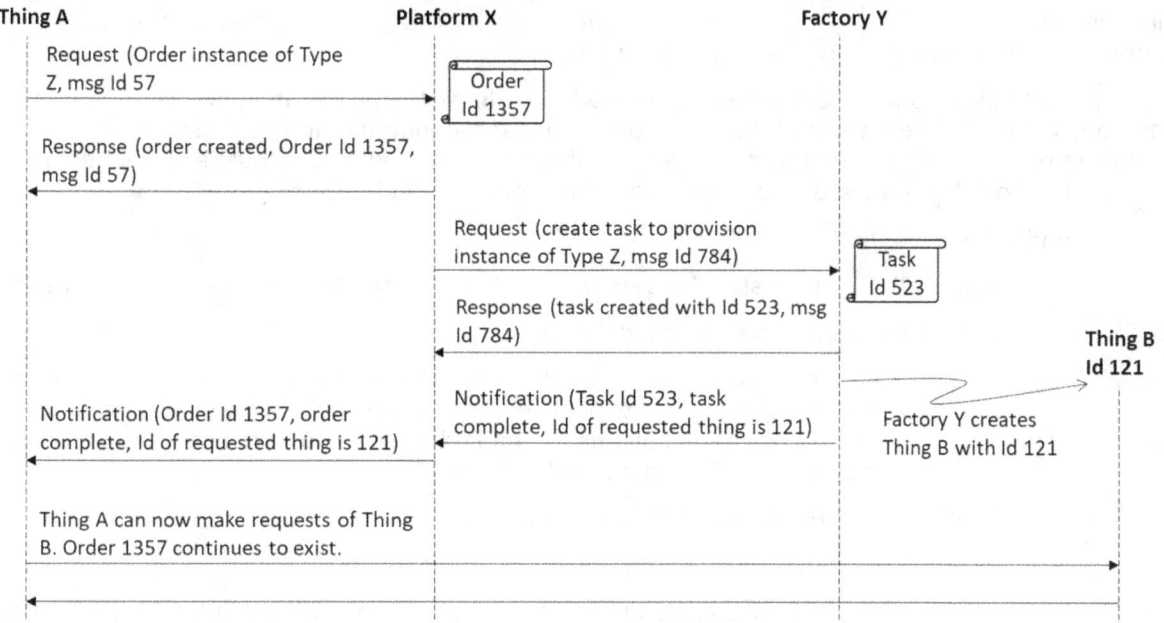

Figure 69. Ordering and Provisioning Relationship

11.9.3 Properties of Tasks and Orders

A given task has some or all the following properties:

- Has a persistent state
  - The persistent state pertains to the task process and not the individual interactions that transpire during the lifetime of the task. The external interactions with the task are based on the Request-Reply or One-way MEPs which are stateless and thus supportive of a RESTful approach [26].

- Can bundle several items (i.e., sub-tasks)

- Can have its processing suspended and subsequently resumed
  - This may also be possible at the sub-task level.

- Can have its processing aborted
  - This may also be possible at the sub-task level.

An order, being a type of task, inherits all of the above properties. An order has the additional property of being able to transfer ownership of a thing from one entity to another.

11.10 Trust and Traceability

[Author's note: I originally intended this subsection to be about distributed ledgers (blockchain) but soon realized that blockchain only solves part of the stated problem. There is a basic issue with the validity of the information that enters the blockchain. If the information is incorrect, it will be persisted forever. So, much of what is written below addresses the issue of information validation.]

11.10.1   Overview

When multiple things collaborate to accomplish some task or set of tasks, a contract is required among the things (as discussed in Section 12.3). In many cases, there is a lack of trust among the things involved in a contract. To address this issue, it is necessary to verify and reliably trace the contributions of the things engaged in the contract.

The bullet list below summarizes the steps needed to address the lack of trust in a contract. The first step is to identify the areas of distrust. Approaches for monitoring and verification are then established. The verified events and transactions need to be stored in a reliable and immutable manner, and possibly retrieved when there are challenges to past happenings.

- Identify Areas of Distrust
    - Identify the various stakeholders (some of whom may be external to the contract).
    - Determine the areas of distrust:
        - This may not be symmetric. There may be trust among some stakeholders in a contract (e.g., a prospective home buyer and the home inspector that he or she hires) and distrust among other stakeholders (e.g., a prospective home buyer and the home seller).
    - Identify what needs to be tracked and when:
        - Pre-contract
            - ✓ For example, when a house is to be purchased in the United States, the seller needs to get a certificate of occupancy from the local government.
            - ✓ Further, the buyer will typically want the house inspected by an independent third party and will purchase title insurance.
        - During contract lifecycle
            - ✓ For example, a Content Delivery Network (CDN) may come with guarantees concerning response times, latency and content storage capacity, all of which need to be monitored to make sure the contract is being faithfully executed by all parties involved.
        - Post-contract – even after a contract is complete, there could still be challenges, e.g., a home repair is found to be faulty after the contract period is over and the contractor who provided the home repair is found to be negligent.
- Verification – the solutions that address the areas of mistrust must support a verification process for the associated events and transactions:
    - Approaches:
        - Mutual agreement among parties in the contract – this approach is used in software development where the parties involved in the development

(designers, code developers and testers) all sign-off on the final software product).

- Trusted third party (in the house purchase example above, the certificate of occupancy, title insurance and house inspection are provided by trusted third parties).

○ Time of Verification: In some cases, the events related to a contract may only be monitored (e.g., by an automated measurement system) and not further verified unless challenged by one of the parties in the contract. For example, there may be extensive monitoring of a CDN. If all is well, the measurements are accepted as-is. If the party leasing the CDN runs into a problem, then the measurements will need to be further analyzed to determine the source of the problem. This analysis is effectively a higher-level of verification concerning the performance of the CDN. There are two relevant timing considerations:

- Concurrent with the event: the exchange of money in payment for a thing such as a house

- Post-event: In some cases, an event that impacts a contract may not be recognized as an issue at the time of its occurrence. For example, a CDN may be encountering problems relative to its guaranteed level of service. The source of the problem may not be detected for several hours or days, and then eventually recorded as a verified event (possibly with billing consequences).

- Recording of Verified Events and Transactions: What needs to be recorded and for how long must be described in the contract. Further, the method of recording (e.g., blockchain) and associated requirements (e.g., immutable and permanent storage) needs to be agreed.

- Searching through Verified Events and Transactions: When problems arise concerning the fulfillment of a contract, it may be necessary to search and analyze past events and transactions.

11.10.2   Requirements

The following requirements are derived from the analysis in the previous section:

- **Trust_R1**: A contract shall identify the various stakeholders (some of whom may be external to the contract) and state the areas of distrust among the stakeholders.

  ○ For example, a CDN consumer (the entity leasing the CDN, not the end-user) may have a strong requirement that its customers (end-users) do not have to wait more than a given number of seconds for requested content to be delivered (e.g., start to stream a movie).

- **Trust_R2**: In support of trust verification, a contract shall indicate the types of events and transactions that need to be tracked and when the tracking is to occur.

  ○ Continuing with the CDN example, the requirement could be "if, during a one-hour period, more than 10% of end-user content requests take longer than 3 seconds to fulfill, then a billing discount is to be granted by the CDN supplier to the CDN consumer." This requirement implies a particular set of measurements need to be taken, evaluated and verified.

- **Trust_R3**: A contract shall describe how the identified events and transactions (from Trust_R2) are to be tracked.

  ○ Trust_R2 is about "what" and Trust_R3 is about "how" (implementation). In the CDN example, the contract may stipulate that the response time is to be measured from the time that the end-user request first reaches the CDN to the time the requested content starts to leave the CDN (in route to the end-user). Further, the one-hour measurement periods are overlapping (with start-times every 5-minutes).

- **Trust_R4**: A contract shall describe how the collected events and transactions (from Trust_R3) are to be verified.
    - o In the CDN example, the consumer of the CDN may want to have simulated end-users at various test points to confirm the measurements from the CDN supplier. The agreement could be that a measure from the CDN supplier is not considered to be verified until the CDN consumer agrees, or 72 hours after the time of measurement (whichever comes first).

- **Trust_R5**: The verified events and transactions, related to a contract, shall be stored in an immutable manner.
    - o Blockchain technology is recommended for this aspect of the contract. However, other options are viable:
        - ▪ A centralized database that only allows for new data to be added with no support. for updates or deletes
        - ▪ A database whose access is managed by a trusted third party.
    - o The "immutable" part of the requirement does present difficulties when information is entered into a blockchain and later found to be incorrect. In such cases, the only option is to add another transaction that references the prior transaction, with an indication that it is incorrect and with some additional information to set the record straight. Another option is to replace "immutable" with "reliable" and allow for changes (but only under strong governance and with the agreement of all parties involved).

- **Trust_R6**: It shall be possible to search, in an efficient way, the verified events and transactions related to a contract.

- **Trust_R7**: For persistent things (e.g., a house or car), it shall be possible to track, verify, record and search events and transactions that cross several contracts.

12 Patterns for Ecosystems of Things

This section covers patterns (e.g., templates and versioning) that can be applied to several of the management areas defined in the previous section. Table 16 and Table 17 shows the applicability of each pattern to the various management areas. An "x" is only placed in a cell where there is strong applicability.

Table 16. Applicability of Patterns to Management Areas – Part 1

	Billing	Capacity mgmt.	Catalog & inventory mgmt.	Discovery	Factories & deployment scenarios
Backward & forward compatibility			x	x	x
Behavior adjustment	x	x	x	x	x
Contracts & contexts	x	x	x	x	x
Intent-based & detailed-based interfaces	x	x	x	x	x
Message exchange patterns	x	x	x	x	x
Metrics	x	x			x
Root cause problem analysis	x	x	x	x	x
Templates			x		x
Versioning			x	x	x
Virtualization & abstraction		x	x		x

Table 17. Applicability of Patterns to Management Areas – Part 2

	License mgmt.	Revenue assurance	Security	Transfer ownership or control	Trust & traceability
Backward & forward compatibility					
Behavior adjustment	x	x	x	x	x
Contracts & contexts	x	x	x	x	x
Intent-based & detailed-based interfaces	x	x	x	x	x
Message exchange patterns	x	x	x	x	x
Metrics	x	x	x	x	x
Root cause problem analysis	x	x	x	x	x
Templates					
Versioning				x	
Virtualization & abstraction					

For more detailed design patterns (mostly based on object-oriented design), see [22] [23] and [24]. Also, see *OSS Design Patterns: A Pattern Approach to the Design of Telecommunications Management Systems* [25], which focuses on design patterns for Operations Support Systems (OSS) for telecommunications networks.

The subsections of this section are listed in alphabetical order and can be read in any order the reader desires. However, as noted in the introduction to this book, there are many cross-references among the subsections in this section and Section 11.

12.1 Backward and Forward Compatibility

For things to communicate, they need to support a common interface version and make use of a common communication infrastructure. The key word here is "version." This section addresses situations where a consumer and provider share a common interface but at different versions.

12.1.1 Terminology

Backward Compatibility – a property where the provider of an interface continues to support consumers using an earlier version of the interface.

An example of backward compatibility is shown in Figure 70. In this situation, Provider X has been updated to support v2.3 of a given interface but continues to support consumers that use earlier versions.

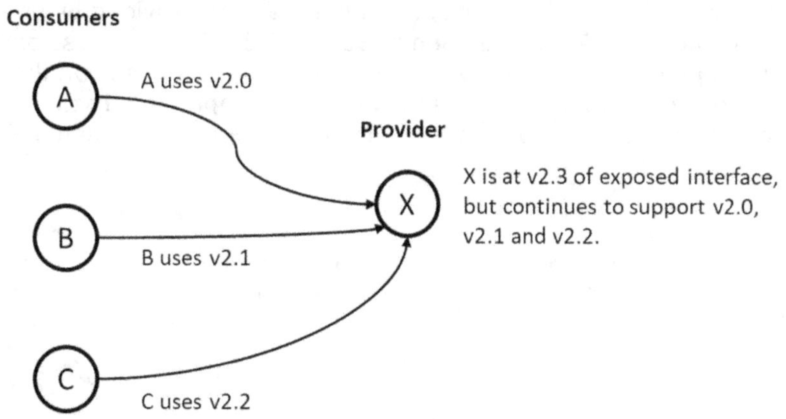

Consumers

A uses v2.0

Provider

X is at v2.3 of exposed interface, but continues to support v2.0, v2.1 and v2.2.

B uses v2.1

C uses v2.2

Figure 70. Backward Compatibility Example

Forward Compatibility – a property where the provider of an interface can support consumers using a later version of the interface.

- This typically entails the provider ignoring conditional features in the later versions of the interface.

Figure 71 shows an example of forward compatibility where Provider X can handle requests from consumers using later versions of the interface from what Provider X supports. For example, if Consumer A requests a new feature (in v2.1 but not in v2.0), Provider X could reject the request or possibly only partially fulfill the request (while ignoring the feature in v2.1 but not v2.0).

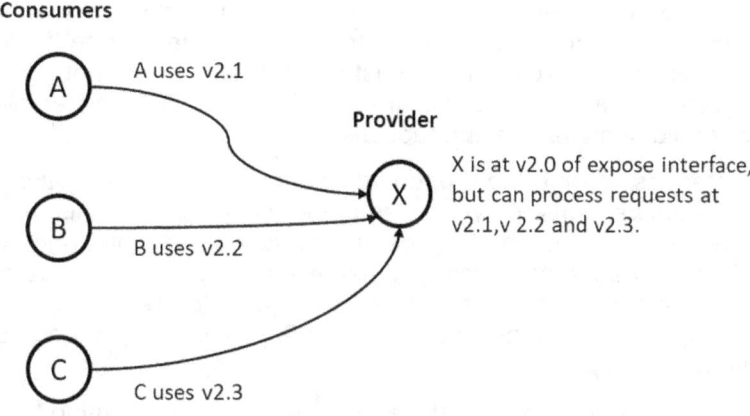

Consumers

A uses v2.1

Provider

X is at v2.0 of expose interface, but can process requests at v2.1,v 2.2 and v2.3.

B uses v2.2

C uses v2.3

Figure 71. Forward Compatibility Example

12.1.2 Compatibility Approaches

The most basic and costly compatibility approach (i.e., brute force) entails multiple versions of an interface being supported by the provider or consumer. There may be no choice but to use this approach if major changes are made to an interface in going from one version to the next (see Section 12.1.2.1). However, if there is significant overlap in functionality between one version of an interface operation and another, less onerous approaches are possible.

The left-hand side of Figure 72 depicts the overlap in the features provided by an operation in two different versions of an interface. As will be seen in Section 12.1.2.2, it is possible to define a methodology for handling forward and backward compatibility in this case. On the right-hand side of Figure 72, there is no overlap in the features provided by an operation in two different versions of an interface. In this case, the brute force method (Section 12.1.2.1) is needed in support of compatibility.

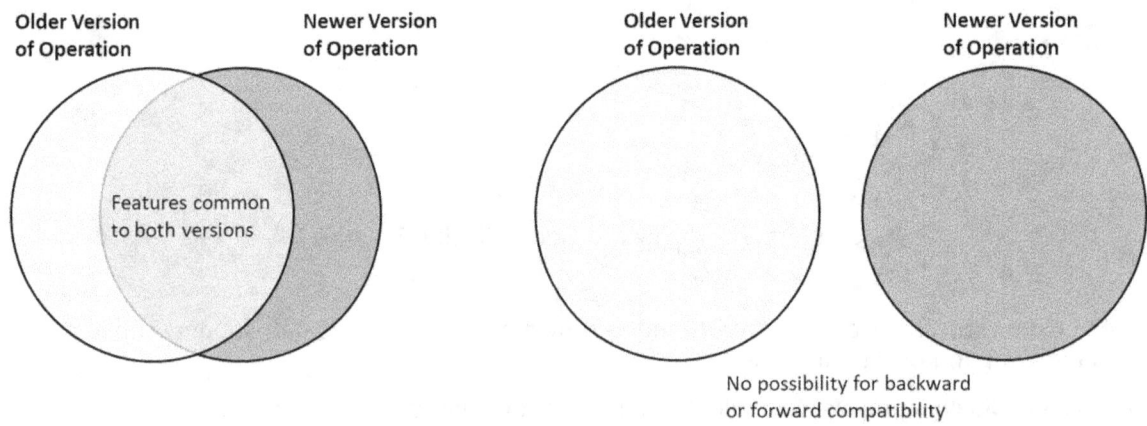

Figure 72. Overlap between Versions of an Interface Operation

12.1.2.1 Simultaneously Supporting Several Versions

For stateless interactions, the migration from one version of a type to another can be handled by simultaneously supporting instances of both the old and new version (also known as the "brute force" method). A very strong form of "stateless" is used here, i.e., the provider does not need to have any memory of past events to fulfill a request from a consumer. There is no state information stored about the interaction and there are no persistent objects created that last beyond an interaction, e.g., this would exclude a RESTful interface (see the Wikipedia article [26]) for ordering since an order object would span several interactions.

In Figure 73, some instances of Type X are updated from one version to another. During the transition, instances of both versions of Type X are made available to consumers. In the middle of the figure, the instances of Type X supporting the old version are in white, and those supporting the new version are in gray. As the consumers of instances of Type X are updated to support the new interfaces offered by instances of Type X, they can direct their requests to the instances of Type X that have been updated to the new version. This is possible since there is no requirement to remember past interactions.

It is possible to update the Management interface of Type X without updating the Capabilities interface, and vice versa. This is highlighted in Figure 73 where the consumer things on the left only use the Capabilities interfaces of instances of Type X and the consumer things on the right only use the Management interfaces of the instances of Type X. So, if only the Management interface of Type X is updated, the consumer things on the left will be unaffected. One can go even further and subdivide the Capabilities and Management interfaces, thus allowing for more focused updates that affect smaller groups of consumers.

"**Microservices**" is a software development approach in which application capabilities are exposed via relatively small and loosely coupled interfaces. One advantage of this approach is to allow form aspects of an application (a thing) to be updated independently of other aspects. All of which fits well with the preceding discussion. The finer-grained interfaces discussed in Section 7.5 is essentially a microservice approach. The finer-granularity in Section 7.5 was focused on security issues. In general, a microservices approach can be used to address multiple issues. From the Wikipedia article on microservices [27]:

> The benefit of decomposing an application into different smaller services is that it improves modularity. This makes the application easier to understand, develop, test, and become more resilient to architecture erosion. It parallelizes development by enabling small autonomous teams to develop, deploy and scale their respective services independently. It also allows the architecture of an individual service to emerge through continuous refactoring. Microservices-based architectures enable continuous delivery and deployment.

While not commonly (if at all) mentioned, a microservices approach can be applied to many types of things outside of the software domain.

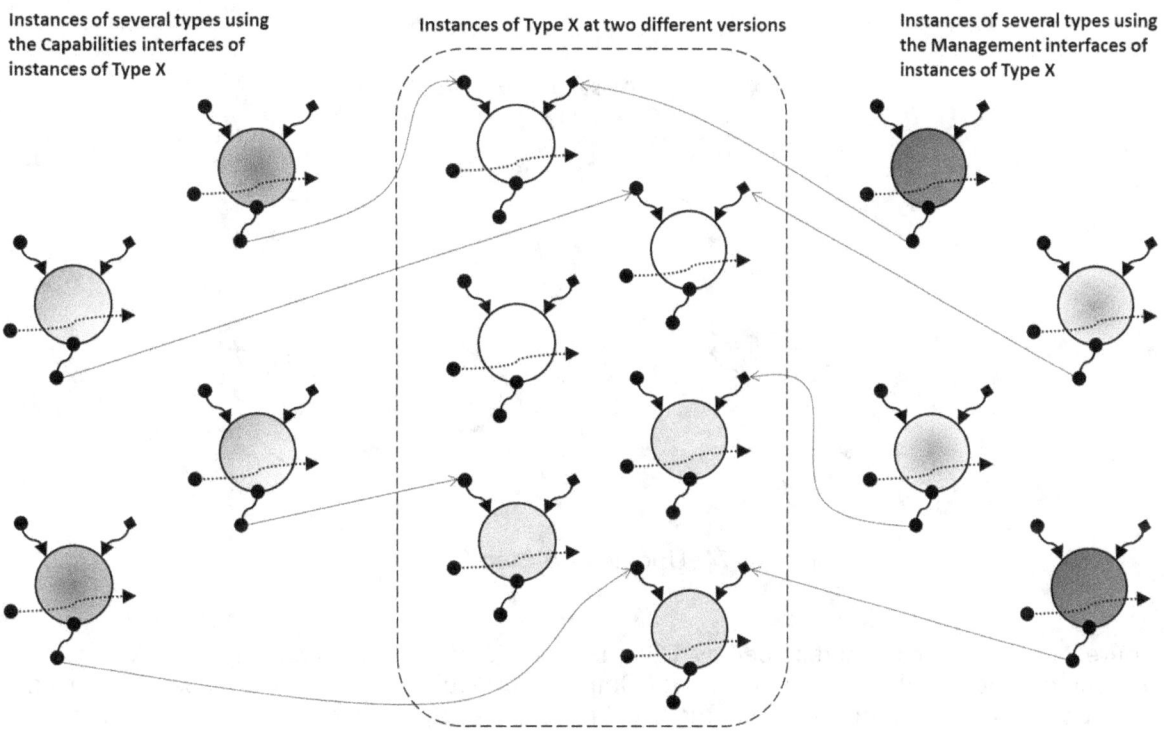

Figure 73. Update of Stateless Things

For stateful interactions, the transition becomes much more difficult. A consumer cannot simply switch from using an instance of a provider at one version to another instance of a provider (of the same type) at another version. The current state information needs to be replicated in order for the transition to be successful. Further, the state information also includes dependencies from the provider to yet other things.

Figure 74 shows an update procedure when the type of thing being updated is stateful.

- Thing A is the consumer relative to Thing B.

- Thing C is of the same type as Thing B but at a later version. The goal in the scenario is to replace Thing B with Thing C as a provider to Thing A.

- Assume that Things D, E and F are dedicated to the capability that Thing B provides to Thing A. So, before the switch, Thing C should reference these things with the intent of using them after the switch; otherwise, there may be a service interruption to Thing A.

- Prior to the switch, the state of Thing C needs to be synchronized with Thing B. This is under the assumption Thing A is the only consumer of Thing B. If Thing B has several consumers, then additional state information would need to be synchronized with Thing C.

- Once the switch occurs, Thing A will be making use of Thing C and no longer associated with Thing B.

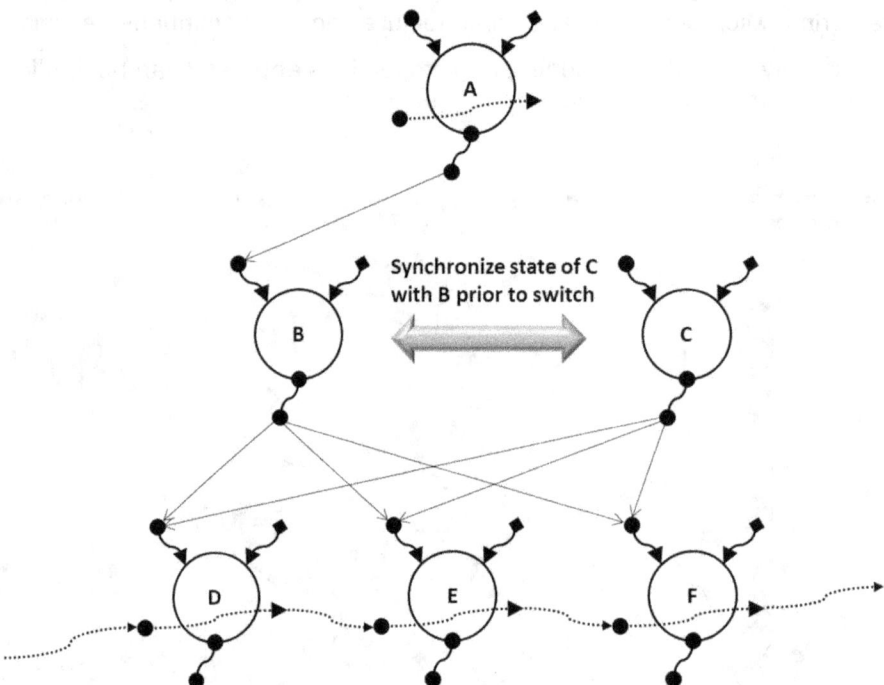

Figure 74. Update of a Stateful Thing

In Figure 75, Thing A is to be replaced by Thing B which is of the same type as Thing A, but of a later version. Since A supports a flow (Input / Output interface), the flow needs to be transferred to Thing B before the switch occurs. In the figure, it is assumed that Thing C can replicate the flow, and send it to Things A and B. This requires some foresight in the design of Thing C. Another possibility would be to insert a thing (e.g. a load-balancer) between C and A that can replicate the flow. Figure 75 shows the arrangement just before the switch.

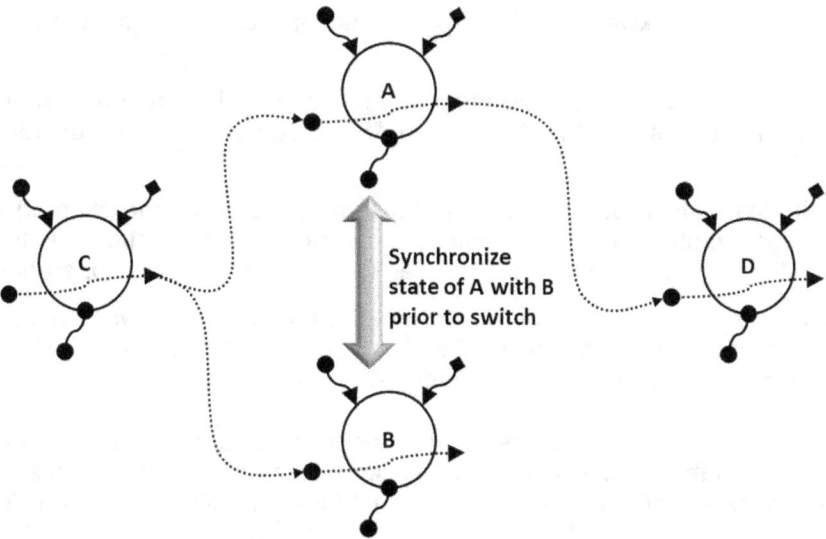

Figure 75. Update of a Thing with a Flow (before switch)

Figure 76 shows the arrangement just after the switch. After the switch, Thing A can be retired, or retained and updated to the new version. Depending on resiliency requirements, Things A and B may be placed in a primary-standby arrangement.

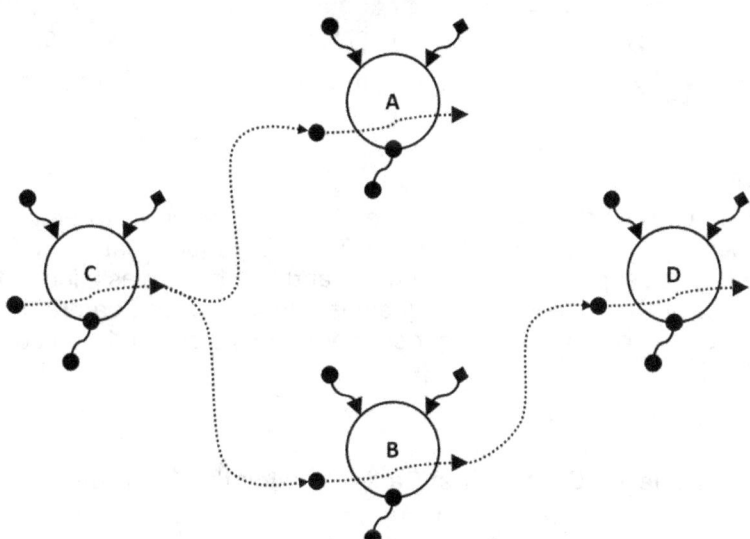

Figure 76. Update of a Thing with a Flow (after switch)

12.1.2.2 Fine-Grained Approach

It is possible to define a fine-grained methodology for handling backward and forward compatibility for any message-based interface offered by a thing. Recall from Figure 14 (and surrounding explanation) that the Capabilities, Management and Requires interfaces of a thing are message-based. The "fine-grained" methodology is applied at the level of the features exposed by the interface elements such as operations and notifications, where "feature" is as defined in Section 2.1. For the discussion here, the focus is on features that are requested by interface operations.

The basic methodology for backward and forward compatibility of an interface is summarized as follows:

- In going from one version of an interface to another, examine each operation and classify the associated features as either Mandatory, "Must Be Fulfilled If Requested," or "Can Be Ignored If Requested."
  - If the Mandatory features are **not** the same for a given operation between two versions, multiple versions need to be supported if compatibility is to be achieved, i.e., the brute force method is needed (at least for the given operation).
  - If the Mandatory features are the same for a given operation between two versions, then compatibility is possible when "Must Be Fulfilled If Requested" features (common to both versions) are requested in an operation.

In Table 18, the features of Operation X are put into the three categories, as noted above. Since the Mandatory features match exactly and there are some common features in the "Must Be Fulfilled If Requested" category, there is some potential for compatibility between Version 1.0 and 1.1.

Table 18. Feature Classification for an Interface Operation X

	Mandatory features (must be present in all requests)	Features (that if requested) must be fulfilled, or the request is to be rejected	Features that can be ignored while partially fulfilling the request
Version 1.0	x, y, z	a, b, c, d, e	f, g, h
Version 1.1	x, y, z	a, b, c, e	f, g
		k, l	m, n

Table 19 shows an example of how to handle requests (of Operation X) when the provider supports Version 1.1 and the consumer supports Version 1.0. The first request can be fulfilled but Feature h will be ignored since it is not supported in Version 1.1 and has been classified in the "Can Be Ignored If Requested" category. The second request is rejected since Feature d is in the "Must Be Fulfilled If Requested" category but is no longer supported in Version 1.1 and so cannot possibly be fulfilled by the provider.

Table 19. Consumer at Earlier Version than Provider

Request	Response
Requested Features: x, y, z a, b, c f, g, h	Request can be fulfilled. However, the response will indicate that Feature h is not supported.
Requested Features: x, y, z a, b, c, d f, g, h	Request will be rejected since Feature d is classified as "Must Be Fulfilled If Requested" for Version 1.0 but not supported at all in Version 1.1.

Table 20 shows how to handle requests (of Operation X) when the provider supports Version 1.0 and the consumer supports Version 1.1. The first request can be fulfilled but Features m and n will be ignored since they are not supported in Version 1.0 and have been classified in the "Can Be Ignored If Requested" category. The second request is rejected since Feature k is in the "Must Be Fulfilled If Requested" category but is not supported in Version 1.0 and so cannot possibly be fulfilled by the provider.

Table 20. Consumer at Later Version than Provider

Request	Response
Requested Features: x, y, z a, b, c f, g, m, n	Request can be fulfilled. However, the response will indicate that Features m and n are not supported.
Requested Features: x, y, z a, b, c, k f, g, m, n	Request will be rejected since Feature k is classified as "Must Be Fulfilled If Requested" for Version 1.1 but not supported at all in Version 1.0.

Variations of the methodology described above are possible. The main idea is to allow for operations to be partially fulfilled when optional features are requested by the consumer but not supported by the provider.

Further, it is possible for a thing to determine supported features at run-time (noting that the above example assumes supported features are determined at design-time). This (i.e., determination of supported features) could be done, for example, by means of a pre-agreed negotiation protocol between the consumer and producer things.

12.2 Behavior Adjustment

12.2.1 Overview

The behavior of a thing may need to change to fit into its environment. Some types of things (humans, other animals, adaptive software) can "self-adjust" to their environment while other things may need help from the outside to determine when and how to adjust. This section covers approaches for behavior adjustment.

12.2.2 Configuration

The behavior of instances of some types of things can be configured at the time of their creation or during their lifetimes. Configuration can be considered a form of behavior adjustment when the characteristics being configured are related to the behavior of the thing under consideration. This approach can be supplemented by the template pattern (see Section 12.8).

Figure 77 shows two versions of a house alarm type on the left, with associated instances on the right. The type definitions allow for a range of behavior selections. The top-right of the figure shows the alarm owner's behavior selections based on Version 1.0 of the house alarm software. Later, the alarm supplier updates the alarm type specification (bottom-left) and associated software. Assume that the alarm unit has Wi-Fi, so its software can be remotely updated to Version 2.0. The homeowner initiates a software update to their alarm unit, and then makes some updates to the behavior characteristics (shown in bold at the bottom-right).

Version update to a type of thing allows for more flexibility in behavior adjustment, but to be clear, it is still possible (in some cases) to modify the behavior of a thing by reconfiguration without any associated version update. For example, the homeowner could have changed the Sound characteristic from "buzzer" to "horn" without updating the alarm to Version 2.0.

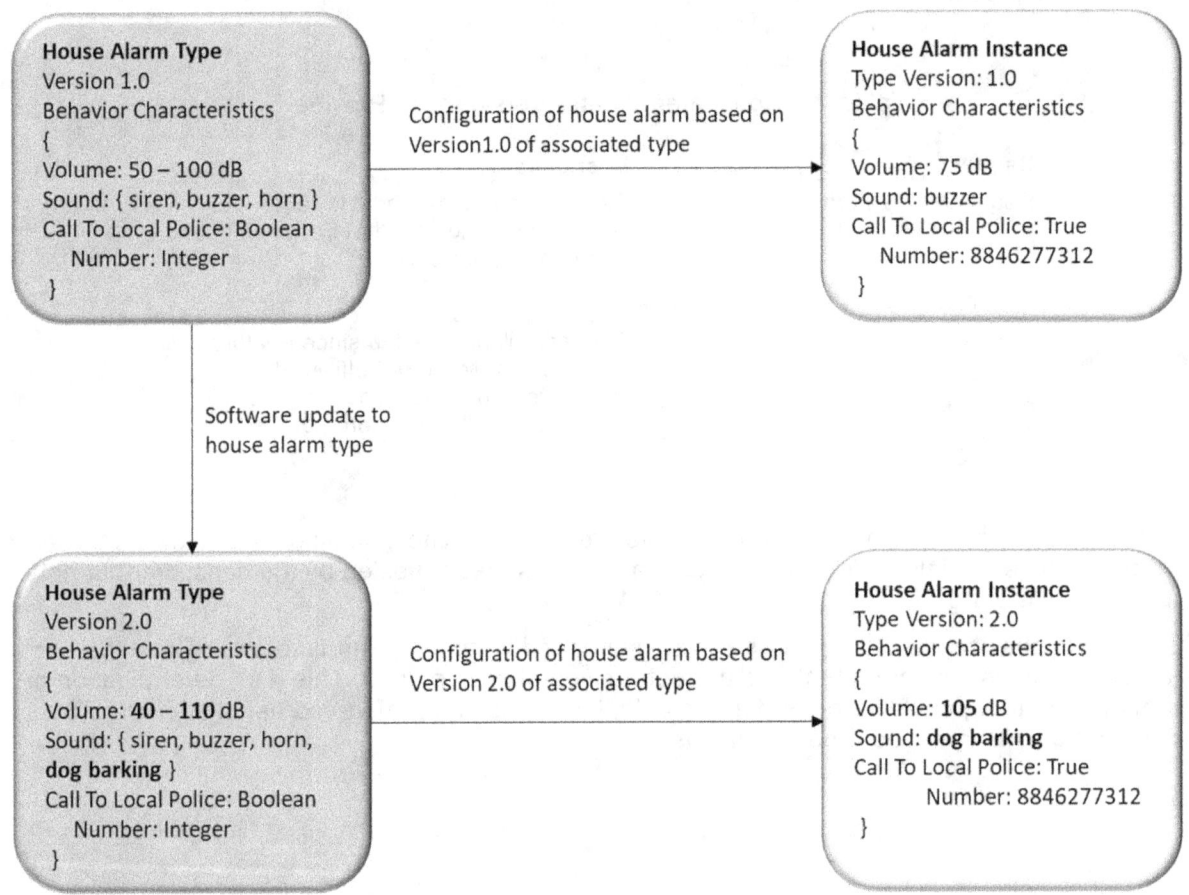

Figure 77. Configuration of House Alarm

In some cases, it is not possible to update an instance from one version of a type to another, e.g., a USB memory stick, a pair of shoes, a ball-point pen. In such cases, the only option is to obtain an instance based on a new version of the type and then configure the characteristics as desired.

12.2.3 Process Breakpoints

In this approach, the internal processing of a thing is designed with breakpoints that allow for the insertion of external logic. The breakpoints are based on predefined conditions. A thing can either stop processing at a breakpoint and wait for further instructions, or continue processing (with the possibility of future input). A good example of this approach comes from the world of telephony where call processing can be stopped at various points, with a notification sent to an external entity which can insert alternative instructions for call processing. This concept is known as Intelligent Network (IN), see ITU-T Recommendation Q.1214 [29]. The rationale is to allow service providers or their agents to add new features beyond or in lieu of the call features provided by the suppliers of the call processing software and associated switching equipment.

IN is based on a standard state machine for the originating and termination side of a phone call. However, the general approach proposed in this book is based on conditions discerned by a thing, with state transitions being only one type of condition.

A simple example of the process breakpoint approach is depicted in Figure 78:

- Thing A determines that some predefined condition is met, stops processing, sends a notification to Thing B and then waits for a response. The notification could also have some information concerning the current state of Thing A.

- Thing B analyzes the notification and determines that additional information needs to be retrieved from Thing A.

- Once Thing B receives the additional information, it can determine a course of action for Thing A.

- Thing B makes one or more requests to Thing A.

- Once Thing A has fulfilled the requests, Thing B returns control to Thing A which resumes normal processing.

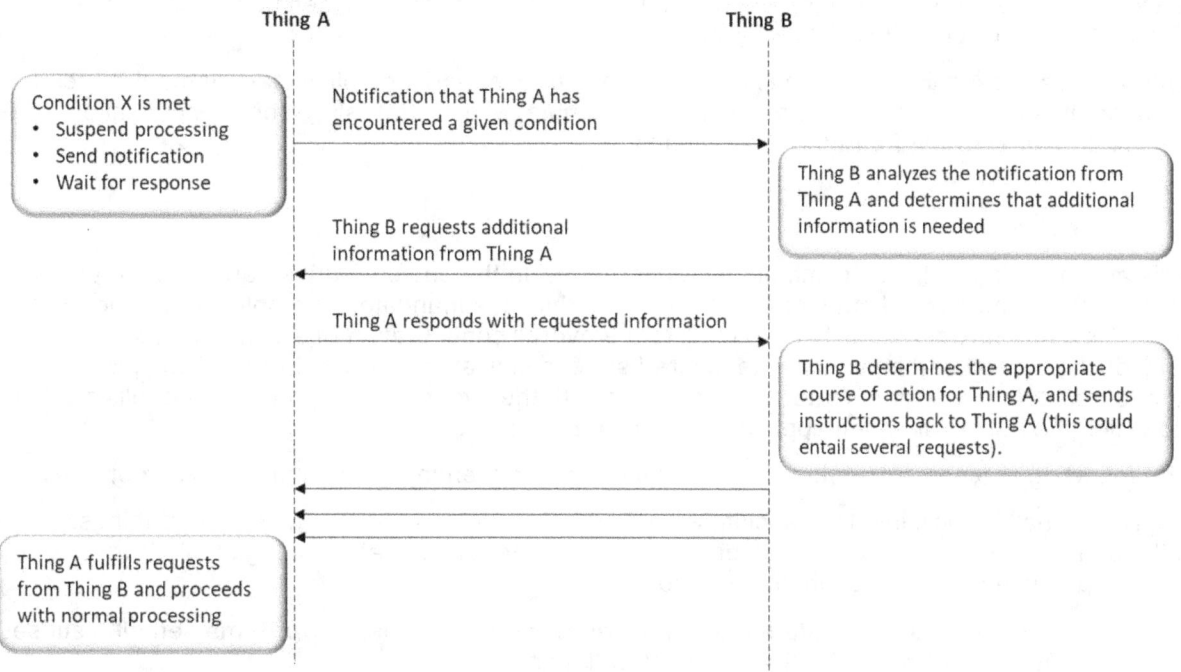

Figure 78. Process Breakpoint Example

12.2.4 Policy Management

Policy management is the process of dynamically enhancing the behavior of things by applying rules, while not modifying the internal composition of those things.

It is assumed that the thing to which a policy rule is applied can perform the desired behavior indicated in the rule. A policy rule depends on and makes use of the native capabilities of a thing – it does not add new capabilities.

A policy rule can be applied to an agent that handles several things. The agent, in turn, may need to issue requests on some or all the things under its purview. In other cases, the agent may not need to interact with the underlying things. For example, consider a firewall that acts as a security agent for several other things. Based on a given policy rule, the firewall may block certain packets from reaching any of the underlying things (who will not even know that the packets have been blocked).

Some alternate definitions of policy:

- Strassner [30]: "Policy is a set of rules that are used to manage and control the changing and/or maintaining of the state of one or more managed objects."

- Sloman [31]: "Policies are rules governing the choices in behavior of a system"

- Verma [32]: "A policy is an administrator-specified directive that manages certain aspects of the desired outcome of interactions among users, among applications, and between users and applications."

   o The definition from Verma is very much focused on IP networks.

12.2.4.1 Event-driven

In the event-driven approach to policy management, policy rules entail the matching of events to predefined conditions. When a match is determined, the thing to which the policy has been applied is expected to perform an action or set of actions. This approach is sometimes referred to as Event-Condition-Action (ECA).

The process breakpoint approach is a special case of event-driven policy management. When a breakpoint is reached, the policy action is, for example, "stop processing, send a notification to a given address and wait for further instructions."

12.2.4.2 Outcome-driven

This approach is much less common in the literature. In the outcome-driven approach to policy management, the desired state of a thing or set of things is mandated in a policy rule. The term "state" is used very generally here to refer to the overall configuration of a thing and its relationships to other things. Only the desired state is indicated, and **not how** the thing is to arrive at and maintain the desired state. This contrasts with the event-driven approach that tells a thing (to which the policy rule been applied) exactly **what** to do.

The following is a non-exhaustive list of requirements concerning the outcome-driven approach:

Ba_R1: It shall be possible to associate a desired persistent state with a given set of things. While a thing may deviate from the desired persistent state, the rule is that the thing shall return to the desired persistent state as soon as possible.

- The desired persistent state (perhaps "configuration" is a better word) may entail a subset of the characteristics for the given set of things.

- The things do not necessarily need to be of the same type. The requirement is that all things in scope have the characteristics defined in the policy rule concerning the desired persistent state.

- The characteristic values associated with a desired persistent state can be exact or one can define ranges. In the latter case, no action is required if the characteristic values are within the set ranges.

- A simple example would be a thermostat in a house. The desired state is the temperature. How the Heating, Ventilation and Air Conditioning (HVAC) system maintains the temperature is outside the scope of the outcome-drive policy (i.e., temperature setting).

Ba_R1a: It shall be possible to request a change to the desired persistent state of a set of things.

Ba_R2: It shall be possible to associate a desired state to a thing when a given set of conditions are met. When the given conditions are no longer met, the thing is free to vary from the desired state.

12.2.5 Learning

Machine-based or natural (human), goal-based learning can be used to achieve behavior changes.

Natural learning can be per instance or at the type level (e.g., evolution). In both cases, the thing or type of thing is attempting to fit better into its environment. For humans, "fitting better into the environment" is not necessarily related to survival. For example, when someone learns to play a musical instrument or to play chess, it is more about fitting socially into an environment.

Regarding behavior adjustments, machine learning can be used to support the outcome-driven policy management approach. The outcome is achieved via machine learning. This could take several iterations with each iteration getting closer to the desired outcome. Even after the desired outcome is achieved, machine learning can continue to find more efficient ways to achieve objectives or even define better objectives.

12.3 Contracts and Contexts

12.3.1 Concepts

For things to collaborate and collectively provide higher-level capabilities, there needs to an agreement as to what each thing will provide in the collaboration. In this book, such an agreement is called a contract.

Contract – an agreement among two or more things to collaborate. The contract shall state what is expected (guaranteed) by each thing regarding the collaboration.

A contract can be viewed from different aspects or facets. Not all aspects will apply to all contracts. The following is a non-exhaustive list of contract aspects:

- Functional aspect – the capabilities that each thing is expected to provide as part of the contract. This is what a thing does – its core capabilities.

- Non-functional aspect – this aspect concerns how well (to what degree) each thing is to provide its functional aspect.

  - For example, a thing that provides an authentication service (functional) guarantees to be able to process 50 requests per second (non-functional).

  - The non-functional aspect can be further divided into categories such as performance, reliability, adaptability (e.g., via machine learning), management capabilities (e.g., support of policy management, auto-diagnostics) and availability (e.g., the proportion of up-time).

- Financial – this aspect concerns compensation (monetary or otherwise) for each thing involved in the contract.

  - Financial considerations are covered in Section 11.1 on billing and Section 11.6 on license management.

In terms of writing a contract, the aspects can be combined into a single statement. For example, consider the contract statement:

Each virtual firewall shall be able to process streams of data up to 100 Mbits/sec at a cost of $100/month regardless of usage.

The functional part is the virtual firewall, the non-functional part is the statement "able to process streams of data up to 100 Mbits/sec" and the financial part is the $100/month price per virtual firewall instance.

Contracts can be classified based on the number of things involved and whether the contract is negotiated.

- Unilateral (take it or leave it) – the contract for a thing is offered on a "take it or leave it" basis. Some examples:
    o An application offered within an ecosystem of applications, where the contract is fixed
    o Produce at a supermarket – the price and guarantees are fixed
    o A "take it or leave it" contract offered by a company to a union representing a collection of people.
- Bilateral (negotiated) – the contract is between two things and negotiation is involved.
    o There could be a preliminary contract that is used as a starting point for negotiations.
    o The contract can be one-directional, i.e., one thing provides capabilities and the other uses the capabilities, or it can be two-ways, i.e., both things provide and use capabilities.
- Multi-party (negotiated) – the contract is between more than two things and negotiation is involved.
    o Each thing in the contract may be a provider of capabilities, user of capabilities or both.

In the case of negotiation, it may not be the things (or type of things) involved in fulfilling the contract that agree on the terms of the contract but rather their agents who agree on the terms. Further, a contract might be applied to an aggregate entity (such as a platform or an organization) that encompasses several different types of things and associated instances.

When a contract is among more complex things (such as platforms), it is sometimes useful to partition the execution (operating phase) of the contract into contexts.

Context – a specification that governs some aspect of a contract's execution.

- Context specifications are part of a contract.
- Contexts involve multiple things, which are referred to as **Context Endpoints**. Each context endpoint plays a role (or possibly multiple roles) in the execution of the contract. A **Role** defines what a context endpoint can and is expected to do within a given context of a contract.

While contexts may encompass more than two endpoints, it is recommended to decompose complex contexts into binary contexts with a single provider and consumer. The examples that follow are restricted to binary contexts.

While the concept of a contract is common in many industries, the concept of a context within a contract is not. The Open Networking Foundation document TR-527 [34] introduces the idea of a context.

In Section 11.10 of this book, trust and traceability with regard to contracts are discussed.

12.3.2 Examples of Contexts

12.3.2.1 *Virtual Content Delivery Network*

In Figure 79, Organization A would like to extend its reach (concerning digital content delivery) into a territory where it does not have distribution facilities. Organization B can provide Organization A with a virtual Content Delivery Network (vCDN) capability and an application gateway via Platform Z. Organization A handles content delivery with its Platform X and application gateways with its Platform Y. There is one contract between Organizations A and B, with two contexts:

- Context #1 is for content delivery. This context covers the interface operations (provided by Platform Z) that are accessible by Platform X. The context also sets boundaries concerning how much capacity Platform X can use (related to vCDN).

- Context #2 is for the application gateway. Like Context #1, this context defines what operations may be used and sets capacity limits (related to the application gateway capability).

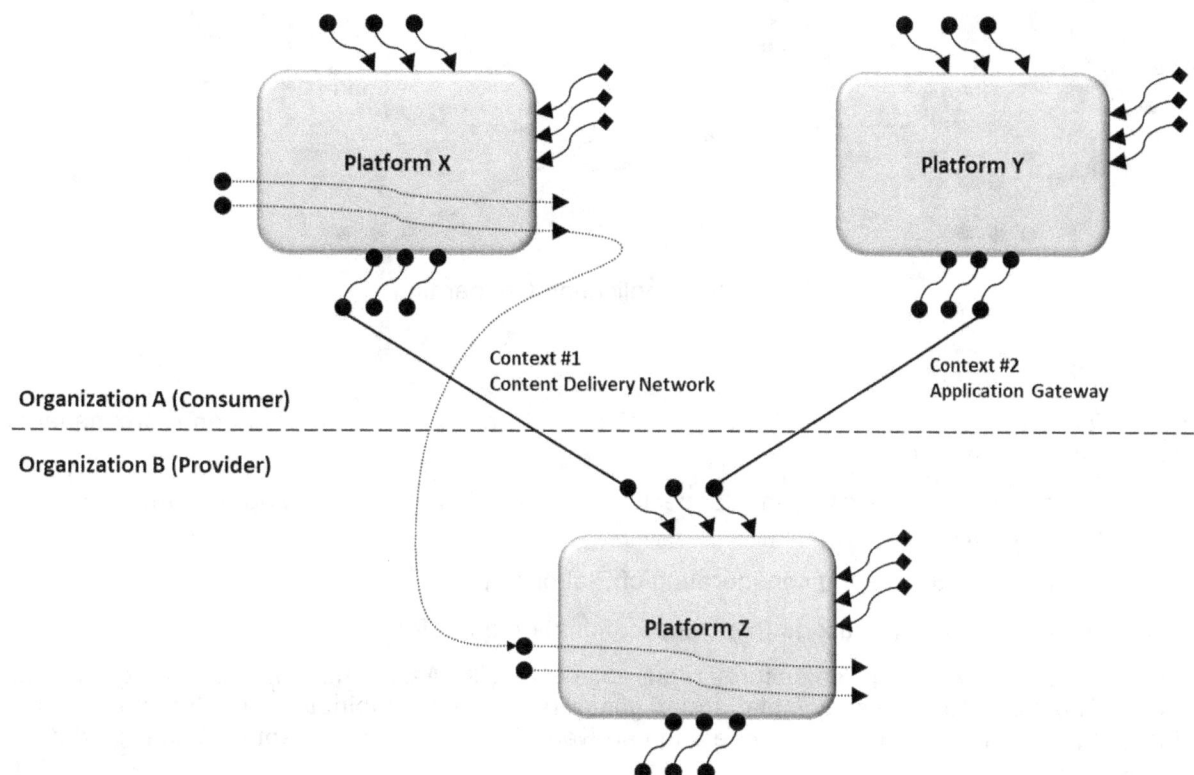

Figure 79. Contexts between Organizations

12.3.2.2 *Onboarding from Internal and External Sources*

Figure 80 depicts the onboarding of applications from internal and external sources. "Onboarding" refers to the loading of application software, catalog descriptions and associated files (e.g., test scripts) onto an execution platform.

In this example, there are two separate contexts, i.e., one for internal sources of new applications and another for external sources. Presumably, the internal source (Platform C) is given additional access to Platform A than is given to the external source (Platform B). In this way, Organization Y can assign the minimum access rights required for Organization X to make use of its Platform A. This is in keeping with the requirement "Sc_R5: Assign Minimum Privileges" (see Section 11.8.1).

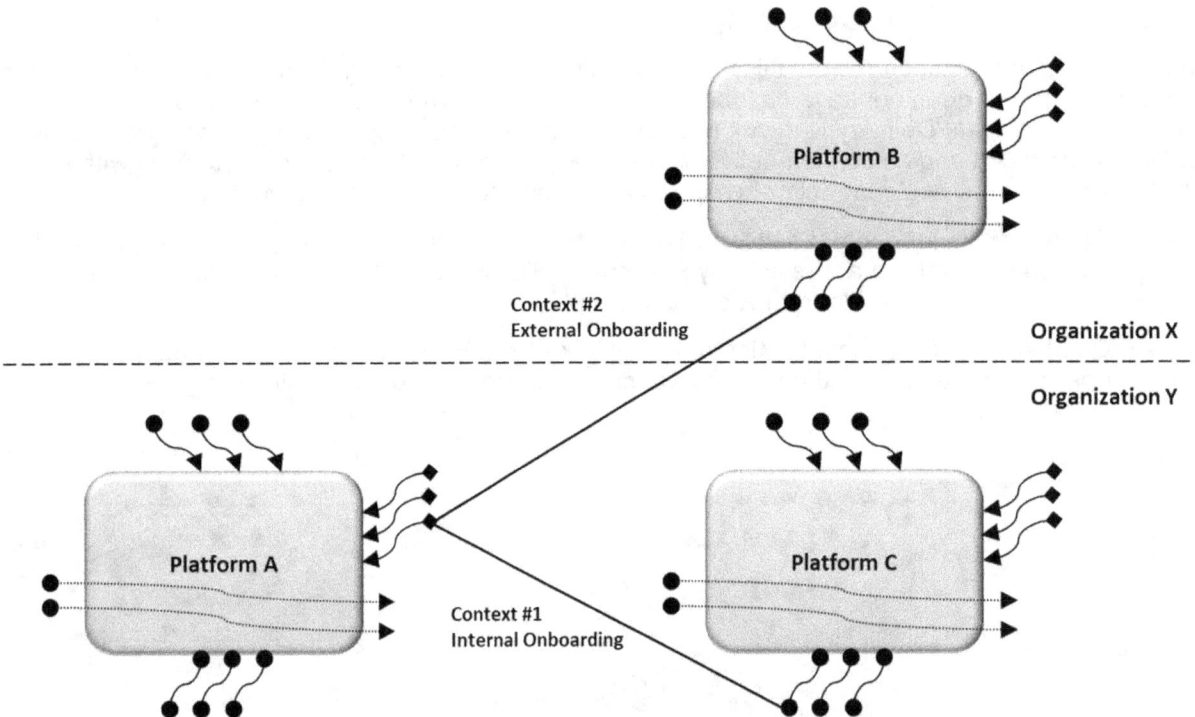

Figure 80. Application Onboarding

12.3.2.3 Contexts per Management Area

The platforms in Figure 81 are within one organization. Various aspects of Platform A are managed by Platforms B, C and D:

- Platform B manages assurance aspects of Platform A (e.g., alarms and performance monitoring).

- Platform C manages the configuration of Platform A.

- Platform D onboards things (e.g., applications) onto Platform A.

This approach is in keeping with security requirement "Sc_R6: Assignment of Roles" (see Section 11.8.1). The platforms in this example (and in general) can be a combination of different types of things, e.g., humans, intelligent software and hardware. This needs to be kept in mind regarding security.

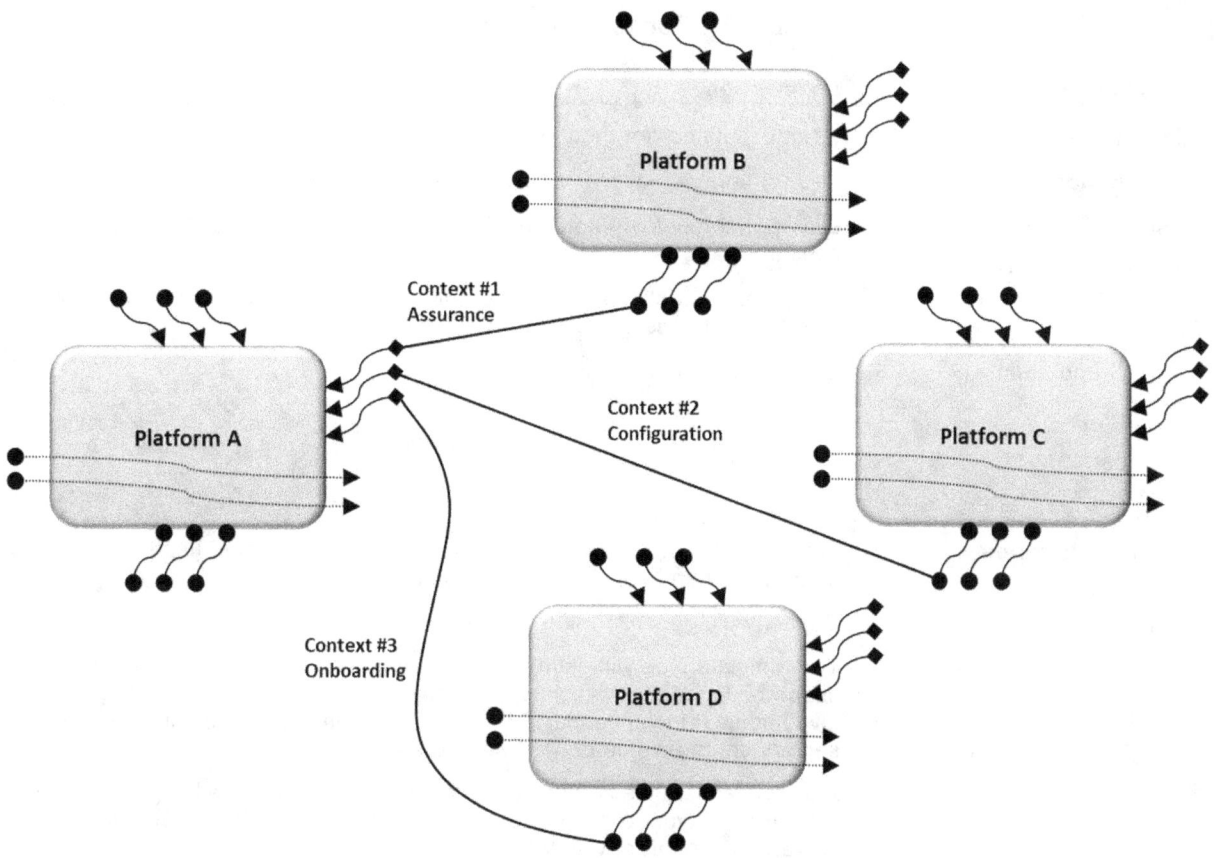

Figure 81. Separate Contexts for Different Management Area

12.3.3 Context Template

Table 21 is a sketch of a context template type. By assumption, there is only one consumer and one provider in the context. The context template type is used to create context instances.

The template is divided into three parts:

- Access Rights – for each interface offered by a type of thing (e.g., a platform), this part of the template indicates what interfaces are available to a consumer within the confines of the given type of context. For each operation, there may be further restrictions.

- Usage Boundaries – the thing playing the role of provider in the context may offer access to and usage of several types of internal things. This part of the template defines the internal things and defines usage limits for the consumer role in the context.

- Non-functional Characteristic – characteristics concerning how well the provider guarantees it will perform. The template type only defines the non-functional characteristics and possible boundary values. Instances of the template type define (i.e., set) specific values for the non-functional characteristics.

Table 21. Context Template Type

Template Item	Description
Identifier	Unique identifier for the template
Access Rights	List of interfaces available for use by the consumer
Interface #1	List of operations in Interface #1 that are available for use by the consumer
Operation #1.1	Operation restrictions, e.g., list of things on which the operation is allowed to act upon in this context
Operation #1.2	Operation restrictions
...	
Interface #2	
...	
Usage Boundaries	For each type of thing whose capacity can be consumed, usage boundaries can be set for the consumer.
Thing Type A	Capacity usage limits relative to a given instance of this context The template type will define the capacity units, and possibly define usage boundaries for each type of thing that can be consumed, e.g., a given context instance must have the maximum number of virtual content servers set to a value between 5 and 25. A template instance can select a specific value within the limits defined in the template type, e.g., set the maximum number of virtual content servers in support of vCDN to 10.
Thing Type B	
...	
Non-functional Characteristics	Each non-functional characteristic can be set individually or there could be "grades of service" that combine settings for several non-functional characteristics
e.g., Grade of Service	Possible values: Platinum, Gold, Silver, Bronze So, for example, a selection of Gold may imply specific value settings for several underlying non-functional characteristics.
e.g., Guaranteed maximum response time	This might be set on a per-operation basis, or perhaps just for the subset of interface operations that are not typically fulfilled immediately.
e.g., Guaranteed minimum time between failure	Could be overall for the context instance, per interface or per operation (less likely)

12.4 Intent-based and Detailed-based Interfaces

12.4.1 Overview

There are several styles for interface design. In an intent-based approach, the consumer (the thing making a request of another) indicates what he, she or it wants, but not how to fulfill the request. In a detailed-based approach, the consumer directs the provider concerning how to fulfill the request. Mixtures of the two approaches are also possible.

Intent-based – an interface approach where the consumer only describes what they want and not how to accomplish the task.

- In the intent-based approach, the consumer indicates what it desires via the selection of features (typically optional) and by providing values for mandatory characteristics. Alternately, one could cast the mandatory characteristic in terms of one or more mandatory features. The second approach is a bit cleaner, since it would then follow that the consumer's intent is based on the selection of features and the setting of characteristics associated with each feature (noting that some features may not have any characteristics).

Detailed-based – an interface approach where the consumer tells the provider how to accomplish a requested task.

- In the detailed-based approach, the consumer must know (at least partially) the detailed structure (e.g., dependencies) and configuration constraints for the supporting things, and how to manage the configuration of the supporting things. This requires close coupling between the information known by the consumer and provider (and possibly subtending providers). This leads to a more complex (and perhaps unnecessary) situation for the consumer.

A related topic, known as Intent-Based Networking (IBN), has taken root in the telecommunication industry. The idea here is for the network administrator to tell "the network" what he or she would like to accomplish rather than how. Current IP networks are still largely managed by very detailed and cumbersome Command Line Interfaces (CLI). For further details on IBN, see the TechTarget article [35] and ONF TR-523, *Intent NBI – Definition and Principles* [36].

12.4.2 Example concerning a Man's Suit

Figure 82 shows two different orders for a man's suit.

On the left of the figure is an intent-based order. The customer (Mr. Gianopulos) indicates what he wants by providing values for required characteristics and by selecting features. For this example, all the features are optional.

On the right of the figure is a mixed intent-based / detailed-based order. The characteristics and features parts of the order are similar to the intent-based order, except that Mr. Gianopulos has left empty the values for Color and Button. In the Directions part of the order, Mr. Gianopulos provides specific details concerning how the suit is to be made.

Intent-based Order
Id 76360347-1
Customer: George Gianopulos
Type: S393775863

Characteristics
    Jacket Size: Medium
    Jacket Length: Regular
    Sleeve Length: 33
    Color: Dark Gray
    Pants (waist, inseam): 35, 33
    Buttons: Black
    Back vents: 2
    Inner pockets: 3

Features:
    Cuffs: No
    Vest: Yes
        Medium
        Back: same as suit jacket interior
    Matching tie set: Yes

Mixed Intent-based / Detailed-based Order
Id 76360347-2
Customer: George Gianopulos
Type: S393775863-C

Characteristics
    Jacket Size: Medium
    Jacket Length: Regular
    Sleeve Length: 33
    Color: -
    Pants (waist, inseam): 35, 33
    Buttons: -
    Back vents: 2
    Inner pockets: 3

Features:
    Cuffs: No
    Vest: Yes
        Medium
        Back: same as suit jacket interior
    Matching tie set: No

Direction:
    Use material supplied by customer
    Use internal lining supplied by customer
    Use buttons supplied by customer
    Use alternate collar design from customer

Figure 82. Different Types of Orders for a Man's Suit

12.4.3 Analysis

This may all seem very simple and straightforward, with the intent-based approach being preferred in most cases. However, that would be far from the case in the area of telecommunications management. Early network equipment lacked intelligence and thus much of the management was done (and still is) by external entities know as Operations Support Systems (OSS). The first generation of OSS was almost totally built using a detailed-based interface paradigm. As network devices have become more intelligent, there has been a slow but steady move toward intent-based interfaces between the OSS and underlying network.

In general, a pure intent-based approach implies that the provider has sufficient knowledge to completely fulfill each of the capabilities that it offers (assuming the consumer has selected the features that it wants and has provided values for the associated characteristics). In the case of a detailed-based or mixed approach, the provider may be able to fulfill all the capabilities that it offers on its own, but it allows the consumer to provide some details concerning how to accomplish a task.

There are cases where a purely intent-based approach is not sufficient. Consider the situation shown in Figure 83:

- There is traffic flow from D to A to F to G, but A is experiencing excessive internal errors.

- F detects the errors and reports the problem to E, which in turn, reports the problem to Platform Z.

- Platform Z has a detailed view of the internals of both Platform X and Y, and knows that the issue can be resolved by replacing A with B (until A can be fixed).

- Using a detailed-based request, Platform Z tells C to rearrange the traffic flow so that D sends to B which will send to F.

- Thing C, in turn, tells D to redirect its traffic to B, and tells B to use an output that goes to F.

- Platform Z then orchestrates the running of a test across Platforms X and Y to ensure that the new flow (D to B to F to G) is functioning properly. The test verifies that the problem has been fixed.

- The point is that neither Platform X nor Y have sufficient knowledge to correct the problem. Platform Z needs an internal view of Platforms X and Y, and and a detailed-based interface to Platform X to provide proper instructions to correct the problem.

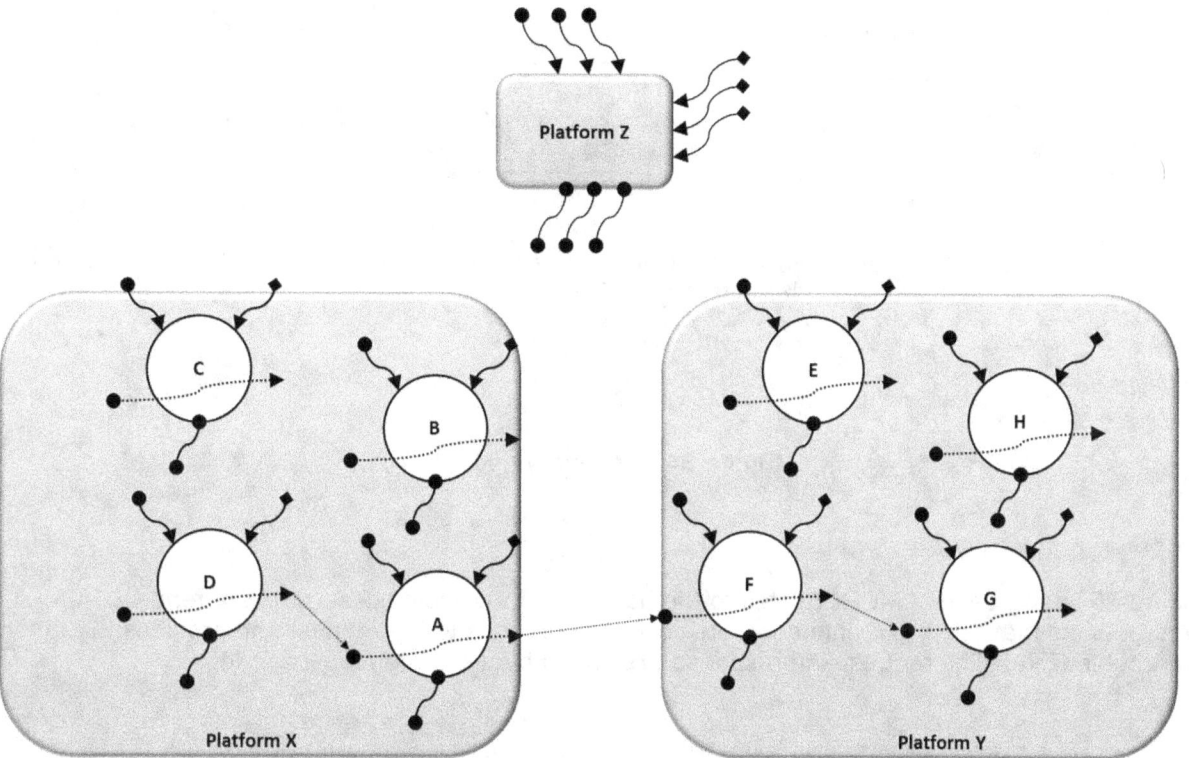

Figure 83. Fault Recovery with Detailed-based Interface

An intent-based approach allows for the internal details of a platform (or other compound thing) to change without changing the external interface, there are cases where the internal details need to be seen by external entities (typically supervisory in nature).

12.5 Message Exchange Patterns

12.5.1 Overview

When things communicate, it is sometimes in the form of a dialog. In some cases, the dialog is very short, e.g., a single command or notification from one thing to another. In other cases, the dialog may be extended over time, e.g., the handling of an order. The structural patterns for such dialogs are referred to as Message Exchange Patterns (MEPs).

Message Exchange Pattern (MEP) – a message-based pattern of communication among several things.

In the examples that follow, the focus is entirely on MEPs between only two things.

12.5.2 Dictionary Retrieval Example

Figure 84 depicts a simple request-reply MEP. A consumer of an online dictionary makes a request to look up the word "pattern". The Online Dictionary responds with a definition of pattern, i.e., "Pattern: noun - a model or original used for imitation or as an archetype." The Message Id (Msg Id 1a2b3c) links the request and response. This is known as the Request-Reply MEP.

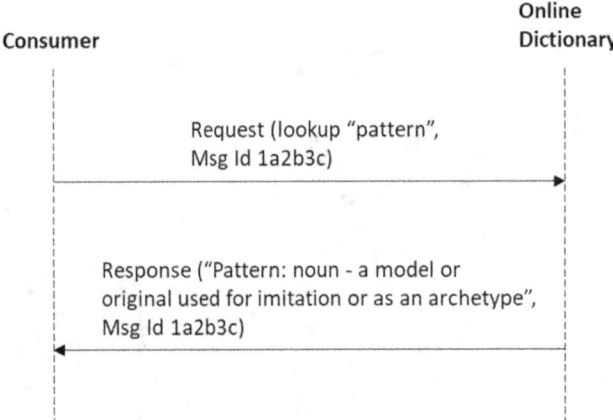

Figure 84. Dictionary Lookup

12.5.3 Trouble Ticket Example

Figure 85 shows several MEPs related to the handling of a trouble ticket (problem report). Thing A first requests that Thing B create a trouble ticket. B responds to the request and provides the Id for the trouble ticket. The request and response are linked by a common message Id.

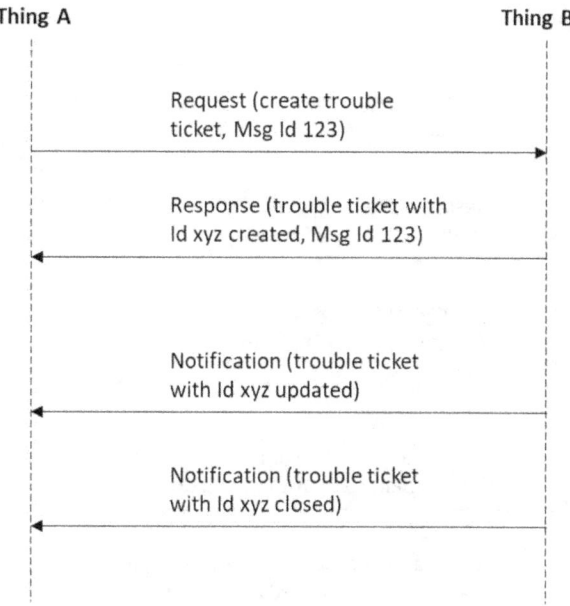

Figure 85. MEPs for a Trouble Ticket

When the trouble ticket is updated, Thing B provides a response to Thing A. This is known as the One-way or Notification MEP. The notification is tied to the Id of the trouble ticket and not to the Message Id from the initial interaction.

Subsequently, Thing B tells Thing A that the trouble ticket is closed via another notification.

Alternately (but not shown in the figure), Thing A could determine that the problem no longer exists and then ask that B close the trouble ticket (using a request-reply MEP).

12.5.4 Ordering Example

Figure 86 depicts a scenario concerning a multi-item order. The first three messages are an example of the Request – Multiple-reply MEP (linked by the same Message Id 456). Thing A requests several items in an order to Thing B. Using the message Id from the initial request, Thing B first acknowledges receipt of the order and then indicates that an order has been created (the implication is that Thing A's request is valid and in the process of being fulfilled).

Subsequently, Thing B provides updates to Thing A concerning expected delivery dates for items in the order. The updates are linked to the Id of the order and not to the message Id of the initial order request.

Once all the items have been delivered, Thing B sends a notification to Thing A, indicating that the order is complete.

The order (with its unique Id) will continue to exist, e.g., so that Thing A can make a return.

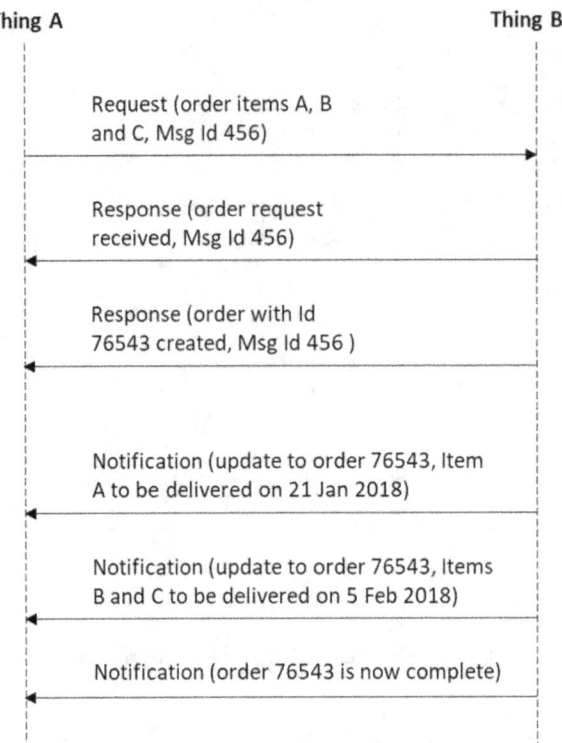

Figure 86. MEPs for an Order

Request-Reply and One-way (or Notification) are the most common MEPs in the literature (e.g., see [43], [44] and [48]) but other more complex patterns are possible such as Request – Multiple-reply and Two-Phase Commit [49].

Mep_R1: It is recommended that the Request – Multiple-reply MEP be avoided since it requires maintenance of an MEP state.

Mep_R2: When a transaction requires several responses, it is recommended that a persistent object be defined (such as a trouble ticket or order). The interactions with the persistent object are via stateless MEPs such as one-way or request-reply. However, the persistent object itself may have a state.

12.5.5 Postal Chess Example and MEP Layering

Figure 87 shows a scenario for a game of postal chess. The pattern entails a chain of responses and requests. However, this pattern is not typical in electronic interactions. The issue is that the running record of the chess game (written on a piece of paper) is sent back and forth with each successive move. In an electronic version of the game, the running record of the game would be stored digitally in some common place, and only the next move would be sent in each request. The record persists throughout the interaction (similar to the trouble ticket and order in the previous examples) and each interaction (i.e., next move, resign, declare checkmate or agree to draw) entails a stateless one-way pattern.

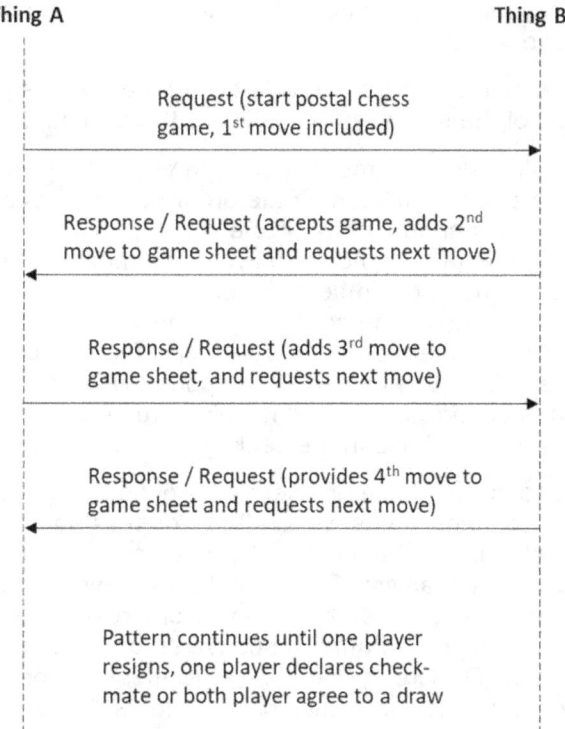

Figure 87. Postal Chess Scenario

The postal chess example exposes another important aspect of MEPs, i.e., they are typically layered. There is one MEP between the players of the chess game and several lower-layer MEP instances concerning the letters going back and forth. The "postal MEP" uses the one-way pattern. Other postal MEPs are also possible, e.g., return to sender if the address is incorrect or insufficient postal is put on the letter, notification to the sender concerning successful delivery of the letter. This analysis gives rise to two types of MEPs, i.e.,

- **Application MEP** – an MEP related to message exchanges that support a distributed task.

- **Transport MEP** – an MEP solely concerned with the transfer of messages between participants in the MEP.

It is possible to have subdivisions of both application and transport MEPs.

As a rule, it is best to keep the application and transport MEPs separate so that a given application MEP can be supported by different transport MEPs.

- **Mep_R3**: Application and transport MEPs shall be defined separately. An application MEP shall not include any details concerning a transport MEP, and vice versa.

When it is decided to support a given application MEP with a transport MEP, a binding between the two needs to be defined. The binding definition is separate from both the application and transport MEPs.

12.5.6 Separation of Control from Request Fulfillment

Aside from the different MEPs used in the previous examples, there is another subtle difference in terms of the manner in which the request is fulfilled.

- In the online dictionary retrieval example, the requested information is returned as part of the response message.

- In the trouble ticket example, the trouble ticket is created on the producer-side and the consumer is informed of the successful creation of the trouble ticket object.

- In the ordering example, the consumer is informed of the order creation (an object on the producer side) but the actual fulfillment of the order (i.e., delivery of order items A, B and C) is done via another exchange pattern. For example, each of the order items (if they are physical objects such as books) could be delivered via postal mail. Alternately, the response to the order request, could be included with the order delivery, e.g., an order summary slip in the box or envelope containing whatever physical item was ordered. In this case, the order exchange pattern and the order fulfillment are combined. Of course, there could be two responses, i.e., one immediate response via, for example, an email that indicates the order has been received and is being processed, and another response in the form of a summary of the purchase in the package in which the order is delivered.

- Video streaming is another example of where control and delivery can be separated. A video streaming protocol (including several MEPs for session creation, pause, resume, session termination, etc.) is used to control the video stream. The video stream is delivered via a separate transport mechanism. There can be two levels of MEPs in this example. For example, when a video is requested, there can be one response to the video display device (e.g., TV, cell phone or tablet) and other response embedded in the video for the human consumer to see on their TV screen (e.g., "video request has been received and will display shortly"). The later response is sometimes referred to as "in-band signaling."

- In-band signally is used for land-line telephones. In this approach, an entered (dialed) telephone number is encoded and transmitted across the telephone line in form of what is called Dual-Tone Multi-Frequency signaling (DTMF). DTMF is audible to the human ear, as anyone who has used a land-line phone knows. The tones are used to instruct the telephone network concerning where the phone call is to be routed. These control tones are sent over the same channel, the copper wire, and in the same frequency range (300 Hz to 3.4 kHz) as the audio portion of the call. In-band signaling is also used on older telephone carrier systems to provide inter-exchange information for routing calls. In this scenario, the MEP (for control of a phone call) and the voice channel (the ordered item) share the same medium.

- Software Defined Networking (SDN) defines a communications architecture where the data plane (information transfer) is separated from the control plane (signaling that directs the data plane), see the Open Network Foundation (ONF) SDN Architecture [50].

In summary, a request (control aspect) and its fulfillment (delivery aspect) can be handled by separate exchange patterns. In some cases, it is natural to combine the control and delivery aspects, e.g., the online dictionary example. In other cases, it advantageous to separate the control and delivery aspects, e.g., ordering of physical items. There are also hybrid cases, e.g., video streaming. The main point is to recognize that the control and delivery aspects of an interaction can be separated if need be, and whether to do so depends on the particular situation at hand.

12.5.7 Publish and Subscribe Pattern

The one-way MEPs in Figure 85 and Figure 86 use notifications in a restricted manner, i.e., each notification is only sent to the requestor of some action. The one-way pattern can be used in a more general manner, where multiple things can subscribe to future notifications that are generated by another thing. In Figure 88, Thing A, B, C and D subscribe to notifications from Thing X (which could be an agent for several things). When a subsequent event occurs (under the purview of Thing X), Thing X generates and publishes the notification to interested parties (i.e., those who have previously subscribed to receive such notifications). In general, the subscribers of notifications from a thing can apply different filters and thus receive only a subset of the generated notifications.

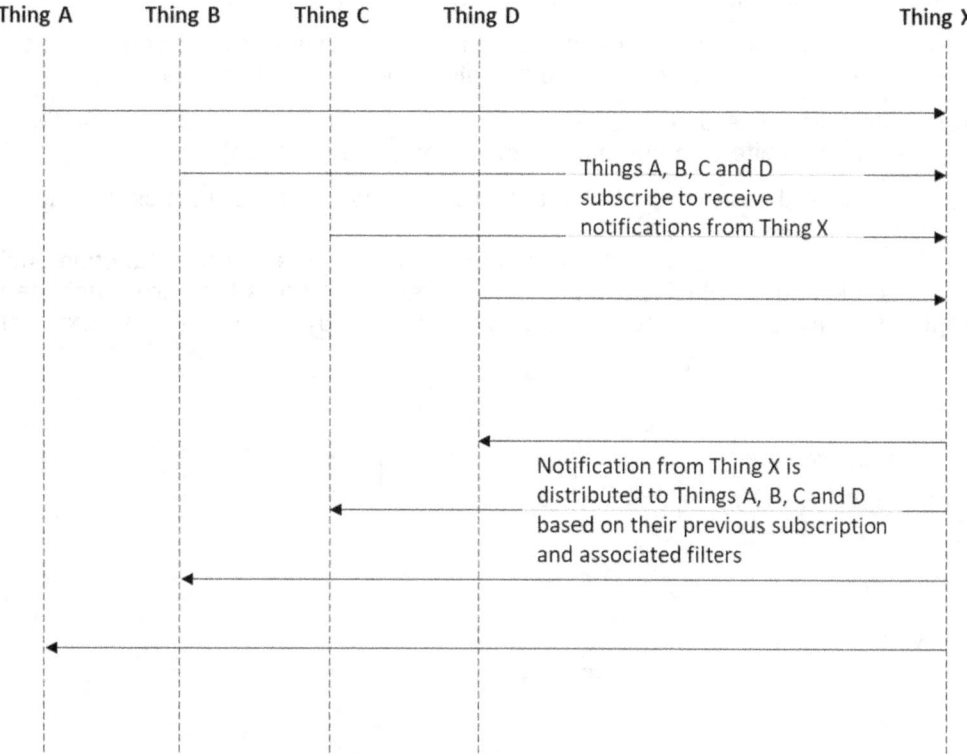

Figure 88. Subscription to and Publication of Notifications (One-way MEP)

12.6 Metrics

This section covers topics related to the collection and reporting of measurements on things. The collected information can be used for multiple purposes, e.g., accounting and billing, detection of performance degradation, big data analytics, and the detection of security breaches. It is recommended that one set of procedures be used to collect and report on metrics regardless of the usage of the collected information.

12.6.1 Terminology

Metrics Management – the process responsible for the collection and reporting of measurements on things.

The following definitions of "counter," "gauge" and "threshold" are inspired by the definitions in ITU-T Recommendation X.721 [51].

Counter – a discrete variable that records the number of occurrences of some type of event related to a thing or set of things.

- The value of a counter increases by 1 each time a particular type of event occurs.

- Some counters can be reset via the management interface offered by a thing. Such counters are called **settable counters**.

- Counters that cannot be reset via management operations are called **simple** or **non-settable counters**.

- Every counter shall have a maximum value. When the maximum value for a counter is reached, there is no valid next value and so a policy has to be defined in advance to deal with this case. Possible policies are as follows:

  o auto wrap when the maximum value is reached, with or without notification (under the assumption that the maximum value is expected to be reached)

  o auto reset to zero on predefined time intervals (under the assumption that the max is set to infinite or a number not expected to be reached)

  o remain at the maximum value until a wrap (reset to zero) request is made.

An example counter is shown in Figure 89. The counter is an increasing step function until its maximum value is reached, at which point the counter value is returned to zero. Each step is 1 unit. The length of each step (measured in time) is determined by the time to the next event of a given type.

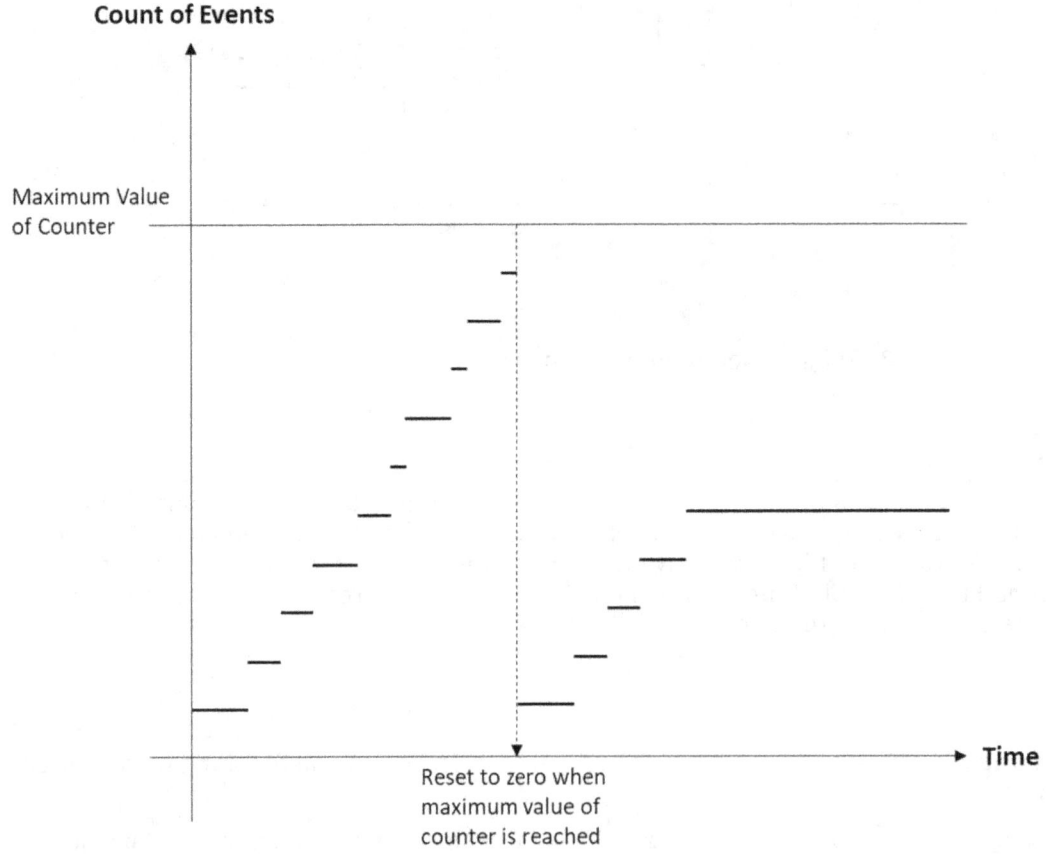

Figure 89. Illustration of a Counter

Gauge – a variable that holds the current value of some measured characteristic of a thing or set of things.

- The value of a gauge can rise and fall by arbitrary amounts.

- A gauge is a not necessarily a continuous function of time.

An example of a gauge is shown in Figure 90. A gauge can take on positive or negative values (e.g., consider the temperature of a thing). ITU-T Recommendation X.721 states that a gauge shall have a maximum and minimum value. However, the value of enforcing such constraints is unclear and is not recommended. If there is a concern about the gauge reaching a particularly high or low value, a threshold crossing notification can be generated.

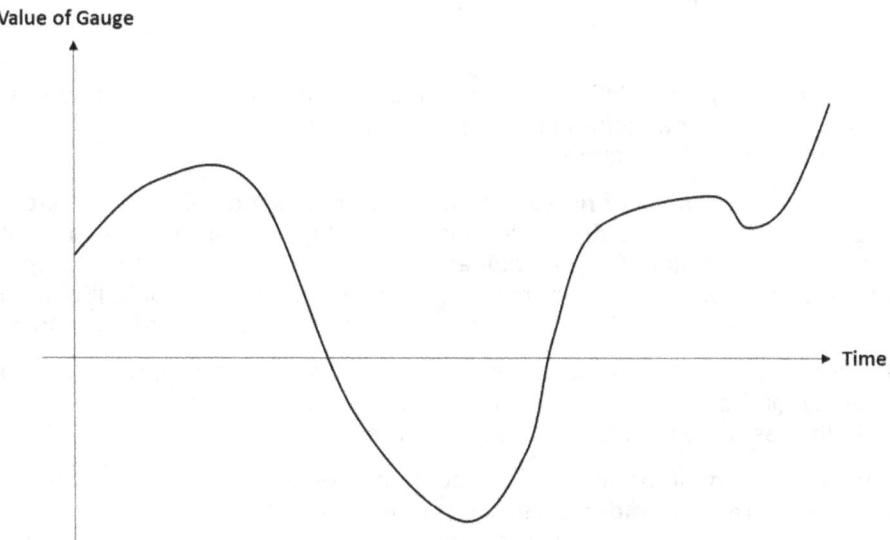

Figure 90. Illustration of a Gauge

Threshold – a measured value (with respect to a given variable) that if crossed, requires some action (e.g., sending a notification to interested parties).

- A given threshold (depending on how it is defined) can be crossed by exceeding a given value or going below a given value.

12.6.2 Concepts

12.6.2.1 Collecting and Reporting

A distinction is made between collecting (producing) measurements and reporting on the measurements. Figure 91 depicts a collection of measurements for a given characteristic (of a thing) and the subsequent reporting of the collected measurements. The measurements are every 5 seconds, and reporting is every 15 seconds. In general, the reporting interval shall be a multiple of the collection interval. Also, notice in the figure that the reporting time is slightly offset from the end of a collection period. This is to give the thing time to prepare the report and not to overload the thing with excess processing at the end of each reporting period.

Mx_R1: The reporting interval for a given variable shall be a whole number multiple of the collection interval.

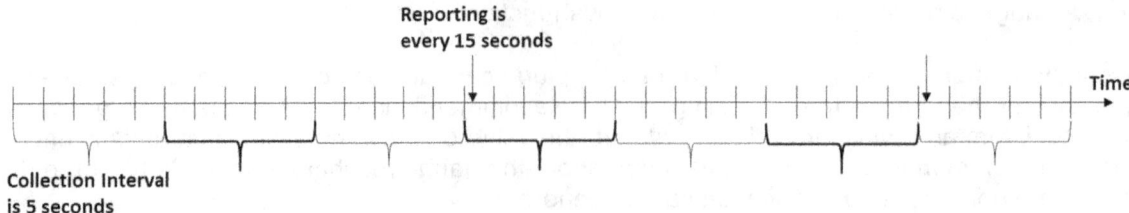

Figure 91. Collection and Reporting Intervals

Reporting can be based on several MEPs, e.g., notifications (including the measurements), notifications (with a pointer to the location of the measurements), retrieval by the consumer of the measurements (basically a polling method).

Retention and subsequent retrieval of **historical measurements** may also be required. In such cases, the consumer's request must identify the monitored thing, desired measurements and the intervals of interest. The retention of historical measurements could be handled by specially designed things (measurement repositories) that store measurements on behalf of many things. An example of this would be an accounting application that stores usage records for many things.

In addition to the regularly scheduled measurements, some things may support the fulfillment of **on-demand** requests for the current value of a variable. This is sometimes needed for emergency situations such as the resolution of faults or security breaches.

There is a distinction to be made between collected measurements vs. calculated indicators (referred to as **Key Performance Indicators** (KPI)) that are generated by performing calculations on the collected measurements. The calculations can be done either by the thing doing the collection or by the consumer of the measurements.

A measurement may represent an **aggregation across several things**. Consider the situation shown in Figure 92. Agent X (via Thing B) provides access to measurements on a collection of similar things (e.g., a collection of authentication applications). Thing A is only interested in how well the collection of things is performing and so only needs to see aggregate measurements for the variables of interest. If the aggregate measurements show there is a problem, Thing A could request measurement on individual things under the supervision of Agent X.

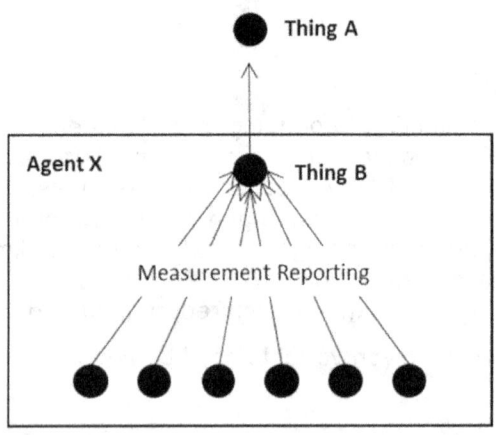

Figure 92. Collecting and Reporting Measurements on a Collection of Things

In some situations, it is convenient to define a set of measurements to be taken on a set of things. This requirement can be handled by the measurement job concept.

A **measurement job** is a specification that identifies a set of measurements to be taken on a given set of things.

ITU-T Recommendation M.3704 [52] defines the following characteristics for a measurement job:

- Measurement Job Id – unique identifier for the measurement job

- Granularity Period – the length of the collection period

- Reporting Period – how often the collected measurements are reported

- Job Status – the state of the job

    o Possible values, as defined in ITU-T Recommendation M.3704, are Scheduled, Active, Off-duty, Suspended and Stopped.

- Measurement Information List – reference to what things are to be monitored and what measurements are to be taken

- Start Time – time when the job is to start monitoring the given set of things

- Stop Time – time when the job and associated monitoring are to be automatically stopped

    o This field can be left empty.

- Schedule – the periods when the job is active, e.g., every weekday from 8 AM to 6 PM the job is active and off-duty at other times.

ITU-T Recommendation M.3704 defines operations to create, suspend / resume, query, stop and delete measurement jobs.

While ITU-T Recommendation M.3704 was written for performance management, the concepts can be applied to any area where measurements need to be collected.

12.6.2.2 Thresholds

Thresholds are used to detect when a variable goes outside of its expected range. For example, some mission-critical computing equipment may be monitored closely to make sure its surrounding environment is within given temperature and humidity ranges.

Figure 93 shows the value of a gauge over time.

- There are two thresholds concerning the upper range, i.e., Thresholds #1 and #2. Threshold #2 is an early warning and Threshold #1 is a critical alarm.

- In some cases, a variable may fluctuate around a threshold (as can be seen at the top of the figure with respect to Threshold #1). This phenomenon is called "hysteresis." To prevent multiple threshold crossings because of fluctuation, one can define a threshold clear value that is different from the threshold. On the upper range of a variable, the threshold clears are less than the threshold, and on the lower range of a variable, the threshold clears are greater than the threshold.

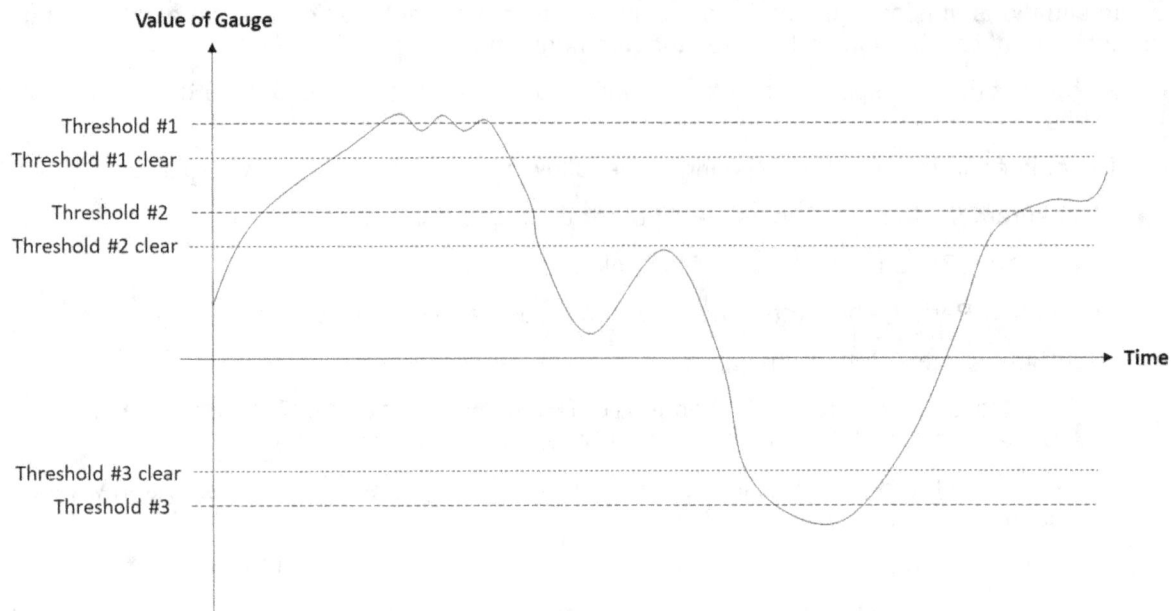

Figure 93. Threshold Crossing and Clears

Thresholds normally apply to gauges. However, it is possible to define thresholds based on counters. For example, it may be useful to know if a counter for a thing crosses a given rate over a given period, e.g., the threshold could be 10 counts / 5 minutes. To measure this, the thing (collecting the measurements) may be designed to compute a rolling (overlapping) rate measurement of length 5 minutes as follows:

- (0, 5 minutes) compute first measurement (in counts / 5 minutes)

- (5 seconds, 5 minutes 5 seconds) compute the second measurement

- (10 seconds, 5 minutes 10 seconds) compute the third measurement

- and so on.

The thing would only report a rate measurement if a given threshold is exceeded.

An alternate approach to counter thresholds is taken in ITU-T Recommendation X.721 where a threshold is raised if the count within an interval exceeds some given value. This is the relative count, i.e., present count minus the count at the start of the interval.

12.6.2.3 Tide-marks and Other Collection Variations

For counters and gauges, the value at the end of an interval is typically what gets recorded and subsequently reported. This may or may not be sufficient information depending on the length of the measurement interval and the volatility of the variable being measured.

One approach to get more information about a gauge during a measurement interval is to use tide-marks. As defined in ITU-T Recommendation X.721, a "**tide-mark**" is a mechanism that records the maximum or minimum value reached by a gauge during a measurement period." Yet another approach is to compute the mean and standard variation of the gauge during each measurement interval. However, neither of these approaches works for counters.

Table 22 provides a summary of the characteristics that pertain to gauges and counters.

Table 22. Summary of Gauges and Counters

	Gauge	Counter
Definition	a variable that holds the current value of some measured characteristic of a thing or set of things	a discrete variable that records the number of occurrences of some type of event related to a thing or set of things
Can rise and fall	Yes	No
Discrete	Possible, but not typical	Yes
Reset / Wrap	No	Yes
Thresholds	Yes	Possible, but not typical
Tide-marks	Yes	No

12.7 Root Cause Problem Analysis

12.7.1 Overview

This section concerns root cause analysis of problems and associated patterns for problem isolation, correction and avoidance.

The following terms and phrases are used in this section:

- **Root Cause Problem Analysis** – the process of identifying the root source (or sources) of a problem in an ecosystem of things.

- **Traceability** – the ability to verify and record the history of a thing, including its relationships to and effects on other things.

12.7.2 Scope

The phrase "root cause problem analysis" typically refers to the process of determining the ultimate sources (or sources) of a fault. This (i.e., focus on faults) is especially true in the telecommunications industry. In this book, a wider perspective is taken. The following is a non-exhaustive list of areas where root cause problem analysis can be applied:

- Fault and performance management – isolating, diagnosing and repairing things that have either failed (not working at all) or are operating in a degraded manner

- Contract guarantees – determining the cause of contract violations (which are not necessarily faults but could be)

- License – analysis of software problems due to the expiration of licenses for components

- Security – determining the cause of security breaches

- Capacity management – determining the cause of capacity depletion problems

- Revenue assurance – determining the cause of revenue leaks.

12.7.3 Example

Figure 94 depicts three platforms, where Platform Z manages Platforms X and Y. Thing A is having performance issues which will eventually affect other things in Platforms X and Y.

Concerning the effects of Thing A's problems on Platform Y, the traffic stream from A to F is experiencing excess latency. The problem is detected by Things F, G and H. Thing F reports the problem to J which, in turn, reports the problem to K. Things G and H directly report the problem to K. K attempts to isolate the problem but can only trace the issue to the boundary of Platform Y (i.e., F's input port). K opens a trouble ticket with Platform Z concerning the unresolved issue.

In Platform X, the problem with Thing A is first noticed by D which sends a request to C for some management information, which in turn, C sends to A. However, the response back to D indicates there is an issue with the operation of A. D does isolate the problem but does not know how to fix the issue, and thus, opens a trouble ticket with Platform Z concerning the issue. Platform Z correlates the problem reported by D with the problem reported by K, and determines the root cause is the same for both problems. Further, Platform Z does have the intelligence to fix the root cause of the problem, e.g., scale-up the processing capability of Thing A.

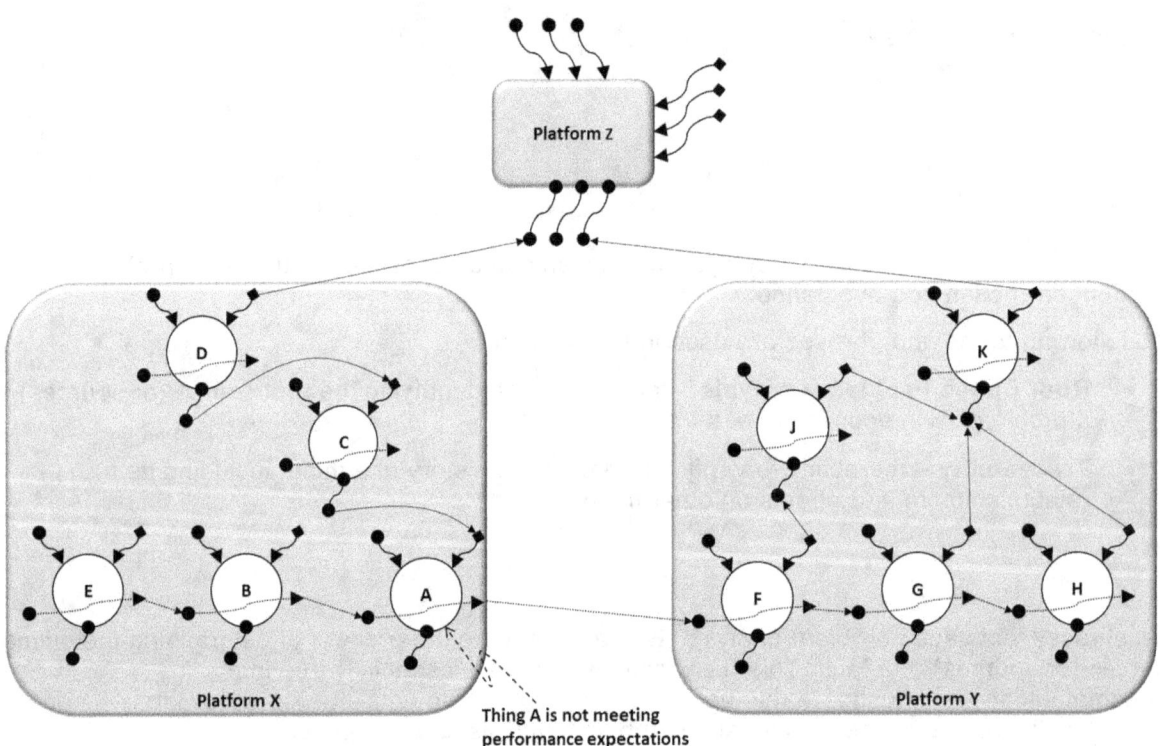

Figure 94. Root Cause Problem Analysis Example

12.7.4 Concepts and Requirements

12.7.4.1 Traceability

Traceability is essential in isolating the source of a problem. Traceability, in turn, depends on having a view of the dependencies among things. In the software world and particularly in the area of virtualization (as discussed in Section 11.6), the dependency relationships are not static. So, when a problem occurs, it may be necessary to construct a dependency graph "on the fly." This is sometimes referred to as dynamic inventory. However, the current dependency graph may not be sufficient if an existing problem was caused by some past event when the dependency graph was different, or if the problem is transient. Creating and storing snapshots of past dependency graphs is likely to be prohibitive in terms of processing time and storage. A partial solution is to at least take snapshots of the dependency graph (of the affected objects) while a given problem is being isolated and diagnosed. Another possible approach is to take dependency snapshots of areas (collections of related things) where a given type of problem is recurring.

For the problem in Figure 94, Platform Z (or more precisely, a problem diagnostic application in Platform Z) creates the current dependency graph for the affected things, and determines that the root cause of the problem is with Thing A. The problem can be solved by adding more computing resources to Thing A (this is known as "scaling-up" in the virtualization vernacular). Platform Z sends (to Thing D) a request to have Thing A "scaled-up." Subsequent tests are performed, and the problem is determined to be resolved. The associated trouble tickets are closed. A better solution would be to not only scale-up Thing A but to add intelligence to Thing A so that it can scale-up and scale-down based on given conditions.

A subtle point worth mentioning is that while Platform Z is attempting to isolate and solve the problem, it is probably best that neither Platform X nor Y attempt further problem resolution procedures as such procedures may interfere with Platform Z. This is a matter of inner control loops interfering with an outer control loop.

Rca_R1: An agent for a set of things (affected by a given problem) shall be able to create a snapshot (real-time) dependency graph.

- In the case of a static relationship among the things, the creation of the snapshot is relatively easy.

12.7.4.2   Defining the Boundary

The agent (e.g., a platform) for a given set of things may not be able to isolate a detected problem because the source of the problem is outside of its field of view. This is the case with Platform Y in Figure 94. Platform Y knows there is a problem with Things F, G and H but can only determine the problem originates at its boundary (in this case, the input port to Thing F).

Rca_R2: An agent for a set of things (affected by a given problem) shall be able to isolate the root cause of the problem or determine that the problem's source is outside of its area of control.

12.7.4.3   Automated Correction and Identification of Patterns

The resolution of the problem associated with the situation shown in Figure 94 can be said to be automated if one assumes Platform Z is software (with no human intervention). Assuming the "scale-up" procedures works, Platform Z should record the successful event. The actions taken to resolve the problem should be part of a learning process to help solve future problems. "Machine learning" was intentionally not used in the previous sentence for the sake of generality, but it is recognized that the trend and worthy goal is towards machine learning regarding problem resolution.

Rca_R3: An agent for a set of things (affected by a given problem) shall be able to automatically correct a problem within its area of control.

- This could entail requests to external agents.

Rca_R4: The steps leading to a successful resolution of a problem (as well as unsuccessful attempts) shall be recorded and subsequently used to help resolve future problems.

12.7.4.4   Preventing the Recurrence of Problems

Even better than automatically learning solutions for problems is preventing the problem in the first place. Learning should be extended to the circumstances leading up to a problem. For the problem in Figure 94, perhaps Thing A is the bottleneck in the traffic flow from E to B to A. Further, assume it has been determined that A gets into performance problems whenever the input at E crosses a known threshold. In this case, it would make sense to scale-up Thing A when Thing E crosses the given threshold or even as E approaches the threshold. This should be the goal of problem handling: determine the patterns that lead to problems and make corrective actions before any problem can occur.

Rca_R5: As part of the problem resolution process, the events leading up to a problem shall be recorded and any detected patterns shall be used to proactively prevent future problems of the same type.

12.8 Templates

This section concerns templates which are a sort of "cookie cutter" that can be applied multiple times to solve the same problem. For example, a factory could use one or more templates to create instances of a given type with the same configuration (at least for the subset of attributes handled by the templates).

12.8.1 Terminology

The following definitions are specializations of the concepts of "instance", "specification" and "type" (as defined in Section 2).

Template Instance – a thing that represents a set of characteristics that can be used to set or modify the characteristics of another thing.

Template Specification – the thing that defines a type of template.

- This may include default attribute values for instances of the given type.

Template Target (or just Target) – a thing to which a template instance is applied.

- The term "**Target Type**" can be used to refer to the type associated with a target.

Template Type – a collection of template instances that share a common set of characteristics.

In Figure 95, Template Type X is specified within the characteristic value boundaries defined for Types A and B. The goal here is to apply an instance of Template Type X to instances of Types A and B. For example, Template Instance X.1 is an instance of Type X and it is applied to Instance A.1 (instance of Type A) and Instance B.2 (instance of Type B). A.1 and B.2 are template targets in this example.

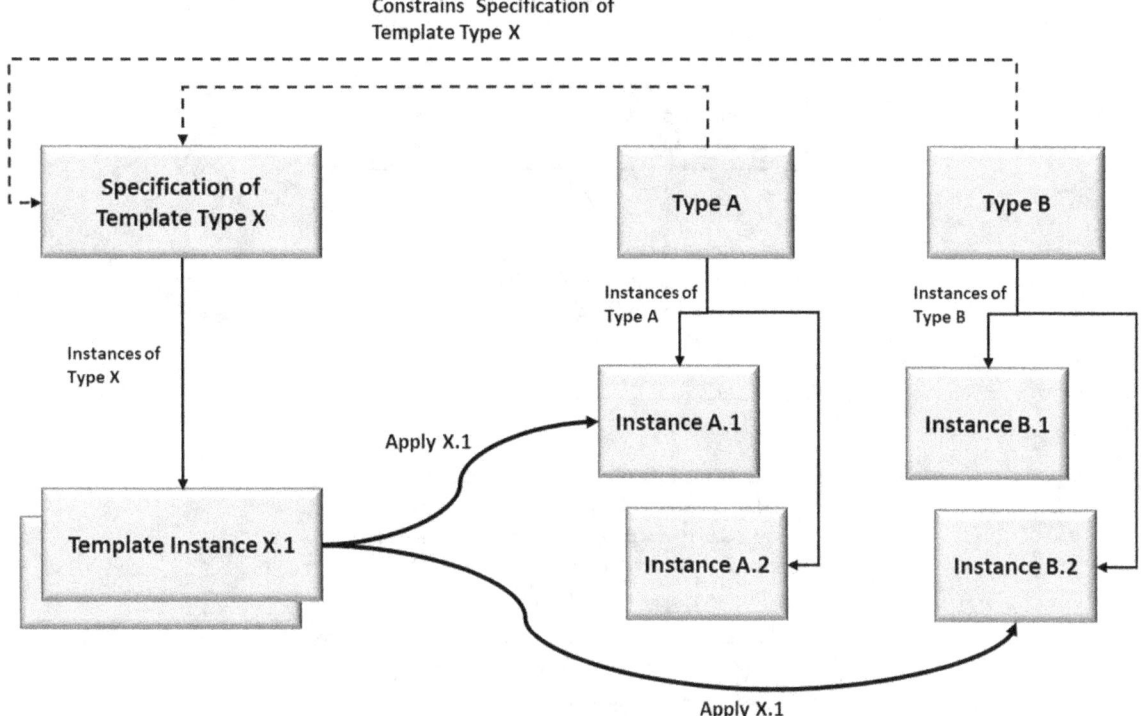

Figure 95. Template Terminology Illustration

12.8.2 Examples

Consider a CSP that needs to configure hundreds of carrier Ethernet switches. The switches have many characteristics, with a subset of the characteristics requiring the same value settings. The CSP can create one template instance (with the desired characteristic values) and apply the template to all the existing switches. As new switches are added to the CSP's network, the template can be applied. This helps to reduce manual configuration errors.

It is also possible to apply a template to instances of several different types, provided the types share the characteristics that are present in the template. Continuing with the example above, assume the CSP has several types of carrier Ethernet switches from a family of similar products offered by the same supplier. Further, the switches have a common set of characteristics. In this case, a single template instance could be used to set the values of the common characteristics for all carrier Ethernet switch instances from the same family of products.

Each template instance is of a given type. It is recommended to first define a specification for the template type before defining template instances.

Figure 96 depicts a flow leading to the creation of template instances. The first step is to decide on what types and associated characteristics are to be handled by the template type. The specifications for the targeted types (to which instances of the template type are to be applied) constrain the definition of the template type and thus need to be considered when defining the specification for the template type. Once completed, the specification for the template type is placed in a repository and is used for the subsequent creation of template instances.

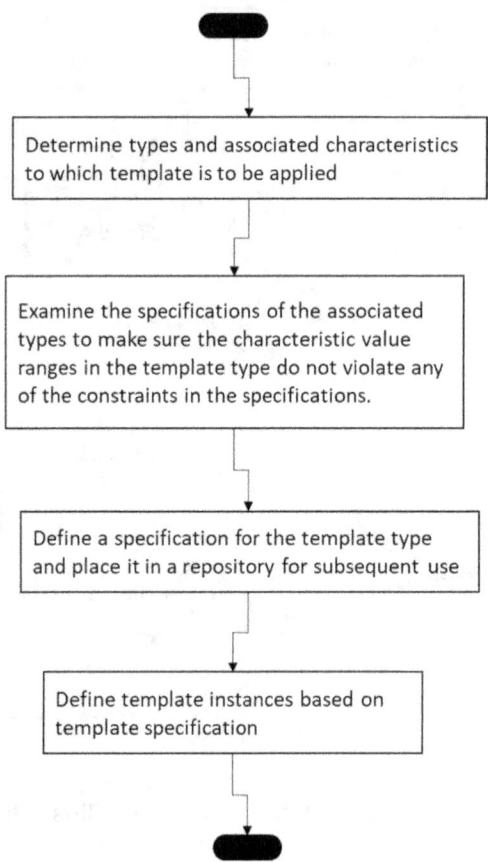

Figure 96. Sketch of Flow for Defining a Template

Figure 97 depicts a scenario where a template instance is created (based on a specification of a template type) and then applied to several targets. The target instances are of two different types: Type X and Type Y. The specification for the template type (Type Z) is constrained by specifications for Type X and Y. For example, if the range of values for color is {red, green, blue, yellow, gray, black, white and purple} for Type X and {red, green, blue, yellow, gray, black, white and pink} for Type Y, then the range of possible colors for Type Z would need to be subset of the intersection of the color ranges for Types X and Y, i.e., {red, green, blue, yellow, gray, black and white}. The specification of Type Z allows for several valid template instances that can be applied to instances of Type X and Y, as shown in Figure 97.

Things of Type X do not have a volume characteristic and so the volume assignment in Template123 can be ignored when applying the template to Things A, B and C.

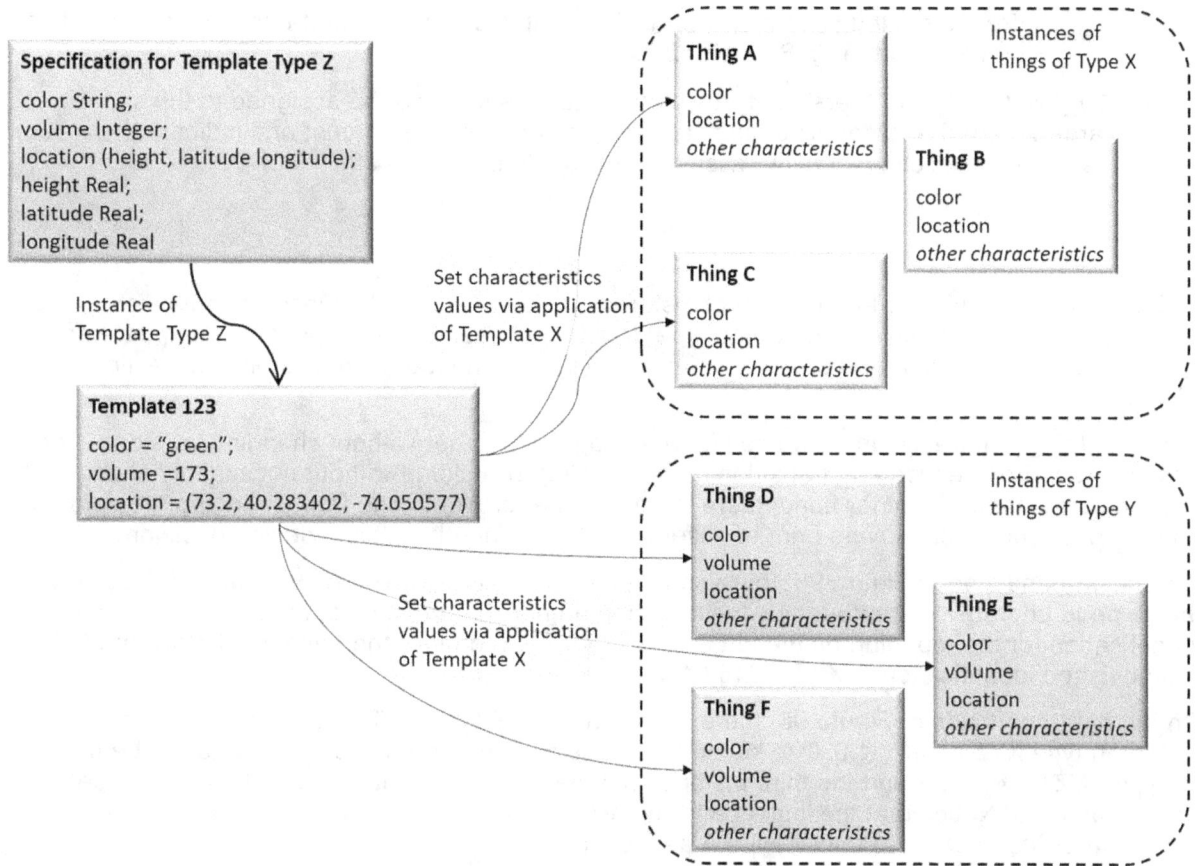

Figure 97. Applying a Template to Modify the Characteristics of Several Things

12.8.3 Requirements

The following requirements apply to template types, template instances and targets:

- **Tp_R1**: It shall be possible to create, modify and delete specifications for template types.

- **Tp_R2**: The specification for a template type shall be constrained (i.e., fit within the boundaries of) the specifications of the associated target types.

  o In other words, a template type should not redefine the target types.

- **Tp_R3**: It shall be possible to create template instances based on a template type.

- **Tp_R4**: It shall be possible to modify and delete template instances.

- **Tp_R5**: It shall be possible to apply a template instance to several targets, where "apply" means the character values in the template are imposed on the associated characteristics in the targets.

- **Tp_R6**: In cases where a template instance has some characteristics that are not present in the target, the request (to apply the template instance to the target) shall be fulfilled for the characteristics that are present in both the template instance and target.

- **Tp_R7**: Application of a template instance to a target can be persistent or not. In the persistent case, the target attempts to stay in lock-step with the template instance even if characteristic values in the template instance change. In the non-persistent case, the template instance is used to set characteristic values in the target, with no further synchronization between template and target.

    ○ Persistent template instance assignment is a form of intent-based policy, which is covered further in Section 12.2.4.

- **Tp_R8**: Conflicting (persistent) template instances shall not be assigned to the same target. If so, the target instance shall reject any conflicting request and indicate the reason as being "conflicting template assignment" (or similar).

12.9 Versioning

In this book, it is assumed that types (not instances) are versioned. Instances of a type are created, based on a given version of the type. In some cases, it may be possible to update an instance to a new version of a corresponding type (see the house alarm example in Section 12.2.2).

A type of thing can transition from one lifecycle stage to another without changing versions. For example, an airplane type can transition from Planning to Building without necessarily changing the version number. On the other hand, there is no rule that prevents one from changing the version number of a type when moving from one lifecycle state to another. It is a design decision.

On the left-hand side of Figure 98, four versions of Type A are shown. All versions of Type A have the same Id and are differentiated by their version number. For example, the fully distinguished identification for the top thing on the left is XYZ12345 / 1.0 and for the thing just below, the fully distinguished identification is XYZ12345 / 1.1.

On the right-hand side of Figure 98, there are instances of Type A. The instance at the top is based on type XYZ12345 / 1.0. The second instance from the top has been updated to be based on type XYZ12345 / 1.1 and the third instance has been further updated to be based on type XYZ12345 / 2.0. Notice that the instance Id remains the same since it is the same instance (but with appropriate updates to follow Type A as it changes).

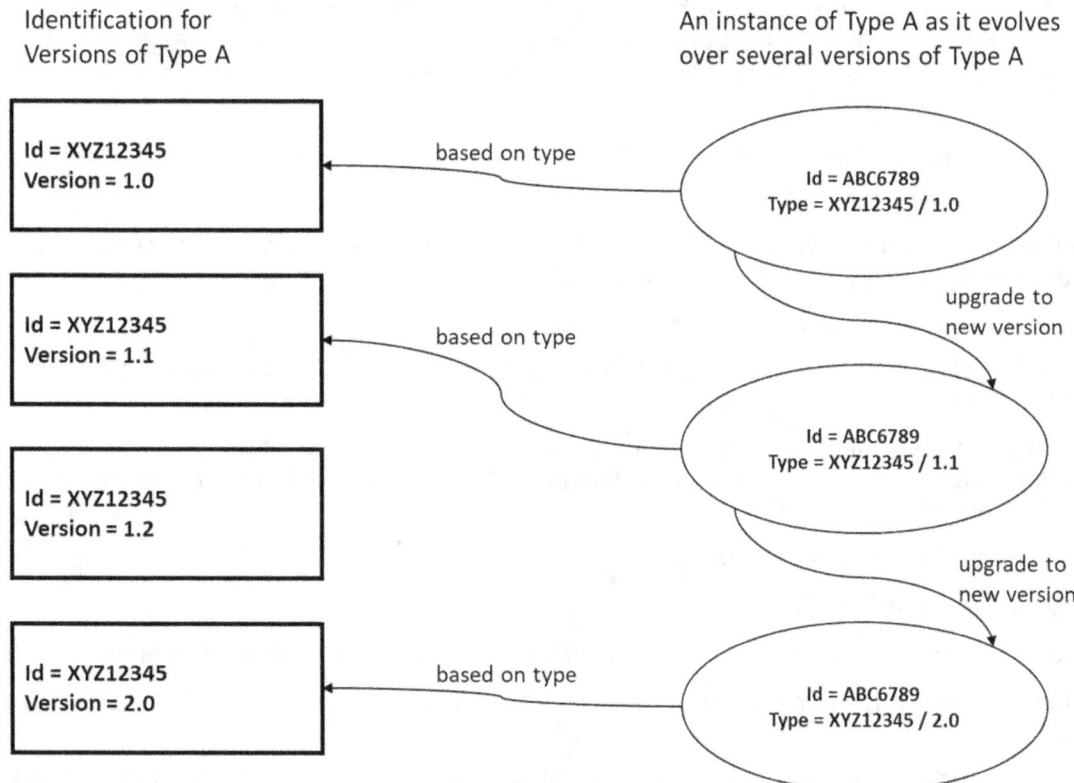

Figure 98. Types, Versions and Instances

In some cases, it will not be practical or possible to make live updates to instances as the associated type evolves, e.g., automobiles, laptop computers, cell phones. Even when it is possible to update an instance to support a new version of the associated type, there may be transition issues if the update requires the instance to be out-of-service for a period.

12.10 Virtualization and Abstraction

12.10.1   Introduction

The terms virtualization, abstraction, partitioning, logical and physical are sometimes used in overlapping and confusing ways. This is particularly true in the IT, telecommunications and computing industries.

For example, looking across several online dictionaries, related but somewhat different definitions of "abstraction" emerge:

- the process of formulating general concepts by extracting common properties of instances

- the act of withdrawing or removing something

- the act of hiding all but the relevant details about a type of thing to reduce complexity and increase efficiency.

The first definition is based on the study of instances to arrive at a generalized thing (this aspect is covered further in Section 12.10.2.1). The second definition assumes there is a starting point (perhaps a draft generalization) that can be further refined (this aspect is covered further in Section 12.10.2.2). The third definition focuses on the omission of unnecessary details for a type of thing based on the needs of a given set of consumers (this aspect is covered in Section 12.10.2.3).

Further, the meaning of "virtualization" has evolved from a partitioning concept (e.g., mainframe computer virtualization) to a concept of substitution or replacement (e.g., virtual reality or NFV [37] in the telecommunications industry). The concept of virtualization is discussed in Section 12.10.3.

12.10.2   Abstraction

12.10.2.1 Generalization

Generalization, a form of abstraction, refers to the extraction of general rules, concepts and structures from the analysis of specific examples.

From the Wikipedia article entitled "Generalization" [55]:

> A generalization is the formulation of general concepts from specific instances by abstracting common properties.

In mathematics, for example, the concept of a Group is defined as a set of things (G) and associated operation (call it *) for combining things from the set, where the operation has the following properties:

- Closure: $a*b$ is also an element of G

- Associativity: $a*b = b*a$

- Identity: there exists an element of G (call it I) such that $I*a = a$ for every element a in G

- Inverse: for every element a in G there exists another element in G (call it a^{-1}) such that $a * a^{-1} = I$.

The concept of a group arose from the study of multiple examples that shared common properties, e.g., the integers under addition, non-zero rational numbers under multiplication, the set of all non-zero complex numbers under multiplication, the set of congruence classes modulo n under addition (a finite group) and the set of permutations S(n) under composition (another finite group).

Further, there are many generalizations (laws) in science, see the Wikipedia article entitled "Laws of Science" [56].

The idea here is that, through the study of many examples, patterns are identified. From the patterns, general structures, rules or laws are proposed. The general structures, rules or laws can be used as a basis for additional discoveries that apply to all the examples that meet the general pattern or structure. For example, the area of Mathematics known as Group Theory provides many theorems based on the simple definition of a group.

With respect to managing things, generalization is the main process in the identification of types.

12.10.2.2 Refinement

Refinement, a form of abstraction, refers to the process of removing, distilling or transforming characteristics of a thing to reduce it to its essence. This aspect of "abstract" fits most closely with the original usage. From the Oxford English Dictionary:

> Middle English: from Latin abstractus, literally 'drawn away', past participle of abstrahere, from ab- 'from' + trahere 'draw off'.

Consider the following quote from Pablo Picasso:

> There is no abstract art. You must always start with something. Afterward, you can remove all traces of reality.

In the case of refinement, there is an implicit assumption that some level of generalization has already occurred and the generalization needs to be further reduced to an essential set of characteristics.

In the context of managing things, refinement concerns the fine-tuning of an already identified type.

When refining a type, it is necessary to define criteria or tests to make sure the refinement is not actually resulting in a new type. This comes down to defining the essential characteristics of a type and the intended "boundary" of a type definition – something of an art.

12.10.2.3 Viewpoints

Closely related to the concept of refinement is the idea of creating viewpoints of a thing. A **viewpoint** is a representation of a thing for a particular purpose and type of consumer. (Viewpoints are covered more generally in Section 7).

For example, consider a detailed representation of the human body. For medical school students, the entire representation would be needed. For a physical therapist, perhaps an "abstracted" version (i.e., viewpoint) with a focus on the muscular aspects of anatomy would be sufficient. Another (less detailed) version could be used for high school students.

Figure 99 relates the various aspects of abstraction. Starting from the left side of the figure, instances of similar things are analyzed with the intent of providing input into the generalization process. The generalization process identifies various types of things. The refinement process fine-tunes the types identified in the generalization process. Based on the needs of different consumers (of instances of a given type), the viewpoint analysis process defines specializations of types (as illustrated in the previous anatomy example). At each step, it is possible to provide feedback to a prior step. For example, the viewpoint analysis process may provide additional examples to be considered by the instance analysis process which could, in turn, provide input to the generalization process. The generalization process might determine that an existing type needs to be subdivided into two types, or perhaps an existing type needs to be further fine-tuned (and thus provide input to the refinement process).

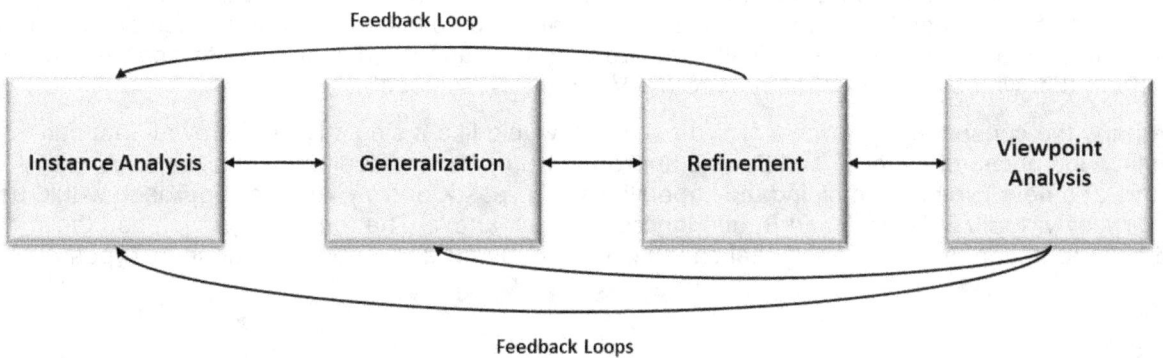

Figure 99. Abstraction Feedback Loop

12.10.3   Virtualization

The concept of virtualization was initially focused on partitioning. For example, in the early computer industry (1960s), virtualization was a method to logically divide the resources of a mainframe computer to support multiple applications. More recently, the concept of virtualization has been expanded to encompass an alternate implementation for a type of thing that can serve as a replacement for the original, where the original is typically closer to something tangible (physical) and the replacement is less tangible (e.g., mostly implemented as software). For example, NFV [37] uses virtualization to define virtualized (software) versions of physical network appliances such as firewalls and load balancers. Another example is the replacement of physical typesetting with its digital equivalent (although the term "virtualized typesetting" is not used).

12.10.3.1 Partitioning

Some things can be partitioned to serve several consumers. The partition can be based on time-slots, e.g., hotel rooms, or the partition can allow for multiple simultaneous consumers, e.g., a computer supporting multiple processes (consumers).

The telecommunications industry has a long history of partitioning transport media into multiple channels, see Plesiochronous Digital Hierarchy (PDH) [57], Synchronous Digital Hierarchy (SDH) [58] and Optical Transport Network (OTN) [59]. However, this is usually referred to as multiplexing or channelization (and not classified as a virtualization method).

12.10.3.2 Virtualization as a Copy or Substitute

More recently, "virtualization" is being used in the sense of a copy or substitute for something, e.g., a virtual tour of a city or some historical site, virtual job fair, and virtual reality.

Figure 100 illustrates the concept of virtualization via a firewall example. At the bottom of the figure, there are four "actual" firewalls, i.e., Firewalls A.1, A.2, B.1 and B.2. The term "actual" is used in the sense that the bottom-level firewalls are **not** a substitute for a more fundamental (lower-level) firewall. Firewall X.1 is an instance of Type X that can be used to replace instances of actual firewalls of Type A. Firewall X.1 can be scaled so that it can replace several instances of Type A firewalls (such as A.1 and A.2 in the figure). It is critical to understand that Firewall X.1 can be used to replace Firewalls A.1 and A.2, but that Firewall X.1 does not use or rely on Firewalls A.1 and A.2. Similarly, Firewall Y.1 can be used to replace instances of firewalls of Type B (such as B.1 and B.2 in the figure).

In general, one type of firewall can replace another firewall (or set of firewalls), if it supports all the features of the firewalls that are to be replaced.

Firewalls of Type A and B bind software with special purpose hardware. Assume the supplier sells instances of Type A and B firewalls as a unit (software and computing platform together). Whereas Firewalls X and Y separate the firewall software from the supporting compute, storage and network platform (known as an NFV Infrastructure (NFVI) in the NFV model).

Perhaps the consumer of firewalls of Type X and Y would like a single type of firewall that can replace instances of Types A and B. One approach would be to virtualize Types X and Y, and arrive at a new Type Z (combining the capabilities of Types X and Y). Another approach would be to directly virtualize Types A and B, and ignore Types X and Y. The former approach has the advantage of capturing any additional capabilities in Types X and Y (beyond those in Types A and B).

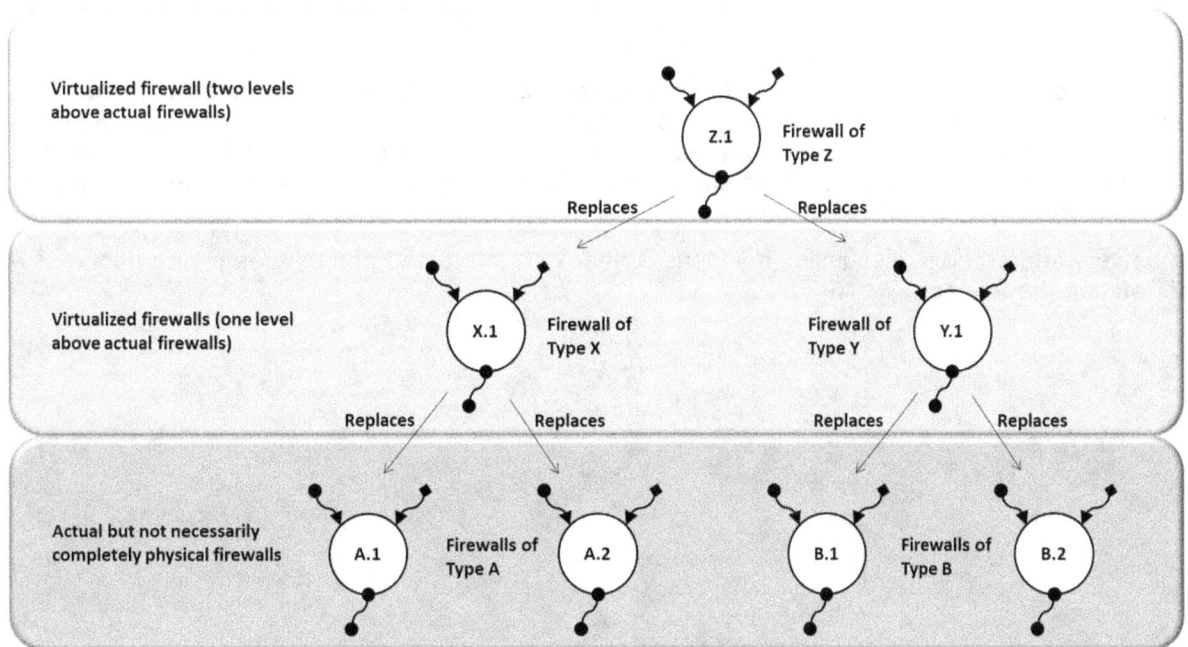

Figure 100. Levels of Virtualization

So, how is this different from the concept of abstraction? Virtualization, as described here, is about replacing one type of thing with another type of thing. There need not be any abstraction in the replacement, but abstraction is not excluded either. The main point is that with virtualization a type is implemented differently (typically using something less concrete such as software versus hardware). It is possible to enhance the original type when it is virtualized. Further, the virtualized type could be abstracted from several similar types.

For the set of terms discussed in this subsection, and in general when terms overlap and conflict, the best approach is to describe exactly what is meant in a given situation rather than endlessly fine-tuning definitions which, in the end, will never fit all possible scenarios.

13 Conclusion

[Author's note: This book is my attempt to put down in writing a foundation, and collection of patterns and concepts for the management of things in general. As noted in the preface, the ideas in this book have grown out of my many years in the telecommunication industry. My intention here was to demonstrate that the management concepts from the telecommunication industry apply to types of things in many other industries.

I'd be very interested in discussing my ideas further with interested parties (see my contact information the Preface).]

Acronyms

B2B – Business to Business

CAD – Computer Aided Design

CDN – Content Delivery Network

CLI – Command Line Interface

CSP – Communications Service Provider

DMV – Department of Motor Vehicles

ECA – Event-Condition-Action

ETSI – European Telecommunications Standards Institute

GMO – Genetically Modified Organism

HDD – Hard Disk Drive

HVAC – Heating, Ventilation and Air Conditioning

IBN – Intent-Based Networking

Id – Identifier

IN – Intelligent Network

IoT – Internet of Things

ISO – International Organization for Standardization

ITU – International Telecommunication Union

KPI – Key Performance Indicator

kWh – kilowatt-hour

LTE – Long-Term Evolution

MEP – Message Exchange Pattern

NFV – Network Functions Virtualization

NFVI – NFV Infrastructure

ONF – Open Networking Foundation

OOD – Object-Oriented Design

OSS – Operations Support System

OTN – Optical Transport Network

PC – Personal Computer

PDH – Plesiochronous Digital Hierarchy

PUR – Product Usage Rights

RAN – Radio Access Network

RCPA – Root Cause Problem Analysis

REST – REpresentational State Transfer

RM-ODP – Reference Model of Open Distributed Processing

SSD – Solid-State Drive

SDH – Synchronous Digital Hierarchy

SDN – Software Defined Networking (or Network)

TPMS – Tire-Pressure Monitoring System

UML® – Unified Modeling Language®

USB – Universal Serial Bus

vCDN – virtual Content Delivery Network

VM – Virtual Machine

VNF – Virtualized Network Function

VPN – Virtual Private Network

References

[1] ITU-T Recommendation X.700 (1992). *Management Framework for Open Systems Interconnection (OSI) For CCITT Applications.* Telecommunication Standardization Sector of the International Telecommunication Union.

[2] M. Atkinson, F. Bancilhon, D. DeWitt, K. Dittrich, D. Maier, and S. Zdonik. *The Object-Oriented Database System Manifesto.* In Proceedings of the First International Conference on Deductive and Object-Oriented Databases, pages 223-40, Kyoto, Japan, December 1989. Also appears in Building an Object-Oriented Database System: The Story of O2. F. Bancilhon, C. Delobel, and P. Kanellakis. (eds.) Morgan Kaufmann, 1992.

[3] "Taxonomy (biology)." *Wikipedia: The Free Encyclopedia.* Wikimedia Foundation, Inc. 12 January 2018. en.wikipedia.org/wiki/Taxonomy_(biology).

[4] OMG® Unified Modeling Language® (OMG UML®) Version 2.5.1 (2017).

[5] ITU-T Recommendation X.731 (1992). *Information Technology – Open Systems Interconnection – Systems Management: State management function.* Telecommunication Standardization Sector of the International Telecommunication Union.

[6] ISO/IEC 7498-1 Second Edition (1994). *Information technology – Open Systems Interconnection – Basic Reference Model: The Basic Model.* International Organization for Standardization (ISO) and International Electrotechnical Commission (IEC).

[7] "Deadlock." Wikipedia: The Free Encyclopedia. Wikimedia Foundation, Inc. 23 December 2018. en.wikipedia.org/wiki/Deadlock.

[8] ETSI GS NFV-IFA 010 V2.3.1 (2017). *Network Functions Virtualisation (NFV) Release 2; Management and Orchestration; Functional requirements specification.* ETSI.

[9] Sloman, M. and Twidle, K., Domains: A Framework for Structuring Management Policy, see www.researchgate.net/publication/2796921_Domains_A_Framework_For_Structuring_Management_Policy.

[10] Parker, G., Van Alstyne M. and Choudary, S. (2016). Platform Revolution: How Networked Markets Are Transforming the Economy and How to Make Them Work for You. W. W. Norton & Company.

[11] Choudary, S. (2015). Platform Scale: How an emerging business model helps startups build large empires with minimum investment. Platform Thinking Labs.

[12] Evans, D. and Schmalensee, R. (2016). Matchmakers: The New Economics of Multisided Platforms. Harvard Business Review Press.

[13] McAfee, A. and Brynjolfsson, E. (2017). Machine, Platform, Crowd: Harnessing Our Digital Future. W. W. Norton & Company.

[14] Innovation Tactics (website with information and analysis on platform-based businesses). www.innovationtactics.com/platform-business-model/.

[15] Taleb, N. (2012). *Antifragile: Things That Gain from Disorder.* Random House.

[16] IG1174 (2018). *Model-Driven Design of Management Interfaces for ODA Components.* TM Forum.

[17] ASTM C62 (2017). Standard Specification for Building Brick (Solid Masonry Units Made from Clay or Shale). ASTM International.

[18] ISO/IEC 10746-1 (1998). *Information technology -- Open Distributed Processing -- Reference model: Overview.* International Organization for Standardization (ISO).

[19] ISO/IEC 10746-2 (1996). *Information technology -- Open Distributed Processing -- Reference model: Foundations.* International Organization for Standardization (ISO).

[20] ISO/IEC 10746-3 (1996) . *Information technology -- Open Distributed Processing -- Reference Model: Architecture*. International Organization for Standardization (ISO).

[21] ITU-T Recommendation M.3400 (2000). *TMN management functions*. Telecommunication Standardization Sector of the International Telecommunication Union.

[22] Gamma, E., Helm R., Johnson R., Vlissides, J. and Grady Booch G. (1994). *Design Patterns: Elements of Reusable Object-Oriented Software*. Addison-Wesley Professional.

[23] Fowler, M. (2002). *Patterns of Enterprise Application Architecture*. Addison-Wesley Professional.

[24] Freeman, E., Bates, B., Sierra, K. and Robson, E. (2004). *Head First Design Patterns: A Brain-Friendly Guide*, O'Reilly Media.

[25] Ashford, C. and Gauthier, P. (2009). OSS Design Patterns: A Pattern Approach to the Design of Telecommunications Management Systems. Springer.

[26] "Representational state transfer." *Wikipedia: The Free Encyclopedia*. Wikimedia Foundation, Inc. 12 January 2018. en.wikipedia.org/wiki/Representational_state_transfer.

[27] "Microservices." *Wikipedia: The Free Encyclopedia*. Wikimedia Foundation, Inc. 21 January 2019. en.wikipedia.org/wiki/Microservices.

[28] "Net metering." *Wikipedia: The Free Encyclopedia*. Wikimedia Foundation, Inc. 12 January 2018. en.wikipedia.org/wiki/Net_metering.

[29] ITU-T Recommendation Q.1214 (1995). *Intelligent Network: Distributed Functional Plane for Intelligent Network CS-1*. Telecommunication Standardization Sector of the International Telecommunication Union.

[30] Strassner, J. (2003). *Policy-Based Network Management: Solutions for the Next Generation (The Morgan Kaufmann Series in Networking)*. Morgan Kaufmann.

[31] Sloman, M. (1994). *Policy Driven Management for Distributed Systems*. Journal of Network and Systems Management (December 1994, Volume 2, Issue 4, pp 333–360).

[32] Verma, D. (2000). *Policy-based Networking: Architecture and Algorithms*. New Riders Publishing.

[33] Klosterboer, L. (2011). *ITIL Capacity Management*. IBM Press and Pearson Plc.

[34] ONF TR-527 (2016). *Functional Requirements Transport API*. Open Networking Foundation (ONF).

[35] "Intent-based Network (IBD)." TechTarget. 23 January 2019. whatis.techtarget.com/definition/intent-based-networking-IBN.

[36] ONF TR-523 (2016). *Intent NBI – Definition and Principles*. Open Networking Foundation (ONF).

[37] ETSI GS NFV-MAN 001 V1.1.1 (2014). *Network Functions Virtualisation (NFV); Management and Orchestration*. ETSI.

[38] ETSI GR NFV 001 V1.2.1 (2017). *Network Functions Virtualisation (NFV); Use Cases*. ETSI.

[39] ETSI GR NFV-EVE 010 V3.1.1 (2017). *Network Functions Virtualisation (NFV) Release 3; Licensing Management; Report on License Management for NFV*. ETSI.

[40] IG1141 (2018). *Procurement and Onboarding Suite*. TM Forum.

[41] "Software license." *Wikipedia: The Free Encyclopedia*. Wikimedia Foundation, Inc. 18 January 2018. en.wikipedia.org/wiki/Software_license.

[42] Tannam, E. (10 December 2018). *O2 and Ericsson to work out compensation over UK data outage*. Silicon Republic. Retrieved from www.siliconrepublic.com/comms/o2-ericsson-network-compensation.

[43] SOAP Version 1.2 Part 1: Messaging Framework (Second Edition), W3C Recommendation, 27 April 2007.

[44] SOAP Version 1.2 Part 2: Adjuncts (Second Edition), W3C Recommendation, 27 April 2007.

[45] TR131 (2012). *Revenue Assurance Overview*. TM Forum.

[46] GB941 (2012). *Revenue Assurance Guidebook*. TM Forum.

[47] GB941D, Release 18.0.1 (2018). *Revenue Assurance: Revenue Leakage Framework and Examples*. TM Forum.

[48] Web Services Description Language (WSDL) Version 2.0 Part 1: Core Language, W3C Recommendation, 26 June 2007.

[49] Raz, Y. (1995). *The Dynamic Two Phase Commitment (D2PC) protocol*. Database Theory – ICDT '95, Lecture Notes in Computer Science, Volume 893/1995, pp. 162-176. Springer.

[50] ONF TR-502 (2014). *SDN Architecture*. Open Network Foundation (ONF).

[51] ITU-T Recommendation X.721 (1992). *Information Technology – Open Systems Interconnection – Structure of Management Information: Definition of Management Information*. Telecommunication Standardization Sector of the International Telecommunication Union.

[52] ITU-T Recommendation M.3704 (2010). *Common management service – Performance management – Protocol neutral requirements and analysis*. Telecommunication Standardization Sector of the International Telecommunication Union.

[53] "Bug bounty program." *Wikipedia: The Free Encyclopedia*. Wikimedia Foundation, Inc. 23 August 2018. en.wikipedia.org/wiki/Bug_bounty_program.

[54] "Open-source software security." *Wikipedia: The Free Encyclopedia*. Wikimedia Foundation, Inc. 5 February 2018. en.wikipedia.org/wiki/Open-source_software_security.

[55] "Generalization." *Wikipedia: The Free Encyclopedia*. Wikimedia Foundation, Inc. 16 February 2018. en.wikipedia.org/wiki/Generalization.

[56] "Laws of Science." *Wikipedia: The Free Encyclopedia*. Wikimedia Foundation, Inc. 16 February 2018. en.wikipedia.org/wiki/Laws_of_science.

[57] ITU-T Recommendation G.705 (2000). *Characteristics of Plesiochronous Digital Hierarchy (PDH) equipment functional blocks*. Telecommunication Standardization Sector of the International Telecommunication Union.

[58] ITU-T Recommendation G.707 (2007). *Network node interface for the Synchronous Digital Hierarchy (SDH)*. Telecommunication Standardization Sector of the International Telecommunication Union.

[59] ITU-T Recommendation G.709 (2016). *Interfaces for the Optical Transport Network (OTN)*. Telecommunication Standardization Sector of the International Telecommunication Union.

Index